SO-FIP-848

Historical Understanding

Past, Present, and Future

EDITED BY
ZOLTÁN BOLDIZSÁR SIMON
AND LARS DEILE

BLOOMSBURY ACADEMIC
LONDON · NEW YORK · OXFORD · NEW DELHI · SYDNEY

BLOOMSBURY ACADEMIC
Bloomsbury Publishing Plc
50 Bedford Square, London, WC1B 3DP, UK
1385 Broadway, New York, NY 10018, USA
29 Earlsfort Terrace, Dublin 2, Ireland

BLOOMSBURY, BLOOMSBURY ACADEMIC and the Diana logo are trademarks of
Bloomsbury Publishing Plc

First published in Great Britain 2022

Copyright © Zoltán Boldizsár Simon and Lars Deile, 2022

Zoltán Boldizsár Simon and Lars Deile have asserted their right under the Copyright,
Designs and Patents Act, 1988, to be identified as Editors of this work.

For legal purposes the Acknowledgements on pp. xvi, 88, 101, 150, 176 and 270
constitute an extension of this copyright page.

Cover image © Julia Filimonova

All rights reserved. No part of this publication may be reproduced or
transmitted in any form or by any means, electronic or mechanical, including
photocopying, recording, or any information storage or retrieval system,
without prior permission in writing from the publishers.

Bloomsbury Publishing Plc does not have any control over, or responsibility for,
any third-party websites referred to or in this book. All internet addresses given
in this book were correct at the time of going to press. The author and publisher
regret any inconvenience caused if addresses have changed or sites have
ceased to exist, but can accept no responsibility for any such changes.

A catalogue record for this book is available from the British Library.

A catalog record for this book is available from the Library of Congress.

ISBN:	HB:	978-1-3501-6861-9
	PB:	978-1-3501-6879-4
	ePDF:	978-1-3501-6862-6
	eBook:	978-1-3501-6863-3

Typeset by Integra Software Services Pvt. Ltd.
Printed and bound in Great Britain

To find out more about our authors and books visit www.bloomsbury.com
and sign up for our newsletters.

Historical
Understanding

CONTENTS

FIGURES

CONTRIBUTORS

Vanessa Agnew is Professor of English at Universität Duisburg-Essen and Senior Researcher at the Australian National University. She directs Academy in Exile's Critical Thinking Program at Freie Universität Berlin. Her *Enlightenment Orpheus* (Oxford University Press, 2008) won the Kenshur Prize and American Musicological Society's Lockwood Award. She co-edited *Settler and Creole Reenactment* (Palgrave Macmillan, 2010), special issues of *Criticism* 46 (2004) and *Rethinking History* 11 (2007), *Refugee Routes* (transcript, 2020), *Routledge Handbook of Reenactment Studies* (2020), and *Reenactment Case Studies* (forthcoming). Her recent exhibitions include *Right to Arrive* and *What We Brought with Us*. Her children's book, *Wir schaffen das—We'll Make It*, appeared with Sefa Verlag (2021).

Franz-Josef Arlinghaus is Professor of Medieval History at Bielefeld University, Germany. His research is focused on urban history, history of literacy, rituals, law, and history of individuality. The Datini archive provided the sources for his dissertation on the relationship of literacy and bookkeeping in *Zwischen Notiz und Bilanz* (Lang, 2000). He analyzed charters of twelfth- and thirteenth-century Milan with the help of a database in *Legitimationsstrategien* (UVK, 2016). His "Habilitation" (*Inklusion/Exklusion*, Böhlau, 2018) deals with legal proceedings in medieval Cologne. He is (co-)editor of two collected volumes on individuality (*Forms of Individuality*, Brepols, 2015, and *Sich selbst vergleichen*, transcript, 2020).

Berber Bevernage is Associate Professor of Historical Theory at the Department of History at Ghent University, Belgium. His research focuses on the dissemination, attestation, and contestation of historical discourse and historical culture in post-conflict situations. He has published in journals such as *History and Theory*, *Rethinking History*, *Memory Studies*, and the *History Workshop Journal*. His monograph *History, Memory and State-sponsored Violence* (Routledge, 2012) is also available in Spanish (Prometeo, 2015) and Portuguese (Milfontes, 2018). Berber is (co-)founder of the International Network for Theory of History (INTH) which aims to foster collaboration among theorists of history around the world.

Jerome de Groot is Professor of Literature and Culture at the University of Manchester, United Kingdom. He is the author of *Consuming History* (2008/2016), *The Historical Novel* (2009), and *Remaking History* (2015). He is currently working on a study of DNA and history.

Lars Deile is Professor of Didactics and Theory of History at Bielefeld University, Germany. His work circles around intellectual and educational history (*Kulturgeschichte als Kulturkritik. Nachfragen bei Georg Steinhausen*, 2008), history didactics (*Geschichtsdidaktische Grundbegriffe. Ein Bilderbuch für Studium, Lehre und Beruf*, co-editor, 2020), history politics (*Historisches Lernen als Rassismuskritik*, co-editor, 2016), and theory of history. Currently he is trying to bring such questions together in a theory of historical learning which is based on a phenomenological approach.

Victoria Fareld is Associate Professor of Intellectual History at Stockholm University. Her current research focuses on history of philosophy, theory of history, historical time, memory, and historical justice. Recent publications include "Time", in *The Routledge Companion to Historical Theory* (Routledge 2021), "Entangled Memories of Violence: Jean Améry and Frantz Fanon" in *Memory Studies* (2021), *From Marx to Hegel and Back: Capitalism, Critique and Utopia* (Bloomsbury, co-editor, 2020), "Coming to Terms with the Present" in *Rethinking Historical Time* (Bloomsbury, 2019), "History, Justice and the Time of the Imprescriptible" in *The Ethos of History* (Berghahn Books, 2018).

Erica Fudge is Professor of English Studies at the University of Strathclyde, Glasgow, Scotland, and is the Director of the British Animal Studies Network. She is the author of *Quick Cattle and Dying Wishes: People and their Animals in Early Modern England* (Cornell, 2018), *Pets* (Acumen, 2008), *Brutal Reasoning: Animals, History and Rationality in Early Modern England* (Cornell, 2006), *Animal* (Reaktion, 2002), and *Perceiving Animals: Humans and Beasts in Early Modern English Culture* (Macmillan, 1999). Her work has appeared in journals including *History and Theory, Angelaki, New Formations, Theory, Culture and Society*, and *Textual Practice*, and in *History Today* magazine.

Stefanos Geroulanos is Professor of History at New York University. He is the author of *Transparency in Postwar France* (2017) and *An Atheism That Is Not Humanist Emerges in French Thought* (2010), and co-author, with Todd Meyers, of *The Human Body in the Age of Catastrophe* (2018) and *Experimente im Individuum* (2014). He has translated two books by Georges Canguilhem and has co-edited, among others, *Power and Time* (with Natasha Wheatley and Dan Edelstein) and *The Scaffolding of Sovereignty* (with Zvi Ben-Dor Benite and Nicole Jerr). He is a co-executive editor of the *Journal of the History of Ideas*.

Jo Guldi is Principal Investigator (PI) of a $1 million NSF grant that funds research into how ideas about property have changed over the *longue durée*. She is currently Associate Professor of History and Data Science at Southern Methodist University, Texas, USA, where she teaches courses on the history of capitalism and on text mining in Python and R. She was formerly a Junior Fellow at the Harvard Society of Fellows. Her second monograph, *The Long Land War*, a global history of occupancy rights in the long twentieth century, will be published by Yale in 2022.

Suman Gupta is Professor of Literature and Cultural History at the Open University, and Honorary Senior Research Fellow, Social Sciences, Roehampton University, United Kingdom. Recent books include *Digital India and the Poor: Policy, Technology, Society* (2020), *What is Artificial Intelligence? Conversation between an AI Engineer and a Humanities Researcher* (with Peter Tu, 2020), and *Social Analysis and the COVID-19 Crisis: A Collective Journal* (with eight co-authors, 2020).

François Hartog is a historian and Professor Emeritus of Ancient and Moderm Historiography at the École des hautes études en sciences sociales, Paris. Among his recent publications are *Chronos, L'Occident aux prises avec le temps* (2020) and *Confrontations avec l'histoire* (2021).

Cornelius Holtorf has been educated in Germany and the UK and is currently Professor of Archaeology at Linnaeus University in Sweden. He also holds a UNESCO Chair on Heritage Futures and runs the Graduate School in Contract Archaeology (GRASCA) at Linnaeus. His research interests include the theory of cultural heritage, heritage futures, and archaeology in contemporary society. Among his recent books are

Culture Heritage and the Future (Routledge, co-edited with A. Högberg, 2021), *Archaeology Today* (Archaeopress, with D. Lindskog, 2021), and *Wow! The Future Is Calling!* (with P. Frid, 2021).

Marnie Hughes-Warrington is Deputy Vice-Chancellor Research and Enterprise at the University of South Australia and Visitor at the School of History at the Australian National University. Her work has expanded the global reach of history theory and is used in primary, secondary, and tertiary classrooms around the world. She is the author of seven books on historiography, including *History as Wonder* (Routledge, 2018) and *History Goes to the Movies* (Routledge, 2007).

Helge Jordheim is Professor of Cultural History at the University of Oslo, Professor of German Studies at the Norwegian University of Science and Technology, and PI of the research project and collective LIFETIMES. His latest books include co-written and edited global histories of the concepts of civility and civilization (*Civilizing Emotions*, 2015) and the world (*Conceptualizing the World*, 2018), as well as a history of universal history (*Universal History and the Making of the Global*, 2018). His work on multiple times, synchronization, and crisis is published in *History & Theory*, *Millennium*, *History of the Present*, and *Time & Society*.

Ethan Kleinberg is the Class of 1958 Distinguished Professor of History and Letters at Wesleyan University and Editor-in-Chief of History and Theory. Kleinberg's scholarly work spans across the fields of history, philosophy, critical theory, comparative literature, and religion. He is the author of *Emmanuel Levinas's Talmudic Turn: Philosophy and Jewish Thought* (Stanford University Press, 2021), *Haunting History: for a deconstructive approach to the past* (Stanford University Press, 2017), and *Generation Existential: Martin Heidegger's Philosophy in France, 1927–61* (Cornell University Press, 2006).

Chris Lorenz was Professor of Historical Theory at Leiden University and Professor of German Historical Culture at VU University Amsterdam. Since 2016 he has been an international research associate at the Ruhr-Universität Bochum. He has published widely on historical theory, historiography, and higher education. His publications include *De Constructie van het Verleden* (Boom, 2008, 9th rev. edn), *If You're So Smart Why Aren't You Rich? Universiteit, Markt & Management*

(Boom, ed., 2008), (with co-editor Berber Bevernage), *Breaking Up Time: Negotiating the Borders between Present, Past and Future* (Vandenhoeck, 2013), and *Entre Filosofía e Historia* (2 vols) (Prometeo Libros, 2015).

Jörg van Norden is Professor of Modern History and Its Didactics at Bielefeld University, Germany. In addition to papers and editorials, he has published monographs on "narrative constructivism" (Habilitation: *Was machst du für Geschichten? Didaktik eines narrativen Konstruktivismus 2011*), "time" (*Geschichte ist Zeit: Historisches Denken zwischen Kairos und Chronos 2016*), and "historical consciousness" (*Geschichte ist Bewusstsein: Historie einer geschichtsdidaktischen Fundamentalkategorie 2018*); he is currently preparing another one on "materiality and historical perception." His research focuses on theory of history, empirical studies on narrative competences, and didactical pragmatics. He is speaker of the section *Geschichtskulturen* (Bielefeld) and of the study-group *Geschichtsdidaktik theoretisch* (KGD).

Moira Pérez is Assistant Professor at the University of Buenos Aires and researcher at the National Council for Scientific and Technical Research, Argentina. Her work focuses on the interplay between violence (including epistemic violence) and identity, and brings together contributions of narrativist philosophies of history, queer theory, and decolonial and postcolonial studies, among others. In relation to the representation of the past, she has worked on narratives of progress in social movements, agency-building through historical representations of marginalized groups, and pinkwashing through official histories. She is currently working on her next monograph, *Identity, Politics and History: Critical Perspectives on Representations of the Past and the "New Subjects" of History* (forthcoming). For more information visit www.aacademica. org/moira.perez.

Joan Wallach Scott is Professor Emerita in the School of Social Science at the Institute for Advanced Study in Princeton, New Jersey. Her most recent books are *Knowledge, Power, and Academic Freedom* (2019) and *On the Judgment of History* (2020).

Zoltán Boldizsár Simon is a Research Fellow at Bielefeld University, Germany. He has been assistant professor at Leiden University and visiting researcher at the Max Planck Institute for the History of Science. His recent work explores the challenges posed by technology and the

Anthropocene to the human condition and modern historical thinking. He has published in journals ranging from *History and Theory* to *The Anthropocene Review*, and he is the author of *History in Times of Unprecedented Change: A Theory for the 21st Century* (Bloomsbury, 2019) and *The Epochal Event: Transformations in the Entangled Human, Technological, and Natural Worlds* (Palgrave, 2020).

David J. Staley is Associate Professor of History at The Ohio State University, where he teaches courses in digital history and historical methods and holds courtesy appointments in the Department of Design and the Department of Educational Studies. Most recently, he has been the author of *Historical Imagination* (2020). His previous books in historical theory include *Computers, Visualization and History* (2002) and *History and Future: Using Historical Thinking to Imagine the Future* (2006).

Marek Tamm is Professor of Cultural History at the School of Humanities, Tallinn University, Estonia. His primary research fields are the cultural history of medieval Europe, theory and history of historiography, and cultural memory studies. He has recently published *A Cultural History of Memory in the Early Modern Age* (Bloomsbury, ed. with A. Arcangeli, 2020), *Making Livonia: Actors and Networks in the Medieval and Early Modern Baltic Sea Region* (Routledge, ed. with A. Mänd, 2020), *Rethinking Historical Time: New Approaches to Presentism* (Bloomsbury, ed. with L. Olivier, 2019), *Juri Lotman—Culture, Memory and History: Essays in Cultural Semiotics* (Palgrave Macmillan, ed., 2019), and *Debating New Approaches to History* (Bloomsbury, ed. with P. Burke, 2018).

Kate E. Temoney is Assistant Professor of Religion at Montclair State University and co-chair of the Religion, Holocaust, and Genocide Unit in the American Academy of Religion. Her research on religion, human rights, and mass atrocities nexuses appears in *Genocide Studies Prevention*, *Religions*, and the *Journal of Religious Ethics*. Recent works include: "Anatomizing White Rage: 'Race is My Religion!' and 'White Genocide,'" *The Religion of White Rage* (Edinburgh University Press, 2020), and "An Assessment of the Plan of Action for Religious Leaders and Actors to Prevent Incitement to Violence that Could Lead to Atrocity Crimes," in *Routledge Handbook on Religion and Genocide* (forthcoming).

Patrícia Vieira is Senior Researcher at the Centre for Social Studies (CES) of the University of Coimbra, Portugal, and Professor of Spanish and

Portuguese at Georgetown University. Her fields of expertise are Latin American and Iberian literatures and cultures, utopian studies, and the environmental humanities. Her most recent monograph is *States of Grace: Utopia in Brazilian Culture* (SUNY Press, 2018). She has published numerous articles in her fields of expertise, as well as op-eds in the media. For more information visit www.patriciavieira.net.

Q. Edward Wang is a Professor of History at Rowan University in the United States and Changjiang Professor at Peking University, China. He has published extensively on the history of historiography and historical theory from a comparative and global perspective. His major publications include *Inventing China through History: The May Fourth Approach to Historiography* (SUNY Press, 2001), *Turning Points in Historiography: A Cross-Cultural Perspective* (University of Rochester Press, 2002), and *A Global History of Modern Historiography* (Routledge, co-authored, 2008 and 2017). More recently, he edited *Historiography: Critical Readings* (Bloomsbury, 2021) in four volumes.

Gary Wilder is a Professor in the Ph.D. Program of Anthropology, with cross-appointments in History and French, at the Graduate Center of the City University of New York, where he is also Director of the Committee on Globalization and Social Change. He is the author of *Freedom Time: Negritude, Decolonization, and the Future of the World* (Duke University Press, 2015) and *The French Imperial Nation-State: Negritude and Colonial Humanism Between the World Wars* (University of Chicago Press, 2005). His newest book, entitled *Untimely History, Unhomely Times: On the Politics of Temporality and Solidarity*, will be published by Fordham University Press in 2021. He is currently working on a manuscript provisionally entitled "More Abundant Life: Black Radical Humanism and the Atlantic World."

Silke Zimmer-Merkle is Postdoctoral Researcher at the Institute of Technology Futures—History Department at Karlsruhe Institute of Technology (KIT). Her fields of expertise and broad-ranging research interests include history of technology and mobility, cultural history, and history of ideas, as well as theory and methodology of history and technology assessment. The latter once sparked her interest in problem-oriented and interdisciplinary research. She is co-editor of *Black Boxes—Versiegelungskontexte und Öffnungsversuche. Interdisziplinäre Perspektiven* (DeGruyter, 2020).

ACKNOWLEDGEMENTS

The idea of this volume grew out of a small workshop held at Bielefeld University in 2018. It took place within the framework of the Center for Theories in Historical Research on the occasion of François Hartog taking up the newly inaugurated Reinhart Koselleck Guest Professorship. The event, called "In and Out of History," had a focus slightly different from this volume and featured only a few participants. It was structured along discussion blocks, in which participants offered brief but strong opening statements (in *c.* 5 minutes) to kick off a debate on different forms of relations to the past, present, and future. As this volume expands on that premise and reaches out to a larger number of participants to explore the current shape of historical understanding, we are very thankful to all participants of the initial workshop and to those who could not join this larger endeavor as well as those who could: Franz-Josef Arlinghaus, Katie Digan, Levke Harders, François Hartog, Silke Zimmer-Merkle, and Jörg van Norden, who was also the co-organizer of the event. At Bloomsbury, our thanks go to Abigail Lane for managing this book project throughout its entire lifecycle. Last but not least, we thank Julia Filimonova for her stunning cover artwork.

INTRODUCTION

Historical understanding today

Zoltán Boldizsár Simon

On the simultaneous crisis and abundance of history

The continuing relevance of modern historical understanding is being questioned today on several grounds; on so many grounds, in fact, that it is almost impossible to keep count. To mention only a few, the dysfunctionality of historical understanding as we came to know it in the last two centuries is equally indicated by the demise of humanities education and a decrease in history enrollments; by the growing sense of memory, trauma, and historical injustice as alternative approaches to the past; and by radical technological, algorithmic, ecological, environmental, and Earth System futures that no longer seem connected to past experiences and past states of affairs.

At the same time, and somewhat paradoxically, a host of historical projects seem to overwhelm us. Despite decades of critique and mistrust concerning ideas of progress, utopia, ideology, modernization, or for that matter, the very idea of history itself, many of the familiar historical projects of the modern world keep on running. Some of them even gain a new life, regardless of how we thought or wished that they might fade away with time, which, needless to say, was also a historical thought or wish in the first place: even wishing history away couldn't happen without having a recourse to history. If you look around, what you see is that the retained political ideologies, the resurfacing nationalisms, the variety of cosmopolitan views, discourses on growth and sustainability (and even degrowth), as well as the continuing emancipatory struggles, have not ceased to imply a historical trajectory over time in the most conventional sense, or very close to it. There are also the many new endeavors springing out of more recent experiential horizons, which, although oftentimes conflicting with one another, qualify as historical ones. Just think of the extension of emancipatory visions to non-humans and to the entirety of planetary life, the accompanying drive to tell multispecies histories, the advent of genealogical DNA testing, or climate engineering aiming to secure the long-term habitability of the planet.

Even better, think of the Anthropocene—a notion emerging in Earth System science, capturing the simultaneity of all aforementioned contradictory attitudes toward an invocation of history and historical understanding. As the proposed geological epoch marked by human activity becoming a natural force and acquiring the capacity to launch radical transformations in Earth System conditions, the Anthropocene appeals to and defies historical understanding at the same time. As a new (although not yet ratified) stage in Earth history, the Anthropocene is 'business as usual' in the historically conceived geological time scale. Yet, as the collision of social (human) and physical (natural) systems, it represents radical novelty that disconnects from past states of affairs, challenging categories of thought and modes of understanding developed in modernity, including assumptions of historical continuity. But, again, does radical novelty not entail a sense of historicity? Sure it does! Except that this sense of historicity, either partly or wholly, may be something completely other than what we have typically referred to as history in the last two centuries while engaging with ideologies, utopias, nationalisms, cosmopolitanisms, and emancipatory struggles—which, like it or not, all stay with us, too.

So here we are, in the midst of contradictory tendencies: on the one hand, we experience a severe crisis of historical understanding on countless fronts; on the other, we face an abundance of history, an overwhelming sense of historicity, and a large variety of historical projects, the character of which oftentimes we cannot even fathom. Something odd, something contradictory, something confusing is happening to history and historical understanding lately, something that no longer allows us to assume that our historical endeavors will somehow converge into a single unified historical project, or to wish that they should. This is not to say that universal histories and grand narratives have vanished, and that none of our historical projects are synchronized. This is only to say that no universal history in currency can meaningfully encompass all historical projects in a single synchronized whole. Equally, we cannot keep on assuming that our many historical endeavors—from reparations for historical injustice through transhumanist aspirations of overcoming our human biological limitations by technological means to historical re-enactment events—are historical in the very same way. Finally, in the midst of such plurihistoricities, we seem to be pulled toward the opposite direction, too. We face the necessity of contending that anthropocenic and technological futures nonetheless require us to think in universal terms about the place and prospects of humans on the planet.

The current shape of historical understanding is defined by a multitude of oftentimes conflicting historicities, temporalities, and relations to past, present, and future that inform our societal, cultural, environmental, technological, and political practices, including scholarly ones. To be able to grasp this as the historical condition and the historical culture of the early twenty-first century, we need to explore their co-existence in their plurality, their peculiar characteristics, their respective scopes, and their potential interactions—as accompanied by the simultaneous and incongruous pull of universality. Even without aiming at a full coverage, we would gain a clearer view on the extent to which modern historical understanding survives, the extent to which it gives way to new forms of historicity in facing new challenges, and the extent to which we should keep our largely unquestioned drive for historicizing the world within narrower confines.

In substantiating the above claims, the coming pages provide a brief introduction to the explorative work of the volume in four very brief steps. The first step clarifies the notion of modern historical understanding; the second one surveys recent challenges posed to such understanding; the third argues that multiple historicities and new scholarly histories spring out of these challenges; while the last step outlines the volume premise.

On modern historical understanding

The notion of historical understanding has several alternatives, with the most popular ones being historical thinking and historical consciousness. While each notion can be aligned with specific intellectual traditions, focusing on historical understanding alone can already be confusing, in that it implies at least two major lineages of intellectual inheritance. First, the German tradition of *Verstehen*—and the distinction between explaining (*Erklären*) and understanding (*Verstehen*) drawn by Johann

Gustav Droysen and substantiated by Wilhelm Dilthey—that exploded into a debate on the respective foundations and methods of the natural and human (and social) sciences (Von Wright 1971; Apel 1984); and second, the Anglo-American discourse on the rational re-enactment of the thoughts of past human actors as initiated by Collingwood ([1946] 1994). The complex interrelation of the two traditions is interpreted today with various emphases put on empathy (Retz 2018) or on the intentionality attributed to past actors (Bevir 2007).

As respectable as these traditions may be, adhering to any of them would significantly limit the scope and potential meaning of the notion of historical understanding. Given that the primary aim here is to come to terms with the richness of existing historical practices, the fitting notion of historical understanding is the one that is able to encompass all potential varieties and forms.

In this spirit, historical understanding will be used here as a broad framing category that refers to the comprehension of ourselves, the world, various phenomena, events, actions, and occurrences as seen together over a temporal plane—that is, as seen being integrated into configurations of past, present, and future. This may seem surprisingly general and quotidian. But the brilliance of Louis O. Mink (1987), whose ideas are reflected in the above working definition, lies in precisely the ability to vest the seemingly self-evident with profundity.

In the heyday of narrative philosophy of history, Mink considered history as a mode of comprehension. Distinguishing between theoretical, categoreal, and configurational modes of comprehension, Mink (1987: 51) argued that the three types are characteristic, respectively, "of natural science, philosophy, and history" (without being identical to these). Modes of comprehension organize experience into larger images through the act of "grasping together" things which cannot otherwise be experienced together (49–50). The theoretical mode of comprehension grasps the general as the common feature of individual instances, the categoreal mode subsumes instances under a conceptual framework, while the configurational one—the one associated with history—comprehends individual elements in their relation to each other inasmuch as they are arranged into a larger configuration (51–3). In each mode, what is comprehended is the larger unit. To Mink, the larger unit in the case of history and the configurational mode meant the whole of the historical narrative—which is the point where this volume takes another route.

While the volume remains indebted to Mink's ideas concerning the configurational mode, it delinks historical understanding and specifically narrative configurations. Instead of assuming a necessary tie between the two, it approaches historical understanding in terms of a variety of temporal configurations between past, present, and future. Although Mink (1987: 55) was right in pointing out that comprehension is not knowledge but "the synoptic vision" and the "human activity by which elements of knowledge are converted into understanding," he was constrained by the preoccupations of his contemporaries. The idea of binding historical understanding to narrative form is far less compelling in the twenty-first century than it was in the second half of the twentieth (Simon and Kuukkanen 2015). While narrative has indeed been the dominant form of configurational comprehension and historical understanding in the modern period—and remains a prominent form inasmuch as it continues to be accommodated by emerging forms of digital media (Rigney 2010)—focusing on specifically temporal configurations helps to explore a much larger variety of historicities than Mink could ever have thought of. And the reason why we need to explore this variety is precisely that narrative and its processual-developmental configuration of events are among the features of modern historical understanding that have been largely challenged in the last decades.

On the multitude of challenges

The intellectual criticism of modern history has been a burgeoning genre in the last decades. From postmodern to postcolonial, gender, and cultural criticism, it yielded indispensable insights into the most problematic assumptions of modern historical understanding and the procedures of professionalized historical scholarship as based on such assumptions (Cohen 1986; Nandy 1995; Trouillot 1995; Smith 1998; Chakrabarty 2000). Yet what seems to effectively transform historical understanding today is less the practice of intellectual critique and more the recent blossoming of a plurality of "new historical practices" in human endeavors—even if, rather evidently, intellectual endeavors contribute to the blossoming of new practices that challenge the fundamental temporal assumptions of modern historical understanding.

What exactly are these "new historical practices"? And how exactly does their emergence challenge modern historical understanding? Briefly put, the challenge is that the sociopolitical, technoscientific, anthropocenic practices of today—the ones briefly surveyed at the opening pages of this introduction—configure the relations between past, present, and future in ways that appear as alternatives to the configuration of a developmental process associated with modern historical understanding. It is the emergence of new temporal configurations, the emergence of new historicities, that increasingly renders modern historical understanding inoperable across various domains.

To bring some concreteness to this highly abstract picture, let's consider a few examples on both larger and smaller scales. As to the largest scale, while the Anthropocene indeed invites us to delve into the deep time of intertwined human and geological and Earth System processes (Chakrabarty 2018), on a more profound level it disturbs assumptions of processual continuity in the first place. When Earth System scientists consider anthropocenic transformations of the Earth System, they seldom talk about developmental processes. The consolidation of the Earth System science as a new knowledge formation has been linked with the view that "Earth-system dynamics are characterized by critical thresholds and abrupt changes" (Steffen et al. 2020: 57). The same applies to the many ways in which technology-induced changes defy the conventional "historical" scenario of developmental processes on the largest scale—be those changes linked with an exponential view (Kurzweil 2004) or be they related to imaginaries of the coming singularity (Shanahan 2015) that I align elsewhere with expectations of "unprecedented change" (Simon 2019).

The collision of social/cultural/political and natural/physical/biological systems through technoscience means that where we previously saw social, cultural, and political practices interacting with the separate sphere of natural practices, today we see what Karen Barad (2007) calls entangled "naturalcultural practices" that demand a redefinition of the human as occupying a less central place when viewed against a larger framework of planetary life. The matching anti- or post-anthropocentric stances developed in the human and social sciences—from approaches to interspecies relations (Latimer and Miele 2013) to critical posthumanism (Braidotti 2013)—oftentimes calibrate their own temporal configurations (Rossini and Toggweiler 2018) as being set against the fundamental tenets of modern historical understanding.

At a more tangible scale, technoscientific changes induce profound transformations in the more narrowly conceived sociopolitical domain— as seen either in itself or within the collision of worlds. Notwithstanding their promises, algorithmic technologies (Benjamin 2019), big data (O'Neil 2016), and human enhancement practices (Clarke et al. 2016) equally appear as threats ranging from the reinforcement of existing modes of inequalities and injustices and the creation of new ones to the erosion of democracy. At the same time, the sociopolitical domain is facing challenges stemming from its own dynamics, too. While François Hartog (2015) claims that a presentist "regime of historicity" is overtaking the future-oriented modern one, the growing recognition of the persistence of historical injustices reconfigures the relationship between past and present (Bevernage and Lorenz 2013), entailing a constellation in which the past does not go away but remains present in the present.

None of this means, however, that the modern form of historical understanding has vanished. It's still around, in the most confusing ways. Its central tenets are explicitly embraced in transhumanist self-mythologies that depict the endeavor as one that carries forward the inheritance of the Enlightenment of gradual improvement of the human condition (Bostrom 2005), despite the fact that its ultimate goal of transcending human biological limitations entails a leap into a "disconnective future" (Simon and Tamm 2021) of other-than-human beings. At the same time, not even practices that call out the global wrongdoings of the modern European/Western world can escape the hold of its modes of sense-making. Decolonial theories (Quijano 2001) and decolonial approaches represent modern historical understanding at its most elemental: decolonizing the Anthropocene (Davis and Todd 2017), for instance, means interpreting it as a colonial legacy, as an emergent phenomenon that develops over the course of deep processes based on a long-term continuity with colonial practices. Or, a history of the complicity of historians and historical imagination in the development of the British Empire (Satia 2020) can hardly abstract fully from the very historical mode of sense-making it calls into question. All in all, although history as we know it has survived in self-contradictory ways, it has also become only one sense of historicity in a plurality of historicities, one mode of historical understanding among the many.

On the plurality of historicities and the new histories

Perhaps it is not too far-fetched to claim that the emergence of "new historical practices" with their new historicities has significantly contributed to the recognition that temporal configurations are manifold, that they are "historical" in multiple ways. By now, it has become the majority view in historical theory and in theoretically inspired historical scholarship that temporalities are multiple (Jordheim 2014); that historical investigations reveal a pluritemporality (Landwehr 2012; Fryxell 2019) and a conflict of temporalities (Edelstein, Geroulanos, and Wheatley 2020); that theoretical examinations could map the new forms of historical time (Tamm and Olivier 2019); that a philosophy of historicities may be a form of a contemporary philosophy of history (Bevernage 2012); or that a hauntology as a theory of multiple temporalities could expose multiple pasts converging in the present (Kleinberg 2017).

With a slightly different emphasis, the recent surge of the notion of "historical culture" in the field of history education (Grever and Adriaansen 2017: 73), broadly defined as a study of "people's relations to the past," conveys a similar sense. It parallels efforts in historical theory to study such relations to the past both in professionalized historiography and the wider society (Day 2008; Paul 2015). Finally, these past-focused efforts are complemented recently by a collective study of modalities of "historical futures" aimed at mapping the ways in which recent technoscientific, algorithmic, naturalcultural, anthropocenic, and sociopolitical practices configure transitions from apprehended pasts to anticipated futures (Simon and Tamm 2021). All this, I believe, testifies to an attentiveness to a plurality of co-existing historicities best captured by the notion of "plurihistoricity" (Simon 2021).

The implications of the above complexities for how history is done in the sense of a scholarly endeavor are, again, extremely intricate. Instead of one overall transformation of the scholarly exercise, what we witness today is the emergence of new histories, reflecting the complexity of the challenges and historicities that sustain them. Who can be the new subjects of today's emancipatory histories, human and more-than-human? Will historical studies, in the end, be included in the larger family of anti- or post-anthropocentric humanities (Domanska 2010)? Will historical approaches play a prominent role in emerging new knowledge formations such as environmental humanities (Robin 2018)? As based on the distinction between climate change and the Anthropocene (Thomas 2019), can a distinct Anthropocene historiography emerge? How would it situate its potential universalism with Amerindian indigenous knowledges (Danowski and Viveiros de Castro 2016) or the Asia Pacific (Simangan 2019)? How profoundly can technological advancements and new scientific tools—from big data (Manning 2013) and the non-textual data recent scientific endeavors reveal about the human past (McNeill

2016) to digital tools (Winters 2018)—alter historical scholarship? Will history as a discipline and a specifically scholarly mode of historical understanding survive the next decades in the first place? Among others, these are questions through which the challenges of the new century and the emergence of new historicities invite the discipline to self-inspect.

On the volume premise

At its most general, this volume attempts to provide a kaleidoscope-like insight into the many shapes of historical understanding today. The insight is kaleidoscope-like not in the sense of showing a static and symmetrical geometrical pattern, but in the sense of exposing the colorfulness and complexity of the current shape of historical understanding, in facing previously unthinkable challenges. In doing so, the volume intends to explore the plurality of historicities and temporalities emerging in a large variety of sociopolitical, technological, scientific, ecological, environmental, and naturalcultural practices, to situate them with the retained forms of modern developmental historicities and with old and new universalisms, and to map their historiographical manifestations.

Differently put, this book is neither a handbook-type introduction to new developments in historiography nor a collection of recent views on the theory and philosophy of history, but an inquiry into an emerging new historical condition. It wants to stimulate reflection and discussion by providing fresh impulses and by addressing the manifold new ways in which we navigate "historically" in coping with present-day challenges—both in the wider society and in historiography. The kaleidoscope-like insight is the means to achieve this goal, through an experimental format of twenty-four short contributions organized into three blocks that represent the elements of the specifically temporal configuration associated with historical understanding: present, future, and past—in this rather unconventional order.

The first block is devoted to contributions that map "historical" relations to the present and to the pressing concerns of our present time, the second one turns to historical relations to the future, while the third block reviews relations to the past. Each block consists of two sections. Contributions that explore larger temporal predicaments or wider societal relations form the section "Historicities," while contributions that explore implications for historiography are included in the section "Histories." The organizational structure means that, for practical and pragmatic considerations of volume composition, the blocks analytically boil down to the constituents of temporal configurations associated with historical understanding. Yet, analytical separation aside, the individual entries constantly address the concerns of the other two blocks and the interrelations of temporal layers, thereby providing an overview of a variety of aspects and forms of historical understanding today.

The ultimate aim is not to capture a definite shape of historical understanding by recounting every possible kind of temporal relation. First, this would be impossible, and second, it would imply having a recourse to unfeasible ambitions and untenable epistemic assumptions concerning totality. Nor does the volume wish to advocate one particular relation and approach, arguing normatively that one temporal configuration or another should be the form of historical understanding everyone is supposed to subscribe to. This does not, of course, mean that the volume is free of normativity; it means only that instead of advocating particular agendas of how historical understanding should be transformed, its primary aim is to explore and, as much as possible, to grasp that which is already the case, the many transformations of historical understanding that are already in effect. Its twenty-four chapters, as seen together, hope to attest to a complexity in our current historical condition that we are as yet struggling to understand.

References

Apel, K.-O. (1984), *Understanding and Explanation: A Transcendental-Pragmatic Perspective*. Trans. Georgia Warnke. Cambridge, MA: MIT Press.

Barad, K. (2007), *Meeting the Universe Halfway: Quantum Physics and the Entanglement of Matter and Meaning*. Durham, NC: Duke University Press.

Benjamin, R. (2019), *Race After Technology: Abolitionist Tools for the New Jim Code*. Cambridge: Polity Press.

Bevernage, B. (2012), "From Philosophy of History to Philosophy of Historicities: Some Ideas on a Potential Future of Historical Theory," *Low Countries Historical Review* 124(7): 113–20.

Bevernage, B., and C. Lorenz (2013), "Breaking Up Time: Negotiating the Borders between Past, Present and Future," *Storia della Storiografia* 63(1): 31–50.

Bevir, M. (2007), "Introduction: Historical Understanding and the Human Sciences," *Journal of the Philosophy of History* 1(3): 259–70.

Bostrom, N. (2005), "A History of Transhumanist Thought," *Journal of Evolution and Technology* 14: 1–25.

Braidotti, R. (2013), *The Posthuman*. Cambridge: Polity Press.

Chakrabarty, D. (2000), *Provincializing Europe: Postcolonial Thought and Historical Difference*. Princeton, NJ: Princeton University Press.

Chakrabarty, D. (2018), "Anthropocene Time," *History and Theory* 57(1): 5–32.

Clarke, S., J. Savulescu, T. Coady, A. Giubilini, and S. Sanyal (eds.) (2016), *The Ethics of Human Enhancement: Understanding the Debate*. Oxford: Oxford University Press.

Cohen, S. (1986), *Historical Culture: On the Recoding of an Academic Discipline*. Berkeley, CA: University of California Press.

Collingwood, R. G. ([1946] 1994), *The Idea of History*. Edited with an introduction by Jan van der Dussen. Oxford: Oxford University Press.

Danowski, D., and E. Viveiros de Castro (2016), *The Ends of the World*. Cambridge: Polity Press.

Davis, H., and Z. Todd (2017), "On the Importance of a Date, or Decolonizing the Anthropocene," *ACME: An International Journal for Critical Geographies* 16(4): 761–80.

Day, M. (2008), "Our Relations with the Past," *Philosophia* 36: 417–27.

Domanska, E. (2010), "Beyond Anthropocentrism in Historical Studies," *Historein* 10: 118–30.

Edelstein, D., S. Geroulanos, and N. Wheatley (eds.) (2020), *Power and Time: Temporalities in Conflict and the Making of History*. Chicago, IL: University of Chicago Press.

Fryxell, A. F. P. (2019), "Time and the Modern: Current Trends in the History of Modern Temporalities," *Past and Present* 243: 285–98.

Grever, M., and R.-J. Adriaansen (2017), "Historical Culture: A Concept Revisited," in M. Carretero, S. Berger, and M. Grever (eds.), *Palgrave Handbook of Research in Historical Culture and Education*, 73–89, London: Palgrave.

Hartog, F. (2015), *Regimes of Historicity: Presentism and Experiences of Time*. Trans. Saskia Brown. New York: Columbia University Press.

Jordheim, H. (2014), "Introduction: Multiple Times and the Work of Synchronization," *History and Theory* 53(4): 498–518.

Kleinberg, E. (2017), *Haunting History: For a Deconstructive Approach to the Past*. Stanford: Stanford University Press.

Kurzweil, R. (2004), "The Law of Accelerating Returns," in C. Teuscher (ed.), *Alan Turing: Life and Legacy of a Great Thinker*, 381–416. Berlin: Springer.

Landwehr, A. (2012), "Alte Zeiten, Neue Zeiten: Aussichten auf die *Zeit-Geschichte*," in A. Landwehr (ed.), *Frühe Neue Zeiten: Zeitwissen zwischen Reformation und Revolution*, 9–40. Bielefeld: transcript.

Latimer, J., and M. Miele (2013), "Naturecultures? Science, Affect, and the Non-human," *Theory, Culture & Society* 30(7–8): 5–31.

Manning, P. (2013), *Big Data in History*. Basingstoke: Palgrave Macmillan.

McNeill, J. (2016), "Historians, Superhistory, and Climate Change", in A. Jarrick, J. Myrdal, and M. W. Bondesson (eds.), *Methods in World History: A Critical Approach*, 19–43, Lund: Nordic Academic Press.

Mink, L. O. (1987), *Historical Understanding*. Edited by Brian Fay, Eugene O. Golob, and Richard T. Vann. Ithaca, NY: Cornell University Press.

Nandy, A. (1995), "History's Forgotten Doubles", *History and Theory* 34(2): 44–66.

O'Neil, C. (2016), *Weapons of Math Destruction: How Big Data Increases Inequality and Threatens Democracy*. New York: Broadway Books.

Paul, H. (2015), "Relations to the Past: A Research Agenda for Historical Theorists," *Rethinking History* 19(3): 450–8.

Quijano, A. (2001), "Coloniality of Power, Eurocentrism, and Latin America," *Nepantla: Views from South* 1(3): 533–80.

Retz, T. (2018), *Empathy and History: Historical Understanding in Re-enactment, Hermeneutics and Education*. New York: Berghahn.

Rigney, A. (2010), "When the Monograph is No Longer the Medium: Historical Narrative in the Online Age," *History and Theory* 49(4): 100–17.

Robin, L. (2018), "Environmental Humanities and Climate Change: Understanding Humans Geologically and Other Life Forms Ethically," *WIREs Climate Change* 9:e499.

Rossini, M., and M. Toggweiler (2018), "Editorial: Posthuman Temporalities," *New Formations* 92: 5–10.

Satia, P. (2020), *Time's Monster: How History Makes History*. Cambridge, MA: The Belknap Press of Harvard University Press.

Shanahan, M. (2015), *The Technological Singularity*. Cambridge, MA: MIT Press.

Simangan, D. (2019), "Situating Asia Pacific in the Age of the Anthropocene," *Australian Journal of International Affairs* 73(6): 564–84.

Simon, Z. B. (2019), *History in Times of Unprecedented Change: A Theory for the 21st Century*. London: Bloomsbury.

Simon, Z. B. (2021), "Domesticating the Future through History," *Time & Society*, online first article, doi: 10.1177/0961463X211014804.

Simon, Z. B., and J.-M. Kuukkanen (2015), "Introduction: Assessing Narrativism," *History and Theory* 54(2): 153–61.

Simon, Z. B., and M. Tamm (2021), "Historical Futures," *History and Theory* 60(1): 3–22.

Smith, B. G. (1998), *The Gender of History: Men, Women, and Historical Practice*. Cambridge, MA: Harvard University Press.

Steffen, W., K. Richardson, J. Rockström, H. J. Schellnhuber, O. P. Dube, S. Dutreuil, T. M. Lenton, and J. Lubchenco (2020), "The Emergence and Evolution of Earth System Science," *Nature Reviews Earth & Environment* 1: 54–63.

Tamm, M., and L. Olivier (eds.) (2019), *Rethinking Historical Time: New Approaches to Presentism*, London: Bloomsbury.

Thomas, J. A. (2019), "Why the 'Anthropocene' is not 'Climate Change' and Why it Matters," *Asia Global Online* (10 January). Available online: https://www.asiaglobalonline.hku.hk/anthropocene-climate-change/ (accessed September 1, 2021).

Trouillot, M.-R. (1995), *Silencing the Past: Power and the Production of History*. Boston, MA: Beacon Press.

Von Wright, G. H. (1971), *Explanation and Understanding*. London: Routledge & Kegan Paul.

Winters, J. (2018), "Digital History," in M. Tamm and P. Burke (eds.), *Debating New Approaches to History*, 277–89, London: Bloomsbury.

PART ONE

The historical present

Historicities

HISTORIES

CHAPTER ONE

The texture of the present

François Hartog

The present is our place and our environment. We are embarked on it, as has always been the case for all human communities. But in order to understand its texture, we must first distance ourselves from it, knowing that it is not the same everywhere or for everyone and that it is very difficult to assign clear boundaries to it. Nevertheless, there are many instruments used for distancing, since this is the very approach of all the social sciences—observing, measuring, evaluating, interpreting, and comparing all help us to understand more and thereby to act better. Indeed, thanks to these multiple questions, we know a lot about the present—or rather, about the different presents. And even more and more so, given the possibilities opened up by the rapid development of big data (the algorithms of the internet giants are a constant testimony to this, for better or worse). But this increase in knowledge is also likely to accentuate fragmentation. Although we might know more and more precisely what it is to live in the present (depending on whether you are a woman, a man, a worker, an executive, unemployed, young, old, a migrant, etc.), we do not necessarily see better what this present is: its texture. To use the example of a picture, we improve our understanding of the details, but not necessarily of what presided over the composition of the painting. At this point, historians can make their contribution, by offering back and forth movements between the present and the past through comparison.

This is what I did almost twenty years ago when I suggested calling the contemporary moment "presentism." This diagnosis was the outcome of maximal distancing, since it was a question of comparing the present with the past by focusing on moments of crises in time (Hartog 2015). What did I—and those who worked before and with me—mean? Just this: that we had gone from a configuration where the future was the dominant category to a new one, where the present had come to be invested with this role. When the future was in the forefront, it illuminated the present and the past, and, driven by progress, it invited and forced us to walk ever faster toward a future full of promise. Accelerating and modernizing were the watchwords. A large part of the nineteenth century was thus intensely futuristic. But two world wars and a few revolutions later, when the brightest promises had turned into nightmares, it became impossible to believe that scientific progress, technological progress, and the progress of mankind went hand in hand. Progress spelled with capital letters had been damaged. Then, the 1970s witnessed the opening up of what was quickly called a crisis of the future—a future that was closing—while, as if in return, the present was occupying an ever greater space. If the occasion was the first "Oil Shock" (1973) and its aftermath on Western economies, the crisis had, in fact, originated long before that. And, for the first time, a decision of global scope escaped the West. This was an important component of the "shock."

The present then became fashionable and, very quickly, an injunction: it was necessary not only to be in tune with one's own time, but also to work and live in the present. The watchwords are never resting, being flexible and mobile, responding to demand, innovating relentlessly, with two keywords: acceleration and urgency. Very quickly, the new information technologies brought, spread, and multiplied the possibilities of exploiting what was called "real time." Paradoxically, while, on the one hand, the present tended to almost abolish itself in the moment, on the other hand, it never ceased to expand in the directions of both the past and the future; eventually, it became omnipresent, cannibalizing the categories of past and future – that is to say, in the first place it devoured daily the past and future which it needed daily, and then at every moment and continuously. Advertisements everywhere trumpeted that the future begins "tomorrow" or, better still, "now." Wasn't "change" also announced for "now" during the 2012 French presidential campaign?[1]

To this present oscillating between almost everything and almost nothing, we must add another dimension. For these decades were also those of the "memory years," to use Pierre Nora's expression. Claude Lanzmann's film *Shoah*, released in 1985, is testimony to this with singular force, while Nora's *Lieux de mémoire* (1984–92) called on memory to rewrite history.[2]

It is in these years that the "demand" for memory, the "duty" to remember, and the "right" to memory were taking an ever greater place in public (media, judicial, cultural) spaces. Soon, memory and its alter ego, heritage, became two obligatory figures in political speeches and agendas. Almost everywhere commemorations were multiplying and became occasions for great mass gatherings (national, patriotic, sometimes chauvinistic, mass protests, too …). Policies of memory are being put in place, often leading to memory laws. Presentism no longer believes in history, but leaves it up to memory, which is, in short, an extension of the present in the direction of the past, by the evocation and convocation of certain (most often painful, hidden, forgotten …) moments of the past into the present. But it does not provide an opening toward the future, except for the "never again," which first of all indicates a return to a past whose closure is proclaimed. Often, the route of memory museums, whose numbers have multiplied throughout the world, ends with this moral injunction: do not forget in order not to begin again.

History, on the other hand, that which the nineteenth century elevated to the rank of major divinity, opened up to the future in a teleological manner—whether its heroes were the Nation, the People, the Proletariat (Hartog 2016). In doing so, it sided with the victors or with those who, temporarily defeated, would be victorious tomorrow, while memory became the instrument or weapon of those who could not speak or were not heard, the forgotten (of history), the minorities, the victims. Memory and presentism, therefore, go hand in hand. But memory allows us to escape from a present—where landmarks are erased at high speed—yet without leaving it. Facing this past which, like I said, does not pass (the past of crimes against humanity and genocides), is therefore also one of the ways of facing the present, since this past is not only still present, but *of* the present. The imprescriptibility of crime against humanity implies that criminals, throughout their life, remain contemporary to their crime. For them, time does not "pass," but, at the same time, neither does time pass for us—as the trials for crimes against humanity since Adolf Eichmann's trial in 1961 have shown.

To diagnose the present (which was for Michel Foucault the very task of the philosopher) is also to perceive that there is not one presentism, the same for everyone, but several presentisms. There are at least two: on the one hand, there is the chosen one, that of those who – connected, mobile, agile – are recognized as the "winners of globalization"; on the other hand, there is the suffered one, that of all those who are banned from plans, who literally cannot project themselves into the future, who live, and survive even, from day to day. Their only universe is "precariousness," or even "great" or "very high precariousness." Today, the most deprived is the "migrant" (neither an emigrant nor an immigrant, but a "migrant," as if he or she were locked in the endless present of migration). Between the most deliberately chosen and the most suffered presentisms there are all the intermediate situations. But we see more and more clearly the dangers of temporalities which are much too out of tune between social groups, age groups, or social classes. If the discordance of time does not produce this, it powerfully fuels social conflict. When contemporaries share the same present while simultaneously being in another time, the gap, if it grows too great, can feed movements of withdrawal, refusal, anger. The spatial distances between center and periphery are at least as many temporal distances. For some years now, Europe has been experiencing this almost daily, translated to the political scene: the success of populist movements. It is not enough to use the same mobile phones to share the same present.

We also hear, here and there, calls to move away from presentism or short-termism (a term borrowed from finance), to reopen history and reinvest in the future. There is a growing awareness that this presentist bubble, so in tune with the globalized economy—that of financial capitalism and the big tech companies for whom every moment (even in the nanosecond range) must generate profits—bears serious dangers. Yet it is impossible to put an end to presentism by decrees! All the more so since, under a presentist regime, historical time as we know it slips or does not get into gear. Historical time, carried by the future, was indeed fed by the gap between the space of experience and the horizon of expectation—to use the categories of Reinhart Koselleck (2004)—and that gap was increasing the more expectations outweighed experience. The outcome is not merely that this time is over now—it is more that it has become impossible to see how it would resume its course in the world that has been taking shape since the beginning of the twenty-first century. Reopening history involves, first of all, the formation of a new concept of history which, while challenging the tyranny of the present, can begin by re-establishing a genuine circulation between the three categories of past, present, and future and thus enable us to properly face the present in order to act on it.

Initiatives to escape the ever-faster rhythms of the metropolises are multiplying. Acceleration and urgency are contrasted with slowdown (slow food, for example, has come to challenge the evidence on fast food). More energy-efficient lifestyles are being sought, with an emphasis on recycling and short economic circuits. In order to break with presentism-induced lifestyles, we see families leaving the big cities. Recently, permaculture has become the banner of these new lifestyles. There have been a multitude of small silent secessions, rather individual, whose number is increasing. Will they aggregate and become an organized political force? One might think that they are inspired by a nostalgia of "things were better before," but what motivates them, is, actually, a concern for the future. For many (particularly for those who are children of presentism, who have known only presentism), it is not the "homecoming," as practiced in the 1960s, that they are reviving. In their choice of a new life, they are confronted with the fact that we are hearing, from various horizons, these increasingly pressing calls to get out of "short-termism." Even politicians are following suit, more or less skillfully, by deploying the term "future" more often in their public interventions and election campaigns. But for some, the most direct path to the future is that of the past—that is to say, of a mythologized past. Such is the case of the winning slogan in 2016: *Make America Great Again* or *Back to the Future Past*!

But, above all, these internal criticisms prompted by presentism itself have been both reinforced and profoundly transformed by the recent outbreak of a threat that brings with it a new era: that of the Anthropocene. We're moving from a concern for the future to a fear of the future. All of a sudden, presentism, which has been shrinking to the point of almost disappearing, is confronted with a time, an ordinary time but one which can be counted in millions and billions of years. Everything happens as if this new *chronos* has burst the presentist bubble, forcing its inhabitants to look past the ends of their noses or their returns on investment. The future is indeed there: a future that simultaneously is no longer and still is in our hands. Beginning in the 2010s, the great swinging movement is still largely in progress. Not without anxiety or excitement at times.[3]

Presentism makes abundant use of the disaster—if we are to view the event in a negative light—but the Anthropocene is not any less mobilizing (Stengers 2015). In this context, it can refer to either the catastrophe in progress (global warming), whose inexorable progress is measured by the Intergovernmental Panel on Climate Change (IPCC) reports or the final catastrophe (the sixth extinction of species). It is also often referred to in terms of collapse and, of course, apocalypse (negative only). Always available, the apocalypse is mobilized by a number of commentators on and around the Anthropocene. In short, the catastrophe passes easily from presentism to the Anthropocene, although with the difference that the Anthropocene catastrophe carries an idea of the end that is ignored by the presentist catastrophe, the latter simply entailing moving from one catastrophe to another.

Yesterday, presentism still believed that it could be its own horizon, but, already contested from within, it suddenly finds itself facing a new abyss of time—a "dark abyss of time," to use the expression of Buffon (2018)—that has confronted the Christian regime of historicity with the deep time of geology and natural history. Today, the configuration is something "other." The confrontation is obviously no longer with the Christian regime of historicity, nor even with the modern regime, but very directly with presentism (Hartog 2020). For while it is certainly being questioned from various sides, presentism is nonetheless still active, insofar as its main operator, namely the digital "revolution," continues to progress. Yet the latter and all the transformations it induces and rapidly provokes in all societal sectors and individual lives are a matter of time (certainly that of *chronos*), even if very short, since we are moving in a universe of nanoseconds. Institutions and individuals are compelled to adjust to instant time, while, at the same time, they are confronted to a new and truly incommensurable time: plain time—ordinary *chronos*, but very long.

The destituted time of presentism is followed by a restituted time of *chronos* that we will have to learn to cope with. On the one hand, the immediate future is to enter a new condition, the "digital condition," by trying to preserve it or giving it a human face; on the other hand, the immediate future seems to be engulfed in a time that cannot be grasped. Like never before in human history, *chronos* is torn between a time so short that it almost disappears and a time so long that it escapes all representation. The new digital condition is also a condition torn or split between two radically incommensurable temporalities. What we need to know is whether it is possible to make a new historical condition out of this one. Between the time of the Anthropocene and that of microprocessors, could there be a historical time or a new historical time (Simon 2019)?

Seeking to grasp the temporal texture of the present, therefore, requires a double distancing movement. The first, ordinary and familiar one consists in taking a step back: observing the present as if we were not in it, to better see what it is made of. But today, extracting oneself from the presentist bubble is no longer enough. We have to make a second, much less familiar move: that of trying to look at the Earth, a planet among the planets, as if we were not part of it. This dual exercise of distanced gaze is somewhat more difficult, but turning away from it or postponing it would be cowardice. This is our task today, without giving in to the apocalyptic turmoil.

Translated by Corentin Marion

Notes

1   "Change is now" ("le changement, c'est maintenant") was the official slogan of François Hollande's presidential campaign in 2012. *[Note from the translator]*
2   For the English translation in three volumes, see Nora and Kritzman (1996–8).
3   In a survey conducted by the *OpinionWay Institute* in March 2019, 48 percent of French people believe it is too late to reverse the course of global warming. Collapsologists and survivalists are getting more and more media attention.

References

Buffon, Le Comte de, G.-LL. (2018), *The Epochs of Nature*. Trans. Jan Zalasiewicz, Anne-Sophie Milon and Matuesz Zalasiewicz. Chicago, IL: University of Chicago Press.

Hartog, F. (2015), *Regimes of Historicity: Presentism and Experiences of Time*. Trans. Saskia Brown. New York: Colombia University Press.

Hartog, F. (2016), *Croire en l'histoire*. Paris: Flammarion.

Hartog, F. (2020), *Chronos, L'Occident aux prises avec le temps*. Paris: Gallimard.

Koselleck, R. (2004), *Futures Past: On the Semantics of Historical Time*. Trans. Keith Tribe. New York: Columbia University Press.

Nora, P. (ed.) (1984–92), *Les Lieux de mémoire*. 7 vols. Paris: Gallimard.

Nora, P., and D. Lawrence Kritzman (eds.) (1996–8), *Realms of Memory: The Construction of the French Past*. 3 vols. Trans. Arthur Goldhammer. New York: Columbia University Press.

Simon, Z. B. (2019), *History in Times of Unprecedented Change: A Theory for the 21st Century*. London: Bloomsbury.

Stengers, I. (2015), *In Catastrophic Times: Resisting the Coming Barbarism*. Trans. Andrew Goffey. London: Open Humanities Press.

CHAPTER TWO

Framing the polychronic present

Victoria Fareld

Introductory remarks

In recent years, there has been an increasing interest among historians
in critically scrutinizing the temporal imaginary at the heart of historiographical practice (Assmann 2020; Tamm and Olivier 2019; Hartog 2015;
Lorenz and Bevernage 2013). In light of this current reworking of the
conceptual space of temporality in history, I will argue for the epistemic
gains to be made by framing the historical present as polychronic. Such a
framing would, I propose, not only help us to examine time conceptions
previously taken for granted and to get a greater understanding of how
time is produced and enacted through historical practices. It would
also direct our attention to the many ongoing pasts in the present and
enable us to analyze the changing presences of historical objects, rather
than assuming their specific location within an already chronologically
determined past. In such a framing, "historical understanding" would
also include "con-temporary" histories in the sense of "joined times" or
"times together"—that is, polychronic and polyphonic histories of the
many times present in the objects and phenomena we study.

Rethinking the practice of contextualization

A core assumption in the fields of historical studies is that historical
understanding requires contextualization. If we want to understand
something historically, we have to consider this something in context.

One doesn't have to adhere to the radical contextualism of Quentin Skinner (1988) and the Cambridge School of the history of ideas to agree upon the basic historicist assumption that if we take historical texts out of their contexts we risk misreading them. An essential task for historians is thus to understand objects, texts, ideas, and concepts within "their" historical contexts. If we fail to do so, we fail as historians.

Historians often argue for the importance of this practice based on a view of the past as something qualitatively different from the present. We who live in the present should be able to correctly situate the objects or phenomena of the past in "their" time and recognize the difference between this other time and our "own" time. Operative in this practice is an idea of temporal belonging, or an assumption that a thing of the past belongs, as it were, to its "own" time, even if it is materially also part of the present. This is why we keep saying that the *Mona Lisa* is a work of art from the sixteenth century, although it is obvious to everyone that it is also a thing of the present. In order to foster a historical understanding of this artwork, we are expected to restore it to its original context, to the context of its creation or first emergence, and recognize the difference between our (present) time and its (past) time. And along these lines, presentism, in the sense of mistakenly looking at the past from the perspective of the present, is understood as a failure to recognize this difference (Hunt 2002).

The historicist practice of contextualization sketched above has in recent decades become the target of critique by more or less explicit constructionist perspectives. Intellectual historian Peter E. Gordon rejects the assumed "holistic fit" between a phenomenon and its age that underwrites the hegemonic contextual practice in which the context is always already there as a "sphere that pre-exists the act of interpretation" (2014: 37, 43). When historicizing becomes tantamount to situating texts in already-defined contexts, we fail, he argues, to recognize that the epistemic potential of historical phenomena is so much greater than the circumstances of their historical emergence.

In a similar vein, literary scholar Rita Felski (2011) criticizes the use of contexts as already-defined temporal boxes, rebooting Bruno Latour's (1988, 2005) criticism of social context as container in favor of his performative idea of context as produced and constantly unfolding. Felski (2011: 581) emphasizes that there is "no compelling intellectual or practical reason why original context should remain the final authority and the last court of appeal"—that is, why epistemic priority should be given to the synchronic context of the studied text or object. And, as intellectual historian Martin Jay convincingly argues, when historical understanding relies upon an idea of context as always already there to give the studied phenomenon its proper historical significance, the temporal logic at play will make us able to recognize the familiar but unable to discover the unexpected, or the unforeseeable events that "can be understood less from the world that precedes them than from the posterity to which they give rise" (2011: 564, quote from Romano 2009: 38). A similar approach, although connected to a broader and more radical project, is that of historian Zoltán Boldizsár Simon, which calls for a new understanding of history that can account for and conceptualize "unprecedented change" (2019).

Despite differences in perspectives, these current articulations share a common interest in challenging hegemonic historical practices by offering alternative temporalities. The remaining pages of this chapter will explore some further manifestations of this ongoing refiguration of historical understanding today, pulling the diverging threads together in the concept of the polychronic historical present.

Understanding the historical present as polychronic

The standard temporal vocabulary of current historiography— chronology, synchrony, diachrony, anachronism—is not sufficient to rethink its temporal structure and analytical resources, nor to grasp the "chrononormativity" of the historiographical practice itself (Freeman 2010). A lot of intellectual effort today is thus invested in reinventing and enriching the temporal terminology, in order to provide historians with a more useful conceptual toolbox. With concepts like "outfluence" (Karlholm 2018), "polychronic assemblage" (Harris 2011), and "chronoference" (Landwehr and Winnerling 2019), it is possible to spot different ways to conceptualize the duration of the past within the historical present.

Let us return to the critical argument, touched upon in the previous section, that the temporal potential of objects is so much greater than what a conventional context-driven historical understanding can account for. In this respect, an urgent question for historians would be: How can the meaning of historical interpretation be transformed in order to also encompass explorations of a present made up of multiple times? Art historian Dan Karlholm uses the word "outfluence" to capture a way of historicizing works of art by focusing not on what they once were but on what they have become. Such an approach works from the assumption that "[h]istory does not predetermine but springs forth from the work of art" (2018: 17). In his words, to historicize a work of art in this way would mean to try "to establish what the work *is* with reference to what it *is in the process of becoming*," rather than to understand its present meaning "with reference to what it *was*" (2016: 45).

Gil Harris (2011: 617–18) articulates a similar critique against his own field, literary history, in which he states blatantly, "we quarantine the past in hermetically concealed necropoles called periods whose organizing principle is context." Instead, he wants to "expand the temporal possibilities" of the contextual work by "elements of the past [that] are always part of the polychronic assemblage that is the present" (618). Harris takes up Manuel De Landa's discussion of exoskeleton in the latter's *A Thousand Years of Nonlinear History* (1997) and uses the figure of the exoskeleton as a trope for the material presence of the past in the present. By referring to the transtemporal character of an exoskeleton as "enduring matter that, even as it asserts borders between body and world, crosses borders of time and period," Harris (2011: 620) articulates a conception of the past as the very *matter* of the present. And in doing so, he also articulates a critique of the epistemic priority given to the original context as the ground of historical understanding. By actualizing Fernand Braudel's notion of the *longue durée* as a concept of temporal infrastructure (1980), Harris argues for a view of historical context as a "transtemporal network that collates multiple periods and multiple organizations of temporality" (2011: 620). Harris's actualization of Braudel has some similarities with Helge Jordheim's (2012) influential reinterpretation of Reinhart Koselleck's theory of historical times as one offering a new way of understanding time as heterogeneous and multilayered rather than being a theory of periodization.

The current interest in questions of multitemporality does not, however, challenge periodization as an essential practice within the field of historical studies, nor does it threaten chronology as a dominant epistemic construct in historical understanding. But it does give rise to a new temporal consciousness which can help us to more clearly articulate the multiple times that the present harbors and, even more importantly, to grasp how these times relate to each other in a polychronic present.

Jordheim's emphasis on the practice of synchronization is essential here to understand the chrononormative underpinnings of the historicist time frame (2014, 2017).

We return to the example of the *Mona Lisa* mentioned above. An alternative way of articulating what we do when we state that the *Mona Lisa* is a sixteenth-century piece of art would be to say that we engage in a practice of bringing the ongoing becoming of this work of art to a standstill, or that we synchronize the multiple accumulated times of its existence into an established chronological temporal standard. Yet another way to express this would be to say—along with Achim Landwehr and Tobias Winnerling (2019) and their concept of "chronoference"— that we engage in a practice of regulating and relating different times in the present. Chronoference would thus refer to our way of establishing, through material objects, relations to times that no longer exist but are nevertheless present to us. This practice of relating times makes visible that we live not only in one time but in many times at once.

The present, defined by Landwehr and Winnerling (2019: 440) as "unpresent within itself because there are always so many other absent times present in it," is undoubtedly the major conceptual site for practices called "chronoferential" or "synchronizing." Let us now turn to this present, "unpresent within itself," and explore how ongoing practices of linking times could be used to further a historical understanding of our contemporary situation.

Understanding time conflicts

In the time of writing this article, statues and monuments in various parts of the world are subjects of mass protest following the global anti-racism demonstrations of the Black Lives Matter movement in the Spring of 2020. Confederate statues and monuments in the United States have been removed by authorities or torn down by protestors. Statutes of historical figures, today associated with oppression, colonialism, and racism, have also become a source of great controversy in the urban memorial landscapes of European cities. And in recent years, we have witnessed recurrent monument controversies raging from the Rhodes Must Fall movement in South Africa to the Ukrainian decommunization laws.

These current conflicts are often framed in an either/or logic: either the statues are removed or they continue to be displayed and commemorated, with or without contextual explanations. UK Prime

Minister Boris Johnson's call in June 2020 to let the statues remain in place, as we shouldn't try to "photoshop" history, or the Speaker of the House of Representatives in the US Nancy Pelosi's call to remove eleven statues in the Capitol Hill as they "pay homage to hate, not heritage," are telling expressions of this logic (Itkowitz 2020; Johnson 2020). The iconoclasts who call for a removal of the statues assert that they are a symptomatic presence of an oppressive past in the present, whereas their critics argue for the need to separate past and present, and to not let the past be kidnapped by present concerns.

In light of the discussion above about linking times, the monument controversies can be conceptually captured in terms of *chronoschisms*— that is, conflicts about how to understand the relationships between different times *in* the present. Let me take as an example the temporal conflicts that arose around the statue of Cecil Rhodes in Cape Town in South Africa in 2015, which launched the international student movement "Rhodes Must Fall." Activists demanded the removal of a statue commemorating Cecil John Rhodes, the British imperialist, mining magnate, and university patron, from the University of Cape Town campus, with the argument that it is a symbol not only of historical colonialism but of the institutional racism that still pervades higher education in South Africa (Chaudhuri 2016). In a statement published by the university's student representative council in support of the movement, the reason for still commemorating Rhodes on campus was heavily questioned:

> Rhodes has been praised for donating this land to the university, building the South African economy, and bringing "civilization" to this country. But for the majority of South Africans this is a false narrative, how can a colonizer donate land that was never his land in the first place? The statue is a constant reminder for many black students of the position in society that black people have occupied due to hundreds of years of apartheid, racism, oppression, and colonialism (Mahapa 2015: 1).

Different public opinions rapidly arose about the removal or non-removal of the Rhodes statue. Well-known author and public figure Eusebius McKaiser supported the removal, proclaiming that the nation's "historical amnesia has [now] come to an end" (McKaiser 2015), whereas public intellectual, Vice Chancellor of the University of the Free State, and President of the South African Institute of Race

Relations, Jonathan Jansen, described the call for removal as "not only anti-educational and anti-progressive, it is in fact to deny ourselves," and called for an engagement with the past that recognized Rhodes's "complex and troubled legacy and our own entanglements within it" (Jansen 2015). After a month of campaigning, the statue was removed from campus after a decision by the University of Cape Town Council (Ndungane 2015).

A productive approach that has the potential to break the temporal either/or logic that frames monument controversies such as Rhodes Must Fall is suggested by art historian Brenda Schmahmann (2016). Her proposal to make public monuments available to artists for temporary creative and critical interventions can, in my view, be seen as a work of relating times, which pays homage not to the past as much as to the polychronic present. And as such, it can actually promote a historical understanding of this present. One example discussed by Schmahmann is an action directed toward the Rhodes statue in question, performed by the cultural activist group Kultural Upstarts Kollective on Heritage Day in South Africa 2007, although removed soon after. In transforming Rhodes to a Black South African soccer supporter equipped with objects associated with working-class soccer fans—a miner's helmet, a plastic horn that fans blow during the games, giant sunglasses that are popular among supporters, as well as a cape with the words "*Whose seat is it anyway?*"—the activists critically engaged with the notion of heritage by unsettling the meaning of the historical claims of the statue. The miner's hat referred to Rhodes's diamond prospecting and a fortune created by forced labor, while the sunglasses in fact blocked his imperialist gaze and exploitative vision of the country.

Through the activists' interventions, the claim of the past on the future, materialized in stone, was transformed into a site of creative and critical engagement. They showed that the future's past of the statue does not have to affirm its claim with reference to what it was. It can productively engage with this claim by turning away from it, directing our attention to what the statue becomes in its shifting presents—by focusing on its outfluence. As one of the activists, Raffella Delle Donne, put it: "symbols like statues don't have to remain static reminders of our oppressive past, but can be reinvented in creative ways to make meaningful statements of the present" ("Recasting Cecil's Shadow" 2007). In such engagements, the present is more than a mirror of our contemporary selves. Rather, it becomes a polychronic space to be explored, with reference to the twofold meaning of contemporaneity—as the present time but also as "con-temporality"; that is, as an accumulation of multiple times or a space of temporal co-existence, highlighting the temporal fusion constitutive of the present. By framing the present as polychronic (rather than homochronic), we can set out to examine the meaning of multitemporality as a structural feature of historiography. In doing so, and by being more attentive to the different voices inhabiting this temporal space, we can hopefully offer more polyphonic versions of historical understanding today.

References

Assmann, A. (2020), *Is the Time Out of Joint? On the Rise and Fall of the Modern Time Regime*. Trans. S. Clift. Ithaca, NY: Cornell University Press.

Braudel, F. (1980), "History and Social Science: The Longue Durée," in F. Braudel, *On History*, 25–54, Chicago, IL: University of Chicago Press.

Chaudhuri, A. (2016), "The Real Meaning of Rhodes Must Fall," *Guardian*, March 16, 2016. Available online: http://www.theguardian.com/uk-news/2016/mar/16/the-real-meaning-of-rhodes-must-fall (accessed June 18, 2020).

Felski, R. (2011), "Context Stinks!" *New Literary History* 42(4): 573–91.

Freeman, E. (2010), *Time Binds: Queer Temporalities, Queer Histories, Perverse Modernities*. Durham, NC: Duke University Press.

Gordon, P. E. (2014), "Contextualism and Criticism in the History of Ideas," in D. M. McMahon and S. Moyn (eds.), *Rethinking Modern European Intellectual History*, 32–55, New York: Oxford University Press.

Harris, J. G. (2011), "Four Exoskeletons and No Funeral," *New Literary History* 42(4): 615–39.

Hartog, F. (2015), *Regimes of Historicity: Presentism and Experiences of Time*. Trans. Saskia Brown. New York: Columbia University Press.

Hunt, L. (2002), "Against Presentism," *Perspectives on History*: *The Newsmagazine of the American Historical Association*, May. Available online: http://www.historians.org/publications-and-directories/perspectives-on-history/may-2002/against-presentism (accessed June 18, 2020).

Itkowitz, C. (2020), "Nany Pelosi calls for removal of Confederate statues in Congress," *The Washington Post*, June 11, 2020. Available online: http://www.washingtonpost.com/politics/nancy-pelosi-calls-for-removal-of-confederate-statues-in-congress/2020/06/10/8c146ede-ab61-11ea-94d2-d7bc43b26bf9_story.html (accessed June 18, 2020).

Jansen, J. (2015), "Erase Rhodes? That Offends Me as a Teacher," *Rand Daily Mail*, March 26, 2015. Available online: http://www.sapeople.com/2015/03/27/erase-cecil-john-rhodes-offends-jonathan-jansen/ (accessed June 18, 2020).

Johnson, B. (2020), "Rather Than Tear Some People Down We Should Build Others Up," *The Telegraph*, June 14, 2020. Available online: http://www.telegraph.co.uk/politics/2020/06/14/rather-tear-people-should-build-others/ (accessed June 18, 2020).

Jordheim, H. (2012), "Against Periodization: Koselleck's Theory of Multiple Temporalities," *History and Theory* 51: 151–71.

Jordheim, H. (2014), "Introduction: Multiple Times and the Work of Synchronization," *History and Theory* 53: 498–518.

Jordheim, H. (2017), "Synchronizing the World: Synchronism as Historiographical Practice, Then and Now," *History of the Present* 7(1): 59–95.

Karlholm, D. (2016), "After Contemporary Art: Actualization and Anachrony," *The Nordic Journal of Aesthetics* 51: 35–54.

Karlholm, D. (2018), "Is History to Be Saved, Closed, or Restarted: Considering Efficient Art History," in D. Karlholm and K. Moxey (eds.), *Time in the History of Art: Temporality, Chronology, and Anachrony*, 13–25, New York: Routledge.

Landa, M. de (1997), *A Thousand Years of Nonlinear History*. New York: Swerve/Zone.

Landwehr, A., and T. Winnerling (2019), "Chronisms: On the Past and Future of the Relations of Times," *Rethinking History* 23(4): 435–55.

Latour, B. (1988), "A Relativistic Account of Einstein's Relativity," *Social Studies of Science* 18: 3–44.

Latour, B. (2005), *Reassembling the Social: An Introduction to Actor-Network-Theory*. Oxford: Oxford University Press.

Lorenz, C., and B. Bevernage (eds.) (2013), *Breaking Up Time: Negotiating the Borders Between Present, Past and Future*. Göttingen: Vandenhoek & Ruprecht.

Mahapa, R. (2015), "UCT SRC Press Release on UCT Student Protest." Available online: http://www.scribd.com/document/258502122/UCT-SRC-Press-Release-on-UCT-Student-Protest (accessed June 18, 2020).

Martin, J. (2011), "Historical Explanation and the Event: Reflections on the Limits of Contextualization," *New Literary History* 42(4): 557–71.

McKaiser, E. (2015), "South Africa's Odious Monument to Cecil John Rhodes," *New York Times*, March 26, 2015. Available online: http://www.nytimes.com/2015/03/27/opinion/eusebius-mckaiser-south-africas-odious-monument-cecil-john-rhodes.html (accessed June 18, 2020).

Ndungane, N. (2015), "UCT Council Votes in Favour of Removing Rhodes Statue," April 8, 2015. Available online: http://www.news.uct.ac.za/article/-2015-04-08-uct-council-votes-in-favour-of-removing-rhodes-statue (accessed June 18, 2020).

"Recasting Cecil's Shadow" (2007), *UCT News*, September 27, 2007. Available online: http://www.news.uct.ac.za/article/-2007-09-27-recasting-cecils-shadow (accessed June 18, 2020).

Romano, C. (2009), *Event and World*. Trans. S. Mackinlay. New York: Fordham University Press.

Schmahmann, B. (2016), "The Fall of Rhodes: The Removal of a Sculpture from the University of Cape Town," *Public Art Dialogue* 6(1): 90–115.

Simon, Z. B. (2019), *History in Times of Unprecedented Change: A Theory for the 21th Century*. London: Bloomsbury.

Skinner, Q. (1988), *Meaning and Context: Quentin Skinner and His Critics*. Edited by J. Tully. Princeton, NJ: Princeton University Press.

Tamm, M., and L. Olivier (2019), *Rethinking Historical Time: New Approaches to Presentism*. London: Bloomsbury.

CHAPTER THREE

Caught between past and future: On the uses of temporal figurations for political exclusion

Moira Pérez

"The radical contemporaneity of mankind is a project."

J. FABIAN, *TIME AND THE OTHER*, P. XXXIX

Introduction

An odd temporal paradox haunts the charming streets of Puerto Williams, Chile, the southernmost city in the world. While various public landmarks such as roads, cultural centers, and even a museum are built around the figure of the late Rosa, the "last member" of the (also late, following her decease) Yagán peoples,[1] visitors are also encouraged to walk around Villa Ukika, a small neighborhood east of town where the Yagán live and strive. How can the Yagán people still be there if the last one of them is gone? Does "Yagán" take on a different meaning in each case, or do they refer to two different forms of existence? Or should we just assume we are facing a perplexing temporal warp? Perhaps all of this is true—after all, identity, temporality, agency, and history work curiously with and against each other.

In this chapter, I will take this and other analogous cases to characterize temporal figurations and illuminate some aspects of how they are used to shape our political present and to select its inhabitants. In analyzing not temporality in itself but temporal figurations, I intend to draw attention to some of the political underpinnings and implications of their production. My aim, inspired by Rosa's case but moving beyond it, is to understand how such figurations are used as instruments to curtail individual and collective agency by pushing certain subjects out of the present, where political agency is possible, and into either an extinct past or an ever-postponed future.

The distribution of events and actors along chronological lines is central to historiographical practice, and the issue of who and what is included and under what terms has been intensely studied by feminist, decolonial, and post-colonial scholars (see Trouillot 1995; Scott 1989; Spivak 1985; de Sousa Santos 2010 for some examples). Temporal figurations—that is, the concrete, varying ways in which time is organized through representations (historiographical or other)—are a key instrument for the differential assortment of subjects and the allocation of agency. By producing these representations, we "figure" time—that is, we give it a concrete shape and contour—and define what is present, what is past, and what is future, and which subjects and social groups inhabit each. When read through the lens I propose here, collectives are not seen as essentially past, present, or future, but rather as being constituted as such through their own temporal figurations and those of others, particularly those occupying hegemonic social locations. The consequences of this are vital for the political configuration of any given society, since political agency involves the capacity to act in the present, an acknowledgement of such capacity by other groups, and the active participation in political decisions as well as in the distribution of life opportunities. In contrast, the social location of certain subjects makes it so that their agency is perpetually pushed away as they are exiled, time and time again, back to the temporal realm of what no longer is, or into what cannot yet be.

The last Yagán

That indigenous communities and cultures in Abya Yala (the region called "Latin America" following colonization) are conceived as something of the past both by the state and by society at large has been amply documented in scholarship both within and beyond said communities (Castanha 2010; Barbosa Becerra 2018; Delrio et al. 2018). In the words of Timoteo Francia of the Qom nation, "the indigenous person is usually seen as a synonym of backwardness, of unculture, or of the remains of a shameful past that should disappear" (Francia and Tola 2018: 56).

This temporal allocation can take the apparently benign form of "preservation," whereby the culture of indigenous peoples is understood as an always-past and static legacy which must be taken care of as a live archaeological site: "we are turned into a tourist attraction, a human zoo the culture of which must be preserved" as unblemished as possible (ibid.). Here, exile to a non-threatening past translates into the denial of historicity and culture through an imperative for purity and authenticity according to an externally allocated identity (Said 1980; Montoya 2017): being indigenous requires being "pure," but this implies being ahistorical, a live anachronism in the present, and this, in turn, will then be used to deny political agency. In these cases, the acknowledgement of a place in history—typically considered as liberatory—turns out to be oppressive in a way that Appiah has called "the Medusa Syndrome": "the gaze of recognition that ossifies what it sees" (2011: 95). Meanwhile, historiography is exempted from its task of historicization, as the study of these subjects and their "static" cultures is outsourced to other fields such as archaeology, anthropology, or area studies (Hamilton 2011).

Still, this is far from being the worse outcome for indigenous peoples regarding temporal figurations. On occasion, they are characterized as extinct, having existed only in the past, and as non-existent, possessing no agency in the present, not even to preserve themselves as "pure." This "primordialism," as Towle and Morgan (2002) have named it, is the case with the Yagán peoples referred to above. It implies ranking the world's societies "on a hierarchy of evolutionary stages from 'barbaric' to 'modern'" and relegating "non-Western" ones to the "primordial slot," defending the idea that "ancient history lives on in the contemporary lives of non-Western peoples, who are then called on to exemplify 'our sacred past'" (ibid.: 482–3). The use of expressions such as "Western" and "non-Western" suggests that these exclusions are fueled not only by temporal figurations but also by spatial ones, and the interplay between both. In fact, post-colonial analyses of cartography and mapping have shown how European cartographic representations "produce a chronologically ordered spatial distribution, in which the margins of the map, that is, all the other areas outside of Europe, are considered as inescapably belonging to the past of civilization, even to barbarity" (Bentouhami-Molino 2016: 21). Therefore, allotting communities to a certain space also entails situating them in a specific temporality, and vice versa.

This understanding of the interplay between spatial and temporal figurations at the service of exclusion owes much to Johannes Fabian's (2014) influential analysis on "allochronism" and Boaventura de Sousa Santos's (2010: 22) thoughts on the "non-contemporaneity of the contemporary"—i.e., the idea that "simultaneity hides asymmetries between the historical times that converge in it." Fabian refers to this as the "denial of coevalness" between the "same" and the "Other"—that is, the epistemic subject producing a certain narrative and those under scrutiny. His notion of "allochronism" reveals that the expulsion of certain subjects from the present is the result of a series of epistemic decisions and mechanisms based on "a system of coordinates (emanating of course also from a real center, the Western metropolis) in which given societies of all times and places may be plotted in terms of relative distance from the present" (Fabian 2014: 26). Through a series of manipulations of time and displacements along its axis, "[t]he Other's empirical presence turns into his theoretical absence, a conjuring trick which is worked with the help of an array of devices that have the common intent and function to keep the Other outside the Time of anthropology" (ibid.: xxxix). Hence the Yagán paradox, which combines theoretical absence (the last one of them died, therefore they are "extinct") and empirical presence (they live just a few steps away).

Needless to say, such temporal figurations are neither objective nor fortuitous, but rather contingent upon power relations and the place allocated to these collectives in our days, as "what to place in the past and what to include in the present does not depend on the time of the events, but on their future expectancies" (Liakos and Bilalis 2017: 209). What is past or present is not a content in itself, but rather a position, "just as I can point to something *over there* because I am *here*" (Trouillot 1995: 15). This is true, first, in a fundamental ontological sense: we describe the past as past because it once was, but is not "here" anymore. And, second, it is also true in a political sense: in this case, the present of those "over there" is produced as the past of those "here," and the present of the latter as the future of the former—one that might never come.

In other cases, subjects seem to jump from "our sacred past" to an unattainable future, always unable to inhabit the present. In the following section, I turn to these.

The first trans man

The past is not the only destination for those exiled from the present: apart from the "no longer," there is also a relentless "not yet" that denies or erases subjects' agency in the present, deferring it to an always-distant future. In his critique of European historicism, Dipesh Chakrabarty characterizes "the modern, European idea of history" precisely as "somebody's way of saying 'not yet' to somebody else," displacing them not to the past but to the future, or, in Chakrabarty's own suggestive expression, to "an imaginary waiting room of history" (2000: 8). History itself is transformed into "a version of this waiting room" (ibid.), as in its historicist version it gives shape not only to the past, but also to the present and the future. By ushering whole populations to such a place, suggesting that they wait for their turn, temporal figurations serve as an instrument that justifies colonization, tutelage, and political exclusion.

One notable example of this can be found in contemporary representations of trans male agency and its iterative birth. In the past decade, we have witnessed a growing number of narratives of "the first trans man" to fulfill a certain accomplishment or achieve a fundamental right, such as being accepted into an all-male institution, competing professionally in some sport, giving birth, or running for public office.[2] The most conspicuous issue with these representations is that they imply that trans men have not been (agents) in the past, erasing a rich history of social life, cultural contributions, and political mobilization. This erasure has direct consequences for the community's political life, since "history often lends legitimacy to a community's claim that it belongs in the here and now" (DeVun and Tortorici 2018: 521). Additionally, "given the frequent citation of history by policy makers, there is no doubt that—at least in certain contexts—we imagine a political value in rendering communities visible within history" (ibid.). On the contrary, novelty is often used to justify political exclusion, with the argument that since trans men have not heretofore been politically active or committed, they now must wait for "their turn" in the political agenda of social movements (Radi 2018).

Still, on a positive note it could be argued that in these cases (unlike those analyzed in the previous section) present individual agency is not denied but affirmed, even celebrated, through the recognition of a given milestone. Nevertheless, it is my contention that by repeatedly locating individual actions in the immediate present, the collective agency (transmasculine, in this case) is erased not only from the past but also from the present, and displaced to a future that is just being inaugurated (and will be, over and over again). Through the reiterated figuration of inaugural temporalities, the repetition of this "pioneering" discourse manages to create an image of novelty for the collective and to perpetuate the idea of the futurity of its agency (and, in some cases, of its very existence). Going back to Fabian's reading of presences and absences, here we find that although empirical presence is explicitly acknowledged, there is nevertheless a conceptual absence built alongside it, through the image of a repeated inauguration (of something that already exists).

This further proves how disenfranchisement can be presented under a celebratory or complimentary guise, just like indigenous nations can be suppressed through a call for the preservation of their "authenticity." At first glance, relegating a social group to the future seems better than consigning it to the past, but both cases imply subjects being located in another time—being denied coevalness, in Fabian's words—and excluded from the present as political agents. The causes for which they mobilize are also affected by this gesture, as their agendas are deemed anachronistic in either sense: "no longer" is it time for a certain cause, and "not yet," for another. The concrete outcome of both is the denial of political participation (past, present, and perhaps future) and the displacement of their agency toward other subjects. Just like discourses about "the last Yagán" assist in the whitening of Latin American societies even while apparently recognizing the contribution and legacy of those communities to it, narratives of "the first trans man" advance cissexist representations of trans experiences and subjects as ontologically and politically derivative in relation to a primarily cis world.

Temporal and political exiles

Temporal figurations, just like causal figurations (White 1999; Tozzi 2006), are effective instruments to "tidy up" events and subjects through time and space. This cleansing task, which is carried out from the present, is continuously reconfigured by disputes for meaning of who we are, who we are not, and who is allowed to be. Kwame Appiah has noted that collective history, including most notably national history, "is a question of what we choose to remember, not just in the sense of which facts we use for our public purposes, but equally in the sense that we choose which facts actually count as ours" (2011: 107). The same can be said, of course, of who we count as "our own" in the present, and who we are willing to include as "our own" in our imagined—and performed—futures. Despite the idea of national homogeneity prevalent in national (and nationalist) rhetoric, "historical processes of national formation involve a number of markings of difference and hierarchy between the populations that in a certain moment can or cannot constitute the nation" (Restrepo 2020: 282). Temporal figurations play a key role in this scenario: just like the past has been said to haunt the present, our ways of understanding and figuring time haunt our visions of present and future, including the places and political possibilities of marginalized groups in them.

In the two operations described above, hegemonic figurations effectively assign politically marginalized subjects and collectives to a deferred temporality, therefore displacing them from the present in which their political identity (that is, their identity as political agents) and perhaps their survival are at stake. We have seen how even in cases where the existence of marginalized subjects is recognized, and when they are, in fact, included in historical narratives (as "the first" or "the last"), they can still be denied an arc able to bring together past, present, and future. Such an arc, however, is vital for the historical understanding of every community, and for the historical consciousness of the people who compose it. Additionally, this erasure through temporal figuration goes hand in hand with exemption from epistemic and political responsibilities for hegemonic groups, since it is not possible to affirm that those who do not exist are being ignored or excluded, and therefore no responsibility can be demanded for said exclusion.

Resisting temporal exiles requires exposing the underpinnings of their figurations and affirming the political agency of these collectives in the past, the present, and the future. As Maya K'iche' scholar and activist Gladys Tzul Tzul has asserted in relation to indigenous community organizing, it is time for non-indigenous subjects to acknowledge the indigenous as political: against that "series of analytical machines that seek to think the indigenous only in the light of the ethnic, the cultural, the Other, or custom," it is time to acknowledge marginalized identities as sources of historical strategies and innovative political structures (2015: 139). If temporal figurations have historically been among those analytical machines used to exclude subjects—indigenous or other—from political agency, building the "radical contemporaneity of mankind" that Fabian imagined entails refiguring our narratives in ways that enable a plurality of trajectories linking past and future, thus bringing agents back into the present.

Notes

1   This is evident, for example, in the documentary film *La última Yagán* by Alfons Rodríguez (2015) and the museological proposal of the Martin Gusinde Anthropological Museum in Puerto Williams, articulated around the contributions of Rosa, "the last Yagán," who allegedly transmitted her knowledge of traditional language and customs before they perished with her. See also Pujals (2014).

2   See, for instance, "Patricio Manuel, the First Trans Boxer to Compete Professionally" (Levin 2018); "Meet Marius Mason, the First Trans Man to Transition in Federal Prison" (Lennard 2016); and "'The First Pregnant Man,' 10 Years Later: Thomas Beatie Reflects On A Difficult Decade" (Wilson 2018), where Beatie is still reduced to being "the first," even ten years down the road.

References

Appiah, K. A. (2011), "Identity, Politics and the Archive," in X. Mangcu (ed.), *Becoming Worthy Ancestors*, 89–108, Johannesburg: Wits University Press.

Barbosa Becerra, J. (2018), "Hijos de la Madre Tierra. Discursos sobre el derecho al territorio ancestral en sentencias de la Corte Constitucional colombiana (1992–2011)," MA diss., Universidad Nacional de La Plata, La Plata, Argentina.

Bentouhami-Molino, H. (2016), *Raza, Culturas, Identidades. Un enfoque feminista y poscolonial.* Trans. J. Lenarduzzi. Buenos Aires: Prometeo.

Castanha, T. (2010), *The Myth of Indigenous Caribbean Extinction: Continuity and Reclamation in Borikén (Puerto Rico).* New York: Palgrave Macmillan.

Chakrabarty, D. (2000), *Provincializing Europe. Postcolonial Thought and Historical Difference.* Princeton, NJ, and Oxford: Princeton University Press.

Delrio, W., D. Escolar, D. Lenton, and M. Malvestitti (eds.) (2018), *En el país de nomeacuerdo. Archivos y memorias del genocidio del Estado argentino sobre los pueblos originarios, 1870–1950.* Viedma: UNRN.

De Sousa Santos, B. (2010), *Descolonizar el saber, reinventar el poder.* Montevideo: Trilce Editorial.

DeVun, L., and Z. Tortorici (2018), "Trans, Time, and History," *Transgender Studies Quarterly* 5(4): 518–39.

Fabian, J. (2014), *Time and the Other. How Anthropology Makes its Object.* New York: Columbia University Press.

Francia, T., and F. Tola (2018), *Filosofía qom. Teoría toba sobre la alteridad.* Buenos Aires: Las Cuarenta.

Hamilton, C. (2011), "Why Archive Matters: Archive, Public Deliberation and Citizenship," in X. Mangcu (ed.), *Becoming Worthy Ancestors*, 119–44, Johannesburg: Wits University Press.

La última Yagán (2015), [Film] Dir. Alfons Rodríguez, Barcelona.

Lennard, N. (2016), "Meet Marius Mason, the First Trans Man to Transition in Federal Prison," *Splinter*, August 19, 2016. Available online: https://splinternews.com/meet-marius-mason-the-first-trans-man-to-transition-in-1793861288 (accessed February 28, 2020).

Levin, S. (2018), "Patricio Manuel, the First Trans Boxer to Compete Professionally: 'It Was Self-Preservation'," *Guardian*, December 21, 2018. Available online: https://www.theguardian.com/society/2018/dec/21/patricio-manuel-trans-boxer-made-history (accessed February 28, 2020).

Liakos, A., and M. Bilalis (2017), "The Jurassic Park of Historical Culture," in M. Carretero, S. Berger, and M. Grever, *Palgrave Handbook of Research in Historical Culture and Education*, 207–24, London: Palgrave Macmillan.

Montoya, L. M. (2017), "¿Quién Construye la Otredad? El rol del Estado en las reconfiguraciones étnicas. Los indígenas Mokaná del Atlántico Colombiano, un estudio de caso," *XVI Colombian Anthropology Congress*, Bogotá, Colombia.

Pujals, J. M. (2014), "La última yámana," *El País*, July 31, 2014. Available online: https://elpais.com/elpais/2014/07/31/planeta_futuro/1406816310_738367.html (accessed February 28, 2020).

Radi, B. (2018), "Political Mythology on Abortion and Trans Men," *Sexuality Policy Watch*, May 29, 2018. Available online: https://sxpolitics.org/political-mythology-on-abortion-and-trans-men/18439 (accessed February 28, 2020).

Restrepo, E. (2020), "Sujeto de la nación y otrerización," *Tabula Rasa* 34: 271–88.

Said, E. (1980), *Orientalism*. London and Henley: Routledge and Kegan Paul.

Scott, J. (1989), "History in Crisis: The Others' Side of the Story," *The American Historical Review* 94(3): 680–92.

Spivak, G. C. (1985), "Subaltern Studies: Deconstructing Historiography," in R. Guha (ed.), *Subaltern Studies IV: Writings on South Asian History and Society*, 330–63, Delhi: Oxford University Press.

Towle, E. B., and L. M. Morgan (2002), "Romancing the Transgender Native," *GLQ* 8(4): 469–7.

Tozzi, V. (2006), "La historia como promesa incumplida. Hayden White, heurística y realismo figural," *Diánoia* 51(57): 103–30.

Trouillot, M.-R. (1995), *Silencing the Past. Power and the Production of History*. Boston: Beacon Press.

Tzul Tzul, G. (2015), "Sistemas de gobierno comunal indígena: la organización de la reproducción de la vida," *El Apantle* 1: 127–40.

White, H. (1999), "Auerbach's Literary History. Figural Causation and Modernist Historicism," in *Figural Realism. Studies in the Mimesis Effect*, 87–100, Baltimore, MD: Johns Hopkins University Press.

Wilson, R. J. (2018), "'The First Pregnant Man,' 10 Years Later: Thomas Beatie Reflects on a Difficult Decade," *Urbo*, July 12, 2018. Available online: https://www.urbo.com/content/the-first-pregnant-man-10-years-later-thomas-beatie-reflects-on-a-difficult-decade/ (accessed February 28, 2020).

CHAPTER FOUR

In sync/Out of sync

Helge Jordheim

Anyone who has ever performed, or moved to the rhythm of music, will know the exhilarating, uplifting, and at the same time reassuring feeling of being *in sync*. Legs shift position at the same time, at the same pace, covering the same distance without ever bumping into each other. Sounds emerge at exactly the right moment and blend into harmony. Should any sound be out of tune, or any movement out of rhythm, they will most likely disappear into the great synchronized whole. Among the few historical studies of "in-syncness" is William H. McNeill's monograph on "dance and drill in human history," entitled *Keeping Together in Time* (1995). One of the most influential US historians, McNeill dedicated his career to understanding the importance of contact and exchange between civilizations in human history, in path-breaking works like *The Rise of the West* (1963) and *The Human Web* (2003). He opens this small and arguably somewhat strange little outlier of a book with a description of his experiences with basic military training when he was drafted into the US Army in September 1941:

> Words are inadequate to describe the emotion aroused by the prolonged movement in unison that drilling involved. A sense of pervasive well-being is what I recall; more specifically, a strange sense of personal enlargement; a sort of swelling out, becoming bigger than life, thanks to participation in collective ritual. … Obviously, something visceral was at work; something, I later concluded, far older than language

and critically important in history, because the emotion it arouses constitutes an indefinitely expansible basis for social cohesion among any and every group that keeps together in time. (1995: 2)

For McNeill (ibid.), the experience came down to "moving big muscles together and chanting, singing, or shouting rhythmically," summed up in the phrase "muscular bonding." The psychological effect of this sort of drill, he argues, gave the modern European armies their superiority. Similar synchronized movements, however, can be traced back to the Late Paleolithic and have as much a religious function as a military and political one. But the social behavior that McNeill traces historically in *Keeping Together in Time* and that I here call "in-syncness," is not limited to dance or drill, and generally to non-linguistic, muscular, and emotional activities; it also involves other forms of social cohesion and communal life. Both dance and drill are embedded in semantic fields and discursive practices, and their meaning cannot be reduced to affective, non-discursive, non-semantic "muscular bonding." Far from the only form of human synchronization, dance and drill are part and serve as emblems of larger social and political processes: revolutions, totalitarian ideologies, or consumer capitalism. This gives us the first hint that "in-syncness" and, by consequence, "out-of-syncness" refer to more general social and political conditions, which themselves have their own history and historicity. In the following, I will sketch a possible way to explore these temporal conditions as well as the work involved in bringing non-synchronous movements of human and non-human life into sync.

Work of synchronization

In McNeill's study of dance and drill, two sets of historical presuppositions stand out. Firstly, the study illustrates how every society, every collective finds itself in a constant, never-ending struggle to achieve "in-syncness" in order to build and maintain social cohesion, or indeed to break with it by means of revolution, or war. Secondly, we are made aware of how "in-syncness" is never a natural or constant condition, but always involves work, which might be muscular, as in the case of dance and drill, or semiotic, in the use of language, signs, or media. History does not come with inherent rhythms or standards—neither on the small or the large scale, neither in the short or the long term; these are always produced and imposed by people who are in a position to do so: drill sergeants, musical conductors, political leaders, or university professors are just a few of these possible rhythm-keepers.

By contrast, a lot of historical work seems to presuppose that there is always a given standard, a kind of "in-syncness" in history, often appearing under the name of "modernization," "civilizing process," or "democratization," that other forms of behavior deviate from what Herder in one of his texts on universal history calls *Maß* (measure) (1997: unpag.). Deviations mostly come in the form of "belatedness," to use Homi Bhabha's term (1994), or in the case of Germany, simply a *Sonderweg* (special path) (Winkler 2006).

In this entry, I want to suggest another approach. Instead of presuming that any historical collective, temporal and spatial, like the nation-state or indeed Western modernity, possesses inherent "in-syncness," marking a temporal and developmental standard, we should take as our analytical starting point the condition of "out-of-syncness." The baseline for human existence on Earth is that we are out of sync with each other, as well as with our surroundings, simply because we live in a condition of multiple, heterogeneous, and diverging times. Everybody is familiar with how the Circadian clock, governing our sleeping patterns, might be radically out of sync with our working schedules; or how four-year election cycles make long-term planning, for example in cutting carbon emissions, all but impossible; or even how the times of technological progress, for instance in the fields of genetic engineering and artificial intelligence, render our ethical views of human life progressively obsolete (Simon 2019). In other words, if human collectives appear to be in sync with themselves and their surroundings. it is due to hard, painstaking work, like when a group of soldiers are learning to march. From the condition of "out-of-syncness," collectives are formed by work of synchronization, using clocks and calendars, but also concepts and narratives, symbols and images. A lot has been written on the synchronization of local and global times, brought about by communication technologies like trains, planes, and phones and supported by the mass production of watches. But other "tools" have been just as efficient, such as concepts like "progress" or "crisis" (Jordheim and Wigen 2018; Jordheim 2019), or narratives of modernization, liberation, and national awakening. As in McNeill's example from his own military training, these acts of synchronization are linked to questions of power and hierarchy, but often not as explicitly as in the case of the yelling drill sergeant.

Conditions of out-of-syncness: Enzensberger's "Norwegian Anachronisms"

If historical subjects act in sync with each other, or if historical processes unfold according to the same rhythm, this is due to "work of synchronization" on the part of historical actors as well as historians. In other words, there is nothing divergent or surprising about societies experiencing conditions of being out of sync, either with themselves, with their surroundings, or with other societies or collectives. Keeping this in mind, we shall return to the considerable literature analyzing "out-of-syncness" in history, inspired especially by German phenomenology and historicism. At the level of language, "out-of-syncness" represents a somewhat hapless English translation of a German expression, *die Gleichzeitigkeit des Ungleichzeitigen*, or in some cases, *die Ungleichzeitigkeit des Gleichzeitigen*, which has enjoyed a mixed career in European intellectual history, having been associated with colonialism, National Socialism, and right-wing revisionism (Landwehr 2012). Previous translations of this "untranslatable," to use Barbara Cassin's term (2004), have included "the contemporaneity of the non-contemporaneous," the "simultaneity of the non-simultaneous," and the "synchronicity of the non-synchronous"—as well as the more polemical and more successful "denial of coevalness," which will be discussed below. At the level of theory, however, "out-of-syncness" allows us to reflect on what I consider to be the basic condition of historicity: multiple times, or temporalities, at work in any historical moment or event, operating at different speeds, rhythms, or intervals (Jordheim 2014).

One of the most succinct representations of "out-of-syncness" is found in an essay about early-1980s Norway by the German poet, novelist, and intellectual Hans Magnus Enzensberger:

> Norway's clocks always ticked differently than those on the continent. This country is the empire of non-synchronicity [*das Reich der Ungleichzeitigkeit*] … On the one hand, [the Norwegian society] loves anachronism and clings to pre-modern ways of thinking and living. On the other hand, it is inclined to thoughtless anticipations of the future. (1987: 310, my translation)

In the style of the essay, Enzensberger associates the time-measuring operations of the clock with particular historical conditions, emotions, mentalities, lifestyles. He wants to grasp a specifically Norwegian kind of historicity, characterized by extreme belatedness and an avantgardeness that is just as extreme, which leaves the country in a condition of non-synchronicity with itself: *Ungleichzeitigkeit*. Enzenberger's use of the clock and the "anachronism" as analytical tools to understand Norwegian society comes with all kinds of problems, among them his choice of the term "pre-modern" to describe people living in what is historically an absolutely modern society, as well as an implied distinction between "thoughtless" and thoughtful "anticipations of the future." Nevertheless, people, both pre- and post-modern, who lived in Norway in the 1980s when social democracy experienced its neo-liberal, oil-fueled makeover will recognize immediately what he is referring to.

Enzenberger, a non-historian, here makes a precise and powerful historical observation, which since then has been accepted by Norwegians as a fair description of this historical moment, and which today can be updated to fit the end of the oil age. But there is nothing specifically Norwegian about a nation being out of sync with itself; on the contrary, out-of-syncness is a crucial part of any society's, any collective's historical existence: in other words, its historicity. What emerges, then, from the sets of arguments and observations presented above, is a different analytics of history, operating from a theory of multiple times and analyzing conditions of out-of-syncness, as well as work of synchronization taking place in specific historical situations and contexts. Rather than attributing historical moments and events to epochs or periods, "temporal regimes" (Assmann 2013), or "regimes of historicity" (Hartog 2015) and making sweeping statements about historical shifts, we could start analyzing the specific ways in which societies, from the very small to the very large, are out of sync with themselves, and what they do to come to terms with their own out-of-syncness. This would take us directly into a history of tensions, conflicts, and struggles—in other words, a history of politics. In particular, this vein of thinking about time and history can help historians of the past, the present, or the future, to break free of different "centrisms"—Eurocentrism, Anthropocentrism, Androcentrism—and include more lives and thus more times in the way we think about history. Theories about the syncing and unsyncing of history have been produced mainly in German historiography, which will be the point of departure for the following theoretical and methodological reflections.

Theories of out-of-syncness: From Pinder to Fabian

Although earlier forays have taken place in fields like theology and philology, attempts to theorize what I call "out-of-syncness" start in German art history. The first to think systematically about *die Gleichzeitigkeit des Ungleichzeitigen*, and to use the term, is the art historian Wilhelm Pinder in the 1926 work *Das Problem der Generation in der Kunstgeschichte Europas* (The Problem of Generation in European Art History). Pinder (1961: 35) developed the trope in order to criticize "die fälschende Idee eindimensionaler geschichtlicher Zeitstrecken" (the false idea of one-dimensional historical time spans), in which one work succeeds another in an endless row. Only anonymous art history, he claims, can proceed this way and postulate the existence of historical epochs and epochal thresholds. As soon as history is populated with people, it dissolves into multidimensional and polyphonic time spaces. To make sense of this populated history, Pinder concludes that historians should replace the idea of epochs or periods with the idea of *generations*. People belonging to the same generation share experiences, styles, and aesthetic and intellectual preferences, which come together into what he terms a *Generations-Entelechie*, an inherent generational goal (155).

In this way, separate generations with their own separate goals come to represent multiple co-existing times. This idea of the co-existence of generations in a specific historical moment is developed in more social, even sociological terms by Karl Mannheim in an essay published only two years after Pinder's book. In this, the later world-famous sociologist concludes that an analysis of history unfolding is impossible without an exploration of the phenomenon of generation, in which he recognizes an entanglement of forces giving rise to historical dynamism (Mannheim 1928: 329). To what extent the concept of "generation" stands up to analytical scrutiny, is not the issue here; rather, "generation" represents one way of pluralizing historical and social times by aligning them with biological aging processes on a collective level.

Following Pinder and Mannheim, there are two other versions of *Gleichzeitigkeit des Ungleichzeitigen* or "out-of-syncness" that need to be mentioned here: one political and one anthropological. In his 1935 book *Erbschaft dieser Zeit*, the German Marxist philosopher Ernst Bloch points out how in Germany between the two world wars "not everybody inhabits the same now." In reality, people have "different times," dependent mainly on their social class (Bloch 1985: 104). National Socialism knew how to exploit these conflicting temporal experiences by mobilizing an "out-of-syncness" characterized by aggression and rage, and linked to a haunting, unredeemed past (ibid.: 122). According to Bloch, only socialism was able to resynchronize the present into a revolutionary now, in which a not-yet-realized future was contained and could be released by revolutionary action (ibid.). In this way, a historical analysis of conflicting temporalities, temporal experiences coming in and out of sync, in the present was mobilized for political purposes.

The scholar who took "out-of-syncness" out into the world, beyond the remits of German history, was the social anthropologist Johannes Fabian. In *Time and the Other* (1983), he launched a systematic and theoretically founded attack on practices of temporalization in anthropology and ethnology. Fabian's concept of "coevalness," which has had a major impact on human and social science scholarship in the post-war era, originated as a translation of the German *Gleichzeitigkeit* and expressed "a need to steer between such closely related notions as *synchronous/simultaneous* and *contemporary*," which correspond to physical and chronological time and typological and historical time, respectively: "*coeval* … covers both ('of the same age, duration, or epoch')." Beyond that, he uses it to connote a common active "occupation, or sharing, of time" (Fabian 2014: 31). "Denial of coevalness," on the other hand, comes down to a willful use of out-of-sync tropes in order to keep people out of the present of Western scholarship. Fabian defines it as "*a persistent and systematic tendency to place the referent(s) of anthropology in a Time other than the present of the producer of anthropological discourse*" (ibid.). That someone can be denied coevalness, however, does not mean that coevalness existed in the first place, other than as a language game, a game of synchronization, practiced by a generation of anthropologists and other Western scholars—who, again, were also in other ways out of sync with each other and with their surroundings.

A new analytics of history: Koselleck

In historiography, the most intellectually challenging version of "out-of-syncness" comes out of the essays by the German historian and theorist of history Reinhart Koselleck. Alongside his relentless work on the eight-volume lexicon *Geschichtliche Grundbegriffe* (1972–92), Koselleck produced fragments of a theory of historical times, though he never pieced them together into a coherent theoretical whole. At the core of this sustained, tireless engagement with times in plural—prompting John Zammito to place Koselleck's scholarly persona in the category of "hedgehog" (2004: 126)—is the idea of *die Gleichzeitigkeit des Ungleichzeitigen*.

In his criticism of Koselleck, Achim Landwehr dismisses *die Gleichzeitigkeit des Ungleichzeitigen* as a trope used by representatives of Western modernity to expel non-Western and non-modern cultures to a place outside of history, with or without the ability to catch up (2012: 20–7). As part of the same move, less progressive aspects of Western history such as the murky origins of sovereignty are suppressed, in order, in Kathleen Davis's words, to "sanitize its politics" (2008: 87). Rather than quarreling with Landwehr and Davis, my argument here is that "out-of-syncness" is not an exception or deviation from a "chronocentric" (Landwehr 2012: 20) standard but, on the contrary, represents an inherent condition in any society and any period of history.

In the works of Pinder, Bloch, and Fabian, "out-of-syncness" is linked to social categories like generation, class, and ethnicity—in other words, to social groups that have their own collective times. Koselleck, on the other hand, theorizes "out-of-syncness" on at least three analytically distinct levels: conceptual history, philosophical anthropology, and natural history. At all these levels, in language, in human behavior, and in our physical surroundings, multiple and conflicting times are operating, coming in and out of sync with each other.

On the first level, the task of conceptual history, or *Begriffsgeschichte*, is to study "the synchronicity of the nonsynchronous, contained in a concept" or, in other words, "die Mehrschichtigkeit von chronologisch aus verschiedenen Zeiten herrührenden Bedeutungen eines Begriffs" (different layers of conceptual meanings with different chronological origins) (Koselleck 1979: 125; see also Jordheim 2005, 2010). Concepts carry with them meanings that originated in another historical moment or period, like the concept of "revolution," most recently applied to the Arab spring, that aggregates within it experiences of other revolutions: the French, the Russian, the Iranian, etc. In this way, concepts might serve as "tools of synchronization" in which different times are aligned and calibrated, brought into sync, in order to act shape or act upon the present moment. "Progress" and "crisis" are other examples of concepts that assemble and synchronize historical events in similar ways (Jordheim and Wigen 2018).

In other texts, Koselleck shifts his discussion of "out-of-syncness" from a conceptual to an anthropological level, drawing on Heideggerian notions of human finitude as well as on Johann Gustav Droysen's *Historik*. At this level, he is not addressing historical events in their own right, but rather their pre-linguistic and pre-phenomenological "conditions" (Koselleck 2000: 98). These "conditions for possible histories" take the form of dichotomies: above/below, inside/outside, sooner/later (Koselleck 2000: 99–110; 2006: 33–6; see also Hoffmann 2010). But the most fundamental of these dichotomies is in sync/out of sync. Even the spatial dichotomies are fundamentally expressions of this underlying temporal dichotomy, since they all represent "tensions, conflicts, discontinuities, inconsistencies" that "cannot be solved in the present, but that all involved parties need to solve diachronically in order to live on or perish" (Koselleck 2000: 110). Anthropologically speaking, instances of "out-of-syncness" are thus the drivers of history, which we as historians need to identify and analyze to understand historical actors, events, and processes.

In a third set of essays, Koselleck increasingly pushes his thinking beyond the scope of human experience and actions and engages with natural conditions for possible histories. In addition to the philological and the anthropological, these texts present a version of *die Gleichzeitigkeit des Ungleichzeitigen* that most of all seems akin to a kind of natural history, signaled by the introduction of the term *Zeitschichten*, "layers of time" (Koselleck 2000). In a recent edition, the alternative English translation "sediments of time" is offered, bringing the concept back into the context of geology (Koselleck 2018). In an often-ignored entry in *Lexikon Geschichtswissenschaft*, Koselleck points out that both in nature and in history "the times pluralize themselves, they are attributed to cosmic, or social and political systems, which each lay claim on their own time" (2003: 334). In thinking about natural history, Koselleck envisions a plurality of times that cannot be reduced to differences of culture, language, and class, but in which geological, biological, and cosmological times introduce other sets of temporal differences that need to be included in historical understanding. In his essays, Koselleck thus paves the way for questions that haunt historians and other scholars at the present time: how can the long-term geological time of the Anthropocene be combined with the ever-accelerating times of local and global politics (Chakrabarty 2009)?

Conclusion: History in the now

In the last decades, a temporal tear has opened up between economic and technological progress and the survival of the planet, due to accelerating global warming, and even more recently between capitalist economy and population survival, brought about by the COVID-19 crisis. These new forms of "out-of-syncness" give rise to new attempts at synchronization, involving new tools and practices. Across the globe, actors find themselves locked in attempts at resynchronizing communities and societies in response to challenges and threats emerging in the *longue-durée* time of natural history. In the case of COVID-19, concepts like "crisis" and "pandemic" are mobilized to make sure that global audiences feel part of the same present and thus feel compelled to follow the same measures of disease control—all while awaiting the next major moment of synchronization: the distribution of vaccines. Historians are also involved in this work to synchronize the present, most prominently by applying well-rehearsed strategies of periodization. By taking on board the period label "the Anthropocene," the multiple times of natural and human history, produced in fields like geology, climate science, biology, and indeed history, are aligned and calibrated to fit ongoing events or processes, in homes, parliaments, and the atmosphere. These acts of synchronization are crucial for bringing about political action, but they are also highly normative, contestable, and political, and thus need to be historicized and analyzed. Rather than sticking to modernist tropes like standard/deviation, before/after, inside/outside, historians could shift their attention to practices and tools of synchronization, others' and their own, especially those that are not as conspicuous and indeed muscular as military drill or religious dance.

References

Assmann, A. (2013), *Ist die Zeit aus den Fugen? Aufstieg und Fall des Zeitregimes der Moderne*. Munich: Carl Hanser Verlag.

Bhabha, H. K. (1994), "Race, Time and the Revision of Modernity," in *The Location of Culture*, 236–56, London/New York: Routledge.

Bloch, E. (1985), *Erbschaft dieser Zeit*. Erweiterte Ausgabe, Frankfurt am Main: Suhrkamp.

Cassin, B. (ed.) (2004), *Vocabulaire européen des philosophies. Dictionnaire des intraduisibles*. Paris: Le Seuil/Le Robert.

Davis, K. (2008), *Periodization and Sovereignty. How Ideas of Feudalism and Secularization Govern the Politics of Time*. Philadelphia, PA: University of Pennsylvania Press.

Enzenberger, H. M. (1987), *Ach Europa! Wahrnehmungen aus sieben Ländern. Mit einem Epilog aus dem Jahre 2006*. Frankfurt am Main: Suhrkamp.

Fabian, J. (2014), *Time and the Other. How Anthropology Makes Its Object*. With a New Postscript by the Author. Foreword by Matti Bunzl. New York: Columbia University Press.

Hartog, F. (2015), *Regimes of Historicity. Presentism and Experiences of Time*. New York: Columbia University Press.

Herder, J. G. (1997), Review of Schlözer's *Vorstellung, Frankfurter gelehrte Anzeigen*, reprinted in August Ludwig Schlözer, *Vorstellung seiner Universal-Historie* (1772/73). Edited by Horst Walter Blanke. Waltrop: H. Spenner.

Hoffmann, S.-L. (2010), "Koselleck, Arendt, and the Anthropology of Historical Experience," *History and Theory* 49(2): 212–36.

Jordheim, H. (2005), "Die 'Gleichzeitigkeit des Ungleichzeitigen' als Konvergenzpunkt von Zeitlichkeit und Sprachlichkeit. Zu einem Topos aus dem Werk Reinhart Kosellecks," *Divinatio. Studia Culturalogica Series* 22: 77–90.

Jordheim, H. (2010), "'Unzählbar viele Zeiten.' Die Sattelzeit im Spiegel der Gleichzeitigkeit des Ungleichzeitigen," in Hans Joas and Peter Vogt (eds.), *Begriffene Geschichte. Beiträge zum Werk Reinhart Kosellecks*, 449–80, Frankfurt am Main: Suhrkamp.

Jordheim, H. (2014), "Introduction: Multiple Times and the Work of Synchronization," *History and Theory* 53(4): 498–518.

Jordheim, H. (2017), "Synchronizing the World: Synchronism as Historiographical Practice, Then and Now," *History of the Present* 7(1): 59–95.

Jordheim, H. (2019), "Making Universal Time. Tools of Synchronization," in Hall Bjørnstad, Helge Jordheim, and Anne Régent-Susini (eds.), *Universal History and the Making of the Global*, 133–50, New York: Routledge.

Jordheim, H., and Wigen, E. (2018), "Conceptual Synchronisation: From Progress to Crisis," *Millennium: Journal of International Studies* 46(3): 421–39.

Koselleck, R. (1979), *Vergangene Zukunft. Zur Semantik historischer Zeiten*. Frankfurt am Main: Suhrkamp.

Koselleck, R. (2000), *Zeitschichten. Studien zur Historik*. Frankfurt am Main: Suhrkamp.

Koselleck, R. (2003), "Zeit," in S. Jordan (ed.), *Lexikon Geschichtswissenschaft*. Stuttgart: Reclam.

Koselleck, R. (2006), *Begriffsgeschichten. Studien zur Semantik und Pragmatik der politischen und sozialen Sprache*. Frankfurt am Main: Suhrkamp.

Koselleck, R. (2018), *Sediments of Time. On Possible Histories*. Trans. Sean Franzel and Stefan-Ludwig Hoffmann. Stanford, CA: Stanford University Press.

Landwehr, A. (2012), "Von der 'Gleichzeitigkeit des Ungleichzeitigen'," *Historische Zeitschrift* 295: 1–34.

McNeill, W. H. (1995), *Keeping Together in Time. Dance and Drill in Human History*. Cambridge, MA: Harvard University Press.

Mannheim, K. (1928), "Das Problem der Generationen," *Kölner Vierteljahrshefte für Soziologie* 7: 157–85, 309–30.

Pinder, W. (1961), *Das Problem der Generation in der Kunstgeschichte Europas*. München: Bruckmann.

Simon, Z. B. (2019), *History in Times of Unprecedented Change: A Theory for the 21st Century*. London: Bloomsbury.

Thompson, E. P. (1967), "Time, Work-Discipline, and Industrial Capitalism," *Past & Present* 38: 56–97.

Winkler, H. A. (2006), *Germany: The Long Road West.* Vol. 1: 1789–1933. Trans. Alexander J. Sager. New York: Oxford University Press.

Zammito, J. (2004), "Koselleck's Philosophy of Historical Time(s) and the Practice of History," *History and Theory* 43(1): 124–35.

CHAPTER FIVE

Favoring an offensive presentism

Lars Deile

Spatiotemporal expansions

If you travel from inland to the North Sea, to Friesland or Holland, at some point you will stand dejectedly in front of a hill and look in vain for the sea. First comes the dike. But even behind it, the waves of the sea do not roar. Instead, one encounters strangely muddy areas (Figure 5.1), an intermediate space that is neither land nor sea, a landscape of constructed ditches and embankments, partly still underwater, partly already overgrown, a tiled landscape of polders and walls.

With the use of wind pumps, a spatial expansion in the North Sea began in the fifteenth century which is referred to as "Landgewinnung" in German, and even more sharply as "land reclamation" in English, and to which one-sixth of the territory of today's Netherlands owes its existence (De Mulder, De Pater, and Droogleever Fortuijn 2019). Water regulation systems already existed in Mesopotamia. But spatial expansion is in a special way a characteristic of Western modernity. What began in the marshlands of the North Sea was later continued overseas. Conquest is a particular trait of modernity (Bartlett 1993), occurring in quite comprehensive contexts which include geographical surveying as well as scientific drive, accompanied by violence as an assumed appropriate means of enforcing claims that are perceived as legitimate.

FIGURE 5.1 Harry H. Zimmermann, *Landgewinnung in Dithmarschen* (2018).

This expansion of modernity is not limited to space. It also characterizes how time is dealt with. To imagine the past, the present, and the future as separate, delimitable (and conquerable) periods—not merely as time that has passed by (*Vergangenes*), is current (*Gegenwärtiges*), or is forthcoming (*Zukünftiges*)—was an innovation of the seventeenth and especially the eighteenth century (Hölscher 1999; Fritzsche 2004: 201; Hölscher 2020: 49). When Johann Christoph Gatterer founded a Historical Academy in Göttingen in 1764, he oriented himself methodologically to early-eighteenth-century geographical surveying techniques—starting from a fixed zero point, dividing into a regular grid, and recording the contents found there—which later became the chronological order of historical studies, too (Gatterer 1775, 1777; Hölscher 2020: 38–41). Once the continuous premodern notion of time had been divided into time periods and sealed in, the relations of these time periods to each other could also be brought into sharper focus.

Reinhart Koselleck, among others (Dux 1989: 350–61; Fritzsche 2004: 11–54), has very plausibly described how these time structures, and, indeed, the "configuration of time" (Gumbrecht 2014: xii), have changed in modernity. Whereas before the *Sattelzeit* people saw themselves in a "seemingly continuous space of experience" (Koselleck 2004: 27) with the past, the accelerating turbulence of events around 1800 generated a new horizon. The future firmed itself as the new temporal power of orientation (ibid.: 40). This was accompanied by a new relationship to the past. The past could be understood as done and closed and different, and thus became accessible. It could be researched, measured, appropriated, or used as a projection screen for desires and losses. It became a political object (Clark 2019). It could be managed and was now actually only available as an object of investigation, because this allowed the investigator to no longer be part of that investigated. David Armitage (forthcoming) has put it better: "A fish may not be able to analyse the medium in which it swims, but humans ... certainly can do so." At the same time, history (in the singular, and in German even with the definite article) acquired the status of a teleological entity with a striving toward the future, as Friedrich Schiller put it in a nutshell in his famous inaugural speech in Jena in 1789. Instead of gathering and documenting fragments of the past, he was concerned with the philosophical shaping of a course of history, of a *Gewordensein* that led to the present and the future (Muhlack 1995; Schiller 2006; Hölscher 2018). In the process, the moment of the present became the decisive, the shapable lapse of time (Landwehr 2014). It was here that a decision could be made about whether humans would rise to their predetermined task or, alternatively, fail to substantiate the future. Schiller's contemporary Herder spelled this out as the "Second Genesis" (1887: 348).

Whereas in the seventeenth and eighteenth centuries this order of time still stood as one possibility alongside other ideas (such as cyclical, continuous, or simultaneous), the expansive model prevailed in the late nineteenth century. The past became an object of historical exploration and the future a meadow to be played on. Those who thought of closing themselves off to this very idea of progress (Koselleck and Meier 1975; Speich-Chassé 2012) were themselves quickly threatened with ending up in the dustbin of history.

The threat of presentism

François Hartog has summarized Koselleck's ideas very succinctly and developed them further by describing ideal-typical dominant forms in which the past, present, and future are related to each other, capturing these forms in the concept "regimes of historicity" (*régime d'historicité*)

(Hartog 1996, 2015, 2016). An old regime (*régime ancien*) and a modern regime (*régime modern*) part ways in the *Sattelzeit* period described by Koselleck (1972). Hartog (2010: 86) claims, however, that at present these modes, the one related to the past and the one related to the future, no longer function:

> But if, as is currently apparent, the future can teach us nothing anymore and disappears from the horizon, the present tends to become its own and only horizon. Then a (previously unknown) regime is establishing: the regime of presentism (le régime du présentisme).

Hartog's concept has rightly received much attention (and criticism as well). It brings the configuration of our time to the point, makes it understandable. With a cool head and intellectual elegance, Hartog analyzes phenomena as diverse as the spreading culture of memory, the growth of nostalgia, or the heritage boom of our days. Increasingly, the only way of dealing with the past seems to be its exploitation for the needs of the present. This presentism eats up everything and digests it according to the rules of its own limitations.

Whereas Hartog almost never criticizes this in severe terms, others more explicitly do. David Armitage (forthcoming), for instance, has taken up Hartog's theorem and states:

> If the present is indeed omnipresent, then it may fall to historians, as students of time and change, to compare this condition with other historical "regimes", and to provide a perspective on our current presentism to cure perspectival presentism. ... Only then might we hope to escape what another contemporary French historian has ominously termed "the tyranny of the present".

Presentism is thus understood as a plague that one should get rid of as soon as possible if one does not want to fall victim to its "tyranny" (Baschet 2018). Aleida Assmann (2013: 320–2) has elaborated that "today one [can] no longer be safe from any past that one once thought one had settled once and for all and laid to rest." She worries about a possible "permanent inundation" and the danger of "general apathy" because at the same time the future is flooding the present, although, and perhaps precisely because, it has nothing more to offer as "the prospect of permanent renewal and progress has become an empty promise." Hans Ulrich Gumbrecht (2014: xiii) also exercises intellectual composure in the face of an almost hopelessly broad present:

> That we no longer live in historical time can be seen most clearly with respect to the future. For us, the future no longer presents itself as an open horizon of possibilities; instead, it is a dimension increasingly closed to all prognoses—and which, at the same time, seems to draw near as a menace. Global warming will proceed with all the consequences that have been foreseen for quite some time; the question remains whether humanity will manage to accrue sufficient credit for a few additional years before the most catastrophic consequences of the situation arrive. … [A]nother problem the new chronotope presents is that we are no longer able to bequeath anything to posterity. Instead of ceasing to provide points of orientation, *pasts* flood our present; automated, electronic systems of memory play a central role in the process. Between the pasts that engulf us and the menacing future, the present has turned into a dimension of expanding simultaneities.

What all authors have in common is a sense of loss of temporal order and the fear (Fritzsche 2004: 215) of losing agency in the process. This becomes clearest in the analogy Assmann uses: like Hamlet, we can move neither forward nor backward and get caught in the self-created torments of deeply felt hopelessness.

The real problem

Whether the presentism thesis is tenable remains to be seen (Lorenz 2019; Hölscher 2020: 55–8). However, it helps us to thoroughly break open common notions of time (Lorenz and Bevernage 2013), to question them, and, if necessary, to develop new modes of historicity in the determination of the relationship between past, present, and future.

More exciting is the critique that the concept of presentism itself is indebted to modern, linear conceptions of time (Lorenz 2019: 27–30). This would explain the cultural-critical undertone that would result from a loss experience of the modern time regime. One would then lament the new time regime primarily because the modernity one is familiar with no longer works. Hartog, Gumbrecht, and Assmann would certainly protest in equal measure. But the idea is fascinating. Are we capable of developing a new way of dealing with time in the face of the obvious and rumbling failure of modernity? Or are we not still modern altogether?

The political answers to the pressing questions of the present—globalization, global warming, mass extinction of species, digitalization, mass migration, pandemics—tend to follow patterns that have been rehearsed for two hundred years. Instead of diesel engines, vehicles are getting electric power. How the electricity for all these cars is generated, with what effort the batteries are produced, is beyond direct experience and is not included in the calculation. Every problem is answered with a bundle of new problems. Every scarcity of resources is countered with the development of new derivatives. Problem-solving is left to engineers. The answers to the pressing questions of a fracturing modernity are sought in the how-to books of modernity. And this is true even for movements like *Fridays for Future*, which—quite honorably—are driven by concern for a false future and have decided to take it into their own hands. All this is entirely modern.

And perhaps, as I wish to claim, this inability to bury modernity with all its devastating problems is the real problem. As long as it is not possible to get rid of the expansive character of modernity, this modernity will only create numerous new problems for itself every time a single problem is solved. The only way out, I would argue, would be to stop always and constantly appropriating things that lie outside our own direct existence. This applies spatially: There are always others who pay for the strawberries on my dish in the winter. And it applies temporally, too: The past should first belong to the dead and the future to those not yet born.

Finally in the finite

Claus Leggewie and Harald Welzer have suggested that the adequate attitude should be thinking and acting in the mode of the future perfect: "I will have lived" (2009: 196–204). With this rather rare construction of time, one gets involved in looking at oneself from the point of view of the future, thereby taking into account the effects of one's own actions now. This is exhausting, but already a gain. What is actually promising here is the suspension of an assumed boundlessness. The future is given a horizon by placing oneself in it, looking back and not permanently living expansively into it and beyond one's own resources.

But it would be even more consistent—and this is my actual proposal—to develop a new presentness: *I plead for a positive occupation of the limits of the present. I recommend an offensive presentism, not in the sense of an ever-widening present, but for a suspension of expansive reaching into the future and the past.* Only in this way could the expansive traits of modernity be trained away.

At the same time, the past should be allowed to remain the past. Nostalgia was diagnosed in 1688 by the Swiss physician Johannes Hofer as pathological homesickness in Swiss mercenaries who were far from home (Becker 2018; Landwehr 2018). The flight into the reconstructions of many cities today is rather a sign of grief and one's own speechlessness in the face of the questions of the present (Welzbacher 2010; Deile forthcoming). But these Potemkin villages will produce nothing but new estrangement. The situation is similar with the mass of monuments that are springing up everywhere and for everything these days. They are an attempt to create memory in cultural form. But it is precisely this sanctioned encroachment that tempts people to close off discussion and debate, leading to the illusion of having learned something even when there is no longer any encounter at all (Knigge 2010).

What, then, would a world look like that is first and foremost content with the present? Valentin Groebner (2020: 13) expressed hopes in this regard, noting a beneficial end to tourism under COVID-19 conditions and pointing out that this activity always promised more pleasure than it delivered anyway:

> Holidays had been the promise that one could order change and surprise, as an unfailing anti-sedation measure against one's own everyday life. It had only really worked when making plans, that is, in theory. In practice, I had often returned from the trip with weariness of anti-weariness.

Groebner combines a recommendation for spatial boundedness with a call to return from the "zone of near-future" where one supposedly spends 12 percent of waking time, "a good two hours a day" wasted (ibid.: 12). And history, too, as an expansive fantasy, is for Groebner a practice of yesterday, at least in its touristic form, as an appropriation of what one thinks one has lost (ibid.: 14; Groebner 2018). For Groebner, this is all "home cinema in the human zoo" (ibid.: 21) in downright ethically degenerate dimensions with only one sensible alternative: stay at home.

Byung-Chul Han (2017)—following principal claims of Nietzsche (1972) and also schooled in Heidegger, Peter Handke, and Zen Buddhism—has pleaded for a rediscovery of the "scent of time." This is meant olfactorily, but also beyond. Above all, Han laments a basic problem that he sees in "temporal dispersal," in the lack of a "rhythm that would provide order," a "dyschronicity[, that] lets time whizz" (ibid.: vi.). Because we are always already exposed to, and expose ourselves to, far too many impressions that we also try to couple together in a meaningful way, a restlessness arises that lacks gravitation. Only a "revitalisation of the *vita contemplativa*" can offer a way out (vii). The "temporal tension" between a vast and possessively appropriated past and future could only be resolved by a driving concentration on the present, which would remove it from "its passing without end or direction and infuse … it with meaningfulness" (3). The "narrative chain" (51) that characterizes modern historiography could then be replaced by a "contemplative lingering" (69), which alone is capable of giving meaning to existence in the moment.

This sounds airy and at the same time very intuitive. The plausibility of Han's very provocatively presented theses and assertions is not necessarily substantiated by the metaphorical nature of his language. And it is precisely this inviting associative quality of his thoughts that has been sharply reproached by his critics (Klaue 2016). But in view of the fact that the modern understanding of time, with its primarily linear, progress-based, and expansive character, now seems almost natural and uniquely valid, it probably needs verbal and intellectual fireworks of the kind Han delivers to get the thinking of alternatives going. Han is more consistent in suspending temporary expansion than almost anyone else. His proposal would offer a solution to many of the social, economic, mental, and global problems of our time. But the exit Han recommends is certainly not easy to achieve, because its ascetic basic mood runs counter to the constant hunger-inducing satiety that we have trained ourselves to with modern consumer behavior, which some would say is so perfectly suited to human nature. At the same time, it has been, and continues to be, demonstrated that alternatives are also possible with consciousness training, meditation, and convergence.

Gumbrecht's works have a different tone, characterized less by asceticism than by serenity infused with cultural criticism, like a muffled voice from the background that rolls out when no one has anything more to say. His notion of *presence* is very close to Han's views. Gumbrecht (2012: 9), too, calls for a "Posthistoire Now," an overcoming of the urge to drive the present into the past in ever-further meanderings. On the other hand, it is part of modern historical thinking that the present, according to Gumbrecht (2014: xiii) is always "the site where the subject, adapting experiences from the past to the present and the future, made choices among the possibilities the latter offered." In the emerging new chronotope, Gumbrecht (2014: xiii) sees the devaluation of a broad present which "has turned into a dimension of expanding simultaneities." As a result, it is as desolate and disordered as a rubbish dump and functions as an illusion only, in the face of a future horizon that has long since been closed and a past that we now know is unreachable: It is the "impression of an intransitive mobilization [that] often reveals itself to be stagnant" (ibid.: xiii). Gumbrecht (xiv) sees two ways out of the impasse of the modern historical chronotope that the broad present brings about: radical spiritualization (as Han probably ultimately recommends) and an "insistence on concreteness, corporality, and the presence of human life." What Gumbrecht (ix) prefers is "presence," by which he means that "things inevitably stand at a distance from or in proximity to our bodies; whether they 'touch' us directly or not, they have substance." Gumbrecht thus pleads for a pause in order to give space to intensive sensual experience of the world without always slipping into interpreting, sensemaking, and cognitive working-through.

In addition to those mentioned above, many other efforts could be mentioned (Lorenz and Bevernage 2013; Jordheim 2014; Runia 2014; Simon 2019; Tamm and Olivier 2019) which are concerned with the search for alternatives to historical, teleologically and linearly directed, and expansive time. Here I have focused on the present-oriented one; those that embrace presentism in one way or another. This came as a surprise even to me, as this article was first supposed to focus on the future. Yet it ended up being a plea for a suspension of modern notions of time in order to give more space and value to the moment of the present.

Objections would be easy to refute. A reactionary proposal? Yes, it is, but not a retreat into nostalgia: instead, a reaction to the impotence of modern time constellations in the same notion as "staying with the trouble" in Haraway (2016: 1). Contrary to the nature of human? This may not be true in view of the fact that the modern approach to time is no more than two hundred years old. Forgetting the future in the face of impending climate catastrophes? Quite the contrary: my proposal would mean that only those resources that would not be taken away from future generations would be consumed in the present.

References

Armitage, D. (2021), "In Defense of Presentism," in D. M. McMahon (ed.), *History and Human Flourishing*. Oxford: Oxford University Press. Available online: https://scholar.harvard.edu/armitage/publications/defense-presentism (accessed October 3, 2021).

Assmann, A. (2013), *Ist die Zeit aus den Fugen? Aufstieg und Fall des Zeitregimes der Moderne*. München: Hanser.

Bartlett, R. (1993), *The Making of Europe: Conquest, Colonization and Cultural Change 950–1350*. London: Allen Lane.

Baschet, J. (2018), *Défaire la tyrannie du présent: temporalités émergentes et futurs inédits*. Paris: La Découverte.

Becker, T. (2018), "The Meanings of Nostalgia," *History and Theory* 57(2): 232–48.

Clark, C. (2019), *Time and Power: Visions of History in German Politics from the Thirty Years' War to the Third Reich*. Princeton: Princeton University Press.

Deile, L. (forthcoming), "Zurück in die Zukunft? Vorwärts in die Vergangenheit? Stadtplanung und Zeitregime," in K. Kranhold and K. Krüger (eds.), *Bildung durch Bilder*, in print, Bielefeld: transcript.

De Mulder, E. F. J., B. C. De Pater, and J. C. Droogleever Fortuijn (2019), *The Netherlands and the Dutch: A Physical and Human Geography*. Cham: Springer International Publishing.

Dux, G. (1989), *Die Zeit in der Geschichte: Ihre Entwicklungslogik vom Mythos zur Weltzeit*. Frankfurt: Suhrkamp.

Fritzsche, P. (2004), *Stranded in the Present: Modern Time and the Melancholy of History*. Cambridge, MA, and London: Harvard University Press.

Gatterer, J. C. (1775), *Abriß der Geographie*. Göttingen: Dieterich.

Gatterer J. C. (1777), *Abriß der Chronologie*. Göttingen: Dieterich.

Groebner, V. (2018), *Retroland. Geschichtstourismus und die Sehnsucht nach dem Authentischen*. Frankfurt: S. Fischer.

Groebner, V. (2020), *Ferienmüde: Als das Reisen nicht mehr geholfen hat*. Göttingen: Konstanz University Press.

Gumbrecht, H. U. (2012), *Präsenz*. Berlin: Suhrkamp.

Gumbrecht, H. U. (2014), *Our Broad Present: Time and Contemporary Culture*. New York: Columbia University Press.

Han, B.-C. (2017), *The Scent of Time: A Philosophical Essay on the Art of Lingering*. Cambridge: Polity Press.

Haraway, D. (2016), *Staying with the Trouble: Making Kin in the Chthulucene*. Durham, NC, and London: Duke University Press.

Hartog, F. (1996), "Time, History and the Writing of History. The Order of Time," in R. Torstendahl and I. Veit-Brause (eds.), *History Making: the Intellectual and Social Formation of a Discipline*, 95–113, Stockholm: Almqvist & Wiksell.

Hartog, F. (2010), "Geschichtlichkeitsregime," in A. Kwaschik and M. Wimmer (eds.), *Von der Arbeit des Historikers: Ein Wörterbuch zu Theorie und Praxis der Geschichtswissenschaft*, 85–90, Bielefeld: transcript.

Hartog, F. (2015), *Regimes of Historicity: Presentism and Experiences of Time*. Trans. Saskia Brown. New York: Columbia University Press.

Hartog, F. (2016), "Toward a New Historical Condition," in M. Baumstark and R. Forkel (eds.), *Historisierung: Begriff – Geschichte – Praxisfelder*, 271–82, Stuttgart: Metzler.

Herder, J. G. (1887), "Ideen zur Philosophie der Geschichte der Menschheit [1784–85]," in B. Suphan (ed.), *Herders Sämmtliche Werke*, vol. 13, 1–441, Berlin: Weidmann.

Hölscher, L. (1999), *Die Entdeckung der Zukunft*. Frankfurt: Fischer.

Hölscher, L. (2018), "Die Zeit des Historikers: Friedrich Schillers Konzept einer perspektivischen Geschichtsschreibung," in H. Hühn, D. Oschmann, and P. Schnyder (eds.), *Schillers Zeitbegriffe*, 253–68, Hannover: Wehrhahn.

Hölscher, L. (2020), *Zeitgärten: Zeitfiguren in der Geschichte der Neuzeit*. Göttingen: Wallstein.

Jordheim, H. (2014), "Multiple Times and the Work of Synchronization," *History and Theory* 53(4): 498–518.

Klaue, M. (2016), "Byung-Chul Han: Wir hatten eine gute Zeit," *Die Zeit*, September 14, 2016.

Knigge, V. (2010), "Die Zukunft der Erinnerung," *Aus Politik und Zeitgeschichte* 60(25–6): 10–16.

Koselleck, R. (1972), "Einleitung," in O. Brunner, W. Conze, and R. Koselleck (eds.), *Geschichtliche Grundbegriffe: Historisches Lexikon zur politisch-sozialen Sprache in Deutschland*, vol. 1, XIII–XXVII, Stuttgart: Klett-Cotta.

Koselleck, R. (2004), "Historia Magistra Vitae. The Dissolution of the Topos onto the Perspective of a Modernized Historical Process [1967]," in *Futures Past: On the Semantics of Historical Time*. Trans. Keith Tribe, 26–42, New York: Columbia University Press.

Koselleck, R., and C. Meier (1975), "Fortschritt," in O. Brunner, W. Conze, and R. Koselleck (eds.), *Geschichtliche Grundbegriffe: Historisches Lexikon zur politisch-sozialen Sprache in Deutschland*, vol. 2, 351–423, Stuttgart: Klett-Cotta.

Landwehr, A. (2014), *Geburt der Gegenwart: Eine Geschichte der Zeit im 17. Jahrhundert*. Frankfurt: S. Fischer.

Landwehr, A. (2018), "Nostalgia and the Turbulence of Times," *History and Theory* 57(2): 251–68.

Leggewie, C., and H. Welzer (2009), *Das Ende der Welt, wie wir sie kannten: Klima, Zukunft und die Chancen der Demokratie*. Frankfurt: S. Fischer.

Lorenz, C. (2019), "Out of Time? Critical Reflections on François Hartog's Presentism," in M. Tamm and L. Olivier (eds.), *Rethinking Historical Time. New Approaches to Presentism*, 23–43, London: Bloomsbury Academic.

Lorenz, C., and B. Bevernage (eds.) (2013), *Breaking up Time: Negotiating the Borders between Present, Past and Future*. Göttingen: Vandenhoeck & Ruprecht.

Muhlack, U. (1995), "Schillers Konzept der Universalgeschichte zwischen Aufklärung und Historismus," in O. Dann, N. Oellers, and E. Osterkamp (eds.), *Schiller als Historiker*, 5–28, Stuttgart: Metzler.

Nietzsche, F. (1972), "Vom Nutzen und Nachteil der Historie für das Leben [1874]," in G. Colli and M. Montinari (eds.), *Nietzsche Werke: Kritische Gesamtausgabe*, vol. 3.1, 239–330, Berlin: De Gruyter.

Runia, E. (2014), *Moved by the Past: Discontinuity and Historical Mutation*. New York: Columbia University Press.

Schiller, F. (2006), *Was heißt und zu welchem Ende studiert man Universalgeschichte? Eine akademische Antrittsrede [1789]*. Stuttgart: Reclam.

Simon, Z. B. (2019), *History in Times of Unprecedented Change: A Theory for the 21st Century*. London et al.: Bloomsbury Academic.

Speich-Chassé, D. (2012), "Fortschritt und Entwicklung," *Docupedia Zeitgeschichte*, http://dx.doi.org/10.14765/zzf.dok.2.270.v1.

Tamm, M., and L. Olivier (eds.) (2019), *Rethinking Historical Time: New Approaches to Presentism*. London: Bloomsbury Academic.

Welzbacher, C. (2010), *Durchs wilde Rekonstruktistan: Über gebaute Geschichtsbilder*. Berlin: Parthas.

Histories

HISTORIES

CHAPTER SIX

Infinite history

Marnie Hughes-Warrington

According to many, history is concerned with the finite. It is not a form of calculus. We do not think of there being an unending number of phenomena between any two other historical phenomena, or an unending number of phenomena before or after any historical phenomenon (Aristotle 1957: 3.4.204a). These are easy things to say, but they are wrong. History is concerned with the infinite, both mathematically and metaphysically. Both serve notions of the ethics of history as wary of absolutes. Moreover, both unravel the rules of the world in ways broader than Emmanuel Levinas (1998a: 103–4) envisaged in his notion of infinite ethics.

In this chapter, I am going to outline the idea of infinite history by showing, first, that the claims for total history by writers such as Fernand Braudel and David Christian are not claims for complete or bounded history. Rather, they are interested in history as unbounded. The second step in my argument is to show that history is not constituted by cleanly discrete or finite "bits" of space and time, but that we talk of the spatiotemporal scales of history in such a way that they can be explored using paradoxes of the infinite, like Zeno's paradox. This leads to the third step in my argument: to show that Levinas's idea of infinite ethics need not be limited to face-to-face encounters between humans. Rather, I conclude that the paradoxes of the spatiotemporal scales of history are a salutary reminder of the fragility of our attempts to bring order to the world, including ethical notions of how it ought to be.

Total history, unbounded history

The idea of finite history is at play in works such as Adrian Moore's *The Infinite* (2019: xi), where he argues that what lies between us and the past "are finite 'bits' of space and time" that are different to the infinite not just in degree, but in kind. It might also be assumed to be at work in the claims for "total history" made by *Annales* historians like Fernand Braudel, and by the "big historian" David Christian. The typical use of the word "total" connotes success in capturing everything, a whole account of the past, or completing or sealing off an account of the past. This is not what Braudel and Christian mean. For Braudel, total history invites the more comprehensive use of methodologies, spatio- and temporal scales and social and individual viewpoints than in other forms of history-making. He used "total" or "globality" to denote *going beyond* routine approaches, or the pushing of history-making beyond its customary or self-imposed limits. This view is clearly at work in his *The Mediterranean and the Mediterranean World in the Age of Philip II* (1996). As he explains in "En Guise de Conclusion" (1978: 245), for example, making total history or globality

> is not the claim to write a total history of the world. It is not this childish, sympathetic and mad pretension. It is just the desire, when we tackle a problem, to go systematically beyond its limits. There is no historical problem, in my eyes, which is surrounded by walls, which is independent.

The self-imposed limits of history Braudel talks of are far from the idea of the ineffable. This reading is supported by the two examples he offers by way of explanation: first, it is not possible to write a history of peasants in isolation, because peasants are not autonomous from the environmental and cultural contexts in which they live; and second, the concept of a peasant does not make sense without the concept of a lord (Braudel 1978: 245). Yet Braudel does not rule out the idea of going beyond limits and he does not talk of an ultimate limit to history-making.

Christian extends Braudel's idea of methodological comprehensiveness, but also makes a case for taking history-making to the limits of our knowledge in what he calls big history. Big history aims to tell the history of the universe, from the big bang over thirteen billion years ago to billions of years in the future. Big history includes the history of humanity but locates it in a wider history of the organization and harnessing of energy, and the eventual deterioration of energy organization as a result of the universal force of entropy (Christian 2004, 2018). This is not simply on account of Braudel's point about our routine inability to separate out phenomena. Christian also sees the expansion of history as *helpful*. Total history is not only feasible, it is desirable. As he writes:

> I know the idea of totality and grand narratives are on the nose at the moment, but that's what it was. The idea was of going to the max on the logic that if a little bit of history is helpful in gaining perspective on the present, perhaps a little more of history is even more helpful and so on. Why not go to the outer limits of history and see what you see? (Hughes-Warrington, Christian, and Wiesner-Hanks 2019: 585)

Yet big history may not have outer limits in the sense of having discrete boundaries. Asking what there was before the beginning of big history—the big bang—does not make any sense, because the big bang means the beginning of space and time. What is to come, according to both theoretical physics and big history, is the endless shift toward entropic disorder without a clear end, too. We might want to characterize the opening and future of big history, therefore, via Einstein's seemingly paradoxical account of the universe as finite unbounded, which can be explained as akin to a 2D object moving over the surface of a 3D sphere (Einstein 2019: 125). This is history with no edges.

Christian's big history is boundless and endless, and Braudel's total history also seems to be without defined limits. Both use the term "total," paradoxically, to remind other history makers that their works have not pushed the limits of their craft. Yet they are united in not fully appreciating that history is infinite both mathematically and metaphysically, and that it serves a notion of infinite ethics beyond what Levinas envisaged.

Infinite history

First, to the idea of history as mathematically infinite. I begin by noting that via his writings on re-enactment, R. G. Collingwood articulated a view of non-numerical identity. Collingwood's contribution to twentieth-century thought is hard to confine to an idea or two. Across his relatively short life, he wrote on archaeology, history, art, myth, religion, politics, and philosophy. For our purposes, his insights on the nature of history and metaphysics are particularly interesting. Collingwood was particularly interested in the idea that history makers can know or share the same thoughts as people from the past. Collingwood noted with some care that the way we speak about the identity of two thoughts is not the same as the way we speak about the identity of numbers, or of geometric entities like lines or triangles. We are comfortable saying that we have the same thought as another person, agnostic as to whether they are precisely the same in all respects (Collingwood 1993: 301). Another way of putting this is to say that historical artifacts are epistemologically vague in the sense that Andrew Bacon (2018) describes, with us unable to understand them precisely in one way or another. This means that they are open to multiple interpretations, and to dispute. Yet they are also held to be discrete enough for us not to be able to rule out the paradox of history being infinite by division or addition.

Many of us will have heard of paradoxes of the infinite like Zeno's story of the tortoise that Achilles cannot catch, which is recounted in general principles in Aristotle's *Physics* (1934). The scales of history can also provide us with paradoxes of the infinite. We could imagine, for example, dividing the period covered in a big history *or* a microhistory in half, and in half again, and so on *ad infinitum*. If we keep dividing, will we have an infinitely small historical period? This is paradoxical, as we cannot have an endpoint with the infinite. The same can be said for thinking about events to come in a big history and a microhistory. We can add *ad infinitum*. That would mean an infinitely big history, but what would that mean in practical terms? It is hard to get our minds around it. History is infinite by division and addition, in Aristotle's sense of the concept. There is nothing absolute to grasp hold of in terms of how small or how big a history can be, and history is not immune from paradoxes of the infinite.

But beyond simply noting this, what would be the point of acknowledging history as calculus? This is where our story switches from talk of history as mathematically infinite to it being metaphysically infinite. Paradoxes threaten the sense of our world, and our discomfort with them can lead us to try to explain them away. They remind us that a history is never total, complete, whole, or perfect. The paradoxical totality of an unbounded big history is for Christian "helpful." Helpful, in Christian's sense, is being able to see a tragedy of the commons in anthropogenic climate change. As he writes, appealing to the idea of humanity,

> For us humans, the next hundred years are really important. Things are happening so fast that, like the slow-motion time of a near accident,

the details of what we do in the next few decades will have huge consequences for us and for the biosphere on scales of thousands of years. Like it or not, we are now managing an entire biosphere, and we can do it well or badly. (2018: 289)

Adding a little more history, as Christian puts it, encourages us to see something new. He invites us to see climate change. His point of adding is to show that the conventional scales used to tell the story of humanity do not capture some of our most profound impacts. But let us pause on this point. He *adds and adds*. The absurdity of us limiting the scales of history becomes apparent in his addition. But where does that adding end, if anywhere? If we add and add to big history, or to any microhistory, for that matter, we confront the paradox of infinite history. Christian reminds us that conventional, human-scale histories are not complete, whole, or total. But Christian's history is not total either. Infinite history lurks as an absurd, unsettling challenge. This is important, for I hold that the scales of history can lead us to confront notions of totality in an infinite ethics.

Infinite ethics

The idea of infinite ethics is most strongly associated with Emmanuel Levinas. Levinas saw the encounter with the human face of others as outside of our subjective thought and perception. That, in his terms, gives the face of the Other the power to challenge our understandings of ourselves, and to recast our understanding of our ethical responsibility (Levinas 1998a: 173). It demands responsibility from us that we cannot evade or escape: a responsibility to act other than in our own interests (87). Indeed, he sees that captivation as so strong as to speak of us being obsessed, in a state of insomnia, held hostage or traumatized, albeit without violence (ibid.: 219; Levinas 1998b: 10–11, 15, 54, 84, 87, 156). In some of his writing he describes the face of the Other as anarchic, but he also talks of it as an infinite phenomenon (Levinas 1987, 1998a: 103–4). It is both within and not from our world of finite entities, overflowing it, and captured by the "in" of infinite (1998a: 195).

Levinas's use of the word "infinite" captures both our being enthralled *in* the *finite* of the face of the Other and our being overwhelmed or humbled at there being something bigger than ourselves. Many questions can be raised about Levinas's account, but one of the most important ones for our purposes is whether infinite ethics concerns only the human face. Jacques Derrida (2008: 106–7), for example, wondered why Levinas was so reluctant to consider the faces of animals in infinite ethics. Peter Atterton (2011) has responded by noting that there is an ambiguity toward animals in Levinas's writings, and that there is no blanket justification that can be made for omitting them from ethical considerations. When it comes to inanimate objects, we perhaps hit more fertile ground. In *Totality and Infinity* (1998a: 110, 114, 187), Levinas describes a "first morality" in which we enjoy the world—not just survive in it—and thereby experience affective vulnerability. We go beyond that first morality in our encounter with the face of the Other, and from there we engage in the dialogue of social life. Importantly, Levinas acknowledges that there is a residual of the initial encounter of the face of the Other in social life. We do not leave it behind (ibid.: 51, 57).

Conclusion

Unlike Levinas, I do not see ethics as hinging on an encounter with the human face. Our encounter with the infinite need not be restricted to our encounter with humanity, and it need not be restricted to the human scale of history. Rather, our experiences of our own finitude accounts for infinite ethics. I do hold that we can enjoy, and be captivated, traumatized, humbled, and overwhelmed by entities other than humans. That encounter can be with animals, as Derrida argued, but I also hold that it can be with a historical timescale that claims to render human faces microscopic—as with big history—or with the selection of non-human, non-living subjects. It can also be with a microhistorical timescale that is smaller than the human. What these things have in common is that they are other than us. We expect history to be about humans, but history is the finite *unbounded*. Moreover, its play of scales is paradoxical, capable of being divided or added to in ways that seem to make no sense, let alone common, human-centered sense. In infinite history we are confronted by what is other than us, and the acknowledgement that we are much more mathematically, metaphysically, and ethically fragile than we—singular and plural—wish to admit.

This is not just *helpful*, as Christian argued, for seeing the large-scale chemical and biological changes to the planet writ by human action in the age of the Anthropocene. It awakens us to the frightening, traumatizing possibility of history made without us, after we are gone, or, more proximately, by artificial agents. History is infinite, but humanity is not.

References

Aristotle (1934), *Physics*. Trans. P. H. Wicksteed and F. M. Cornford, vol. 2. Cambridge, MA: Harvard University Press.

Aristotle (1957), *Physics*. Trans. P. H. Wicksteed and F. M.Cornford, vol. 1. Cambridge, MA: Harvard University Press.

Atterton, P. (2011), "Levinas and our Moral Responsibility toward Other Animals," *Inquiry: An Interdisciplinary Journal of Philosophy* 54(6): 633–49.

Bacon, A. (2018), *Vagueness and Thought*. Oxford: Oxford University Press.

Braudel, F. (1978), "*En Guise de Conclusion*," *Review* 1(3–4): 243–61.

Braudel, F. (1996), *The Mediterranean and the Mediterranean World of Philip II*, 2 vols. Berkeley, CA: University of California Press.

Christian, D. (2004), *Maps of Time: An Introduction to Big History*. Berkeley, CA: University of California Press.

Christian, D. (2018), *Origin Story*. London: Penguin.

Collingwood, R. G. (1993), *The Idea of History*. Revised edn. Edited by W. J. Van Der Dussen. Oxford: Oxford University Press.

Derrida, J. (2008), *The Animal that Therefore I Am*. Trans. D. Wills. New York: Fordham University Press.

Einstein, A. (2019), *Relativity: The Special and General Theory*. Princeton, NJ: Princeton University Press.

Hughes-Warrington, M., D. Christian, and M. Wiesner-Hanks (2019), "The Big and the Small of It: A Conversation on the Scales of History between David Christian, Merry Wiesner-Hanks and Marnie Hughes-Warrington," *Rethinking History* 23(4): 520–32.

Levinas, E. (1987), "Humanism and An-Archy," in *Collected Philosophical Papers*. Trans A. Lingis, 127–40, Dordrecht: Martinus Nijhoff.

Levinas, E. (1998a), *Totality and Infinity: An Essay on Exteriority*. Trans. A. Lingis. Pittsburgh, PA: Duquesne University Press.

Levinas E. (1998b), *Otherwise than Being, or Beyond Essence*.Trans A. Lingis. Pittsburgh, NJ: Duquesne University Press.

Moore, A. W. (2019), *The Infinite*. 3rd edn. Abingdon: Routledge.

CHAPTER SEVEN

History of the present: Or, two approaches to causality and contingency

Stefanos Geroulanos

As names go for particular varieties of historical inquiry, "history of the present" is a deceptively simple moniker. It trades on the pleonasm it names. Should not historians use their work, it asks, to wrangle with the questions prevalent today, just as anthropologists speak of current affairs, and political scientists and humanists also, and for that matter pretty much everyone else? Doesn't history—at least *some* history—give us a leg up for surveying the present? The term is then used to designate two related endeavors, which may deserve clear distinction. Yet neither quite captures the flag under which it fights.

The first of these receives the lion's share of attention. In this instantiation, "history of the present" is a metonym for contemporary history, and in particular for history-writing that drives to the articulation of current concerns. This is partly a pedagogical pursuit, partly an answer to "How did it all come to this?" partly a search for lines of derivation for the "present" time (what used to be called the "modern" or the "contemporary"). Key here is the building of a configuration that explains "today" and often demands political action. Consider the jacket copy for Pankaj Mishra's book *Age of Anger: A History of the Present* (2017):

> How can we explain the origins of the great wave of paranoid hatreds that seem inescapable in our close-knit world—from American shooters and ISIS to Donald Trump, from a rise in vengeful nationalism across the world to racism and misogyny on social media? ... Mishra answers our bewilderment by casting his gaze back to the eighteenth century before leading us to the present.

For this kind of history of the present, if we are to recover the origins of current attitudes and problems, or to assert the historicity of the present, we must displace the historian's conventional reticence toward teleology, we must explain successive movements by which "the now" has emerged. Historicism leads to "our" moment or, more bluntly, to presentism. This is an activist sense of history, and at times it adorns the historian with every laurel she or he may have desired: the laurels of justice, of truth, of moral superiority.[1] More prosaically, it validates an inquiry that demands that history be useful—that, in the words of Kathleen Belew, it "defin[e] issues relevant to the current moment ... and explor[e] the long stories required to understand the present."[2]

In the second, often more formalized and theoretically oriented sense, history of the present is a way of demonstrating the instability and contingency of the present. It does this by drawing counter-historicities; by confronting a contemporary social or conceptual problematic with an earlier one; by showing the way in which particular forms of knowledge or power developed but were also thwarted, and others took over. In other words, the histories it proposes stop short of the present time and contrast with it. Most directly, "history of the present" in this sense presents the past as grounds for a *criticism* and not an *explanation* of present attitudes or ideas. In this second interpretation, the history of the present is entwined with the approaches known as critical history and historical epistemology.

In both senses, "history of the present" is history-writing as critique. In both, the goal is the organization of a historically minded hermeneutic for "today" (Steinmetz-Jenkins 2020). The ontology each assumes is quite different, and the link to historicism quite contrary. The first variety draws a direct line to the now; the second gives the present *ex negativo*, by countering it with a past that did *not* lead to today. In what follows, I will focus on the second sense, and I will eventually consider a conundrum posed by a conceptual instability of this second sense.

Genealogy

As a term, "history of the present" is generally attributed to Michel Foucault's *Discipline and Punish* (1977). Foucault offered it as a name for thinking about the link between the early-nineteenth-century core of his genealogical studies, notably on the emergence of the penitentiary, and the contemporary intervention he sought to make. His formulation is pithy, paradoxical: "Why? Simply because I am interested in the past? No, if one means by that writing a history of the past in terms of the present. Yes, if one means writing the history of the present" (Foucault 1977: 30–1). Intended as the opposite of a monumentalizing endeavor— and Foucault echoed Nietzsche on this point (Barzilay 2019: Chs. 6–7)— such an effort was counterproductive if it remained a disinterested gaze into the past. Worse, genealogy as an advent story would have been anachronistic and irrelevant: an intellectual who could direct a historical argument toward current results needed to dethrone, dismantle, other, and reconstruct the present out of her study. This was key to Foucault's commitment to prison reform, his effort to find a standing point from which to unravel power relations involved in the punitive society and to alter these relations. As he further noted in texts and interviews from that period, the entire point was to undercut ideological functions of history-writing and presentness by demonstrating that the present was an effect of structural shifts that could not be promptly historicized. Every narrative would mute important elements by generating a convenient direction to the present,[3] and this present was contingent on particular forms that had arisen "historically" and whose story (e.g., surveillance, imprisonment, and punishment as the basis of social organization in *Discipline and Punish*) retained the structure set in place during the period discussed *even though that structure had been rendered invisible by other developments* (the improvement of prison conditions, prison activism, etc.).

Foucault's attempt to design structural contrasts to the present predates *Discipline and Punish*—it is a characteristic of the "archaeological" method of *The Order of Things* (2002).[4] But it was a post-68 practice in the broader sense of a refusal of continuities, with philosophical affinities to the critique of history by Gilles Deleuze and the deconstruction of presence proposed by Jacques Derrida (1982) and Louis Marin (1988). Other 1970s critics of progressivist thinking in history in France concurred: Georges Canguilhem's essays on medicine in the 1960s and

1970s intervened in contemporary debates in medicine, sometimes through short asides citing policy proposals, but more frequently by showing how the guiding concepts of medicine (health, disease, cure, the psyche, nature, and individuality) generated problems whose history remained implicit, even repressed, but which complicated the ostensibly natural contemporary uses of such terms. For Canguilhem, the historian of science was an agent in her own right; if her truths and axiological investments were reflected in her practice, at the same time the urgency of a historical moment demanded a historical excavation of concepts and practices that inflected, even deformed, contemporary practices and goals (Canguilhem 2005, 2008, 2012). Canguilhem's own practice, as a history of the present, shows the political dimension of his rationale—political in the sense that it concerns the place and politics of medicine in a world increasingly dominated by a far-fetched rationalism—and its rejection.

It matters that Canguilhem and Foucault were not historians by discipline or training, not least because this allowed them to avoid some internal debates in post-war history-writing. Where phenomenologists, anthropologists, and philosophers of science were questioning the stability of "the present," historians were finally treating it as available to them. In France, the category of *histoire contemporaine* pointed to the post-1789 period, but, as Pierre Bourdieu (1988) argued, with the transformation of the university underway, a sociology of knowledge and of the *homo academicus* was essential for generating the necessary meta-position for scholars. This context allowed Foucault to present his genealogical or even archaeological work as urgent.

The development of the category of "contemporary history" in the United Kingdom and the United States was considered a historicist achievement—a way of breaking the "50-year rule" which was by then clearly obsolete. In the UK, the *Journal of Contemporary History* was founded in 1966. In its opening "Editorial Note" (1966: iii–iv) it declared:

> The idea that contemporary history could not and should not be written, prevalent between, roughly, the last third of the nineteenth century and the end of the second world war, no longer has many vigorous proponents. A more liberal view has prevailed; or is it perhaps only that the limitations of historiography have become more obvious? ... The *Journal of Contemporary History*, unlike its more distinguished predecessors, while not actively looking for

controversy will certainly not eschew it; it will not shy away from the still unresolved questions of the recent past. "Academic" is not, or at any rate should not be, a synonym for "neutral," "non-controversial," or "irrelevant to today's world."

In Germany, the whole problematic, abbreviated to *Vergangenheits-bewältigung* (the demand of coming to terms with and mastering the recent past), also conditioned many of the efforts to think of the present. The post-war establishment of *Zeitgeschichte* (contemporary history) as an engagement aimed at mastering and engaging with the Nazi and post-Nazi periods coincided with—even crashed against—the persistence of norms, institutions, and even ideas of witnessing that until roughly the 1970s remained strongly attached to an exculpation of Germans' lived experience under National Socialism.[5] Yet, as Reinhart Koselleck (2004: 26–42) noted—and other post-war conservative German historians agreed—history had long ceased to be a teacher of life lessons. Koselleck nonetheless used this note to establish his arguments both on the *Sattelzeit* (the period 1650–1850, which Koselleck identifies with the coalescence or hardening of modern political concepts) and the modern accumulation of temporalities. More to the point for our discussion here, he also used it to conceptualize the present time as bound by a space of experience and an increasingly limited horizon of expectation. Meanwhile, German thought also witnessed a persistent discussion of *"post-histoire"* concerning once more the status of the contemporary.

In more recent years, the question morphed somewhat. Even as "contemporary" history became standardized in equal measure as it atrophied in English-speaking historiography, the problematization of "the present" persisted (Lorenz and Bevernage 2013; Edelstein, Geroulanos, and Wheatley 2020). The category of the present has played an ambiguous role in recent years—and it is this ambiguity that orients discussions of a "history of the present." Some historical theorists—notably François Hartog (2015; Stocking 1982)—have expressly dilated the category, both with an eye to casting the "presentist regime of historicity" as overwhelming and often inescapable, but also with a distinct critical intent. In this approach, presentism "has reigned" since 1989, and the dominant regime of historicity distinguishes the current moment quite forcefully from all that preceded it. Crucially, Hartog's presentism-concept names a cultural diagnosis, according to which modernity's future-oriented "regime of historicity" had been overtaken by one that anchors all viewpoints in the present. According to him (2015: 203), "we are always looking both backwards and forwards, but without ever leaving this present that we have made into the limits of our world." Hartog's approach, influenced by Koselleck's understanding of temporal regimes accelerating in modernity, displaces "end-of-history" approaches (whether from Germany or from Francis Fukuyama) and has the distinct advantage of thinking of *presentism* before *the present*; it stages the present in the midst of a temporal/historical ideology that overdetermines its meaning. By the same token, Hartog's is an approach that perhaps underestimates the anti-normative contestations and political engagements involved in history-writing in the past couple of decades.

Recent uses

It is against this background that recent uses of this second brand of "history of the present" have emerged, often inspired by feminist writing and gender history, but also by legal history and history of science. By 2010, "history of the present" had come to signify a specific critical endeavor inimical to the sense that the present time was foreordained. The most direct and influential definition was offered by Joan W. Scott (2007: 34–5):

> Critique is never satisfied with the regimes that claim to fulfil its desire; futurity is guaranteed only by the persistent dissatisfaction of critique. This is where history-writing comes in ... It is not a question of judging whether the actions of men and women in the past were good or bad from some contemporary ethical perspective ... Critique ought to make us uncomfortable by asking what the sources of those values are, how they have come into being, what relationships they have constituted, what power they have secured ... The attempt is to make visible the premises upon which the organizing categories of our identities (personal, social, national) are based and to give them a history, so placing them in time and subject to review. This kind of history-writing takes up topics not usually considered "historical" because they are either objects taken to be self-evident in their meaning (women, workers, fever, incest) or categories of analysis outside of time (gender, race, class, even postcolonial). The object of critical history-writing is the present, though its materials come from the archives of the past; its aim is neither to justify nor to discredit, but to illuminate those blind-spots ... that keep social systems intact and make seeing how to change them so difficult.

In this account, critique involves precisely the refusal of the historian's *Standpunkt* as stable or predetermined (see also Kleinberg 2017). Translating Derrida's critique of presence in his essay "Différance" into historical practice, Scott posits the dismantling of the now as the purpose of knowledge and the effect of critique. To deny identity and continuity with the past, to deny moralism over the past is to impose an ethics on the present. To Scott's we might add a second self-description, by historian of trauma and critic of emotion theory Ruth Leys, who writes

> in the mode of what I call the "genealogy of the present," by which I mean that I tend to write about contemporary developments or paradigms in the human sciences that have a relatively recent (also a relatively dense) history or lineage. My aim is simultaneously to write the history of those developments or paradigms (or concepts or issues) that interest me and to make an intervention in the present by situating current debates genealogically and critically commenting on them. (Leys and Goldman 2010: 656–7)

Leys's account, a response to both contextualist intellectual history and histories seeking to participate in current neuropsychological studies, foregrounds the need for intervention in contemporary debates using not the achievement but the instability of the present. For her, the genealogical effort unlocks forms of critique particular to history, because it demonstrates the establishment of experimental protocols and conceptual systems. Scott has pursued just as strongly. Together, the two show how lessons of deconstruction and psychoanalysis matter for historical-epistemological inquiry. Whereas the category of the witness, the trust in a veracity and adequacy of oral history and of history from below, and the transparency of subjective experience and its articulation have been important in recent history-writing, here these categories are confronted with a pressure that historical agents are fashioned by history not to the extent that they recognize, but to an extent that precisely *requires* historical research to deny our comfort in the sufficiency of our thinking, feeling, acting selves. Leys's histories of trauma and guilt have relied in part on a psychoanalytic approach, with its concomitant refusal of the primacy of a fully conscious witness or even the sufficiency of interpretation of experimental results. In Scott's understanding as in Leys's, what allows historiographical possibility and intervention is our sense that current categories appear inevitable.

Four years after Scott's essay, the editors of the new journal *History of the Present* (Scott among them) opened its opening issue as follows:

> *History of the Present* is a journal devoted to history as a critical endeavor. Its aim is twofold: to create a space in which scholars can reflect on the role history plays in establishing categories of contemporary debate by making them appear inevitable, natural, or culturally necessary; and to publish work that calls into question certainties about the relationship between past and present that are taken for granted by the majority of practicing historians. We seek to encourage the critical examination of history's influence on politics *and* the politics of the discipline of history itself ... The point is to link the present to the past not as its inevitable outcome, but as the contingent product of changes in relationships of power and in the ideas through which such relationships are conceived. (2011: 1)

This imperative has been taken up by legal historians, historians of political imaginaries, and conceptual historians. Judith Surkis (forthcoming), who identifies as a historian of the present, celebrates recent legal histories: they "unsettle the self-evidence of contemporary legal claims and categories— about state sovereignty, secularism, human rights, and the 'free' market, rather than simply interpreting and contextualizing them. They share a clear sense of the present-day stakes of legal historical argument and a certain genealogical sensibility in disrupting the apparent inevitability of its contemporary configuration." Similar efforts in recent years to rethink the midcentury political and conceptual imagination, "the paths not taken, the dead ends of historical processes, the alternatives that appeared to people in their time" (Cooper 2005: 18), have even gone so far as to showcase transformations as broad as decolonization: how they could well have turned out otherwise, how categories taken for granted in its decolonization—as in others—deserve rethinking (Wilder 2015; Getachew 2019: 4–5). Perhaps the most successful recent case of the historical destabilization of the present is that of Samuel Moyn (2010), whose early work on human rights was aimed at undercutting-by-historicizing what he presented as a hegemonic paradigm in current ideas.

The present as copy

By comparison to this trajectory, the value of the first variety of "history of the present" is attached to its claim on an explicit justification of history's role in contemporary debates and its promise to restore voices unheard and problems that can no longer be ignored. It legitimizes the historians' yearning for intellectual relevance, their hope for a certain justice—and it sometimes appeals to the righting of historical wrongs. Nonetheless, the linearity it commandeers, and the dilation of the historian's judgment, cannot be justified. In more extreme cases, it amounts to an anti-method that openly shackles historical inquiry to the arrogant sense that what matters is the historian's own conclusion *in the present moment* and in the genealogy of that present, but not a systematic, empirically thorough, theoretically sophisticated approach to the object itself, well aware that what appears clear may be ridden with obstacles and opacities.

Do we have any assurance that the "second" variety of "history of the present" does not simply reconfirm our own moral values but, per Scott, asks "what the sources of those values are, how they have come into being, what relationships they have constituted, what power they have secured?" No, in brief, the *mise-en-abyme* is not guaranteed any more than its freedom from moralism. Articulating the contingency of the present does not hinder the historian from passing judgment. But this "second variety" is not a mirror image of the "first": it obliges the historian to operate without their own present as guarantee (Geroulanos 2017: Ch. 1). Nor does it block them from confronting injustice, present or past.

Ethan Kleinberg accounts for the past as both presence and absence, as spectrality. He writes, in *Haunting History* (2017: 114), "like the Great Wall, the past is and is not, or better yet it i̶s̶. The past comes and goes, and the pieces we do have are shot through with the nonsynchronicity of prior historical tellings." Kleinberg's argument doubles as an ontological questioning of the present. As the past becomes spectral, what kind of present can now be reconceived? The present does not exist as a direct extension of the past, just as historical inquiry cannot treat the past as ontologically given. In returning to the now, inquiry must approach it (and the intervention it seeks to make in the present) first of all as the fundamental *détournement*, even hijacking, of a past it can account for. The problem with the first variety of "history of the present" is not anachronism—it is that the present it reimagines *is itself anachronistic*. In the name of a certain subjectivism, problems visible *now* are projected and sources for them derived in the past. In turn, the present becomes a simulacrum of that past's future, just as that past is essentialized as the past of the historian's reinvented today.

"History of the present" should instead take hold of the multiplicity and conflict of temporal regimes characteristic of any moment in history (Edelstein, Geroulanos, and Wheatley 2020). Through them it can retain the urgency of current concerns, folding and unfolding them across a past whose ontological consistency is not guaranteed, and a present forced to exist and ready to disintegrate.

Acknowledgements

I am most grateful to Ethan Kleinberg, Zoltán Simon, and Judith Surkis for discussion and advice on this theme.

Notes

1   David Armitage (forthcoming) takes this to the extreme, endorsing a moralizing, activist presentism. The essay begins with a rather Napoleonic passage where Armitage crowns and miters a very special practitioner. "It is the rare historian who asks herself what the discipline of history can contribute to human flourishing. How human beings can live more fulfilling lives; how they can best use their various capabilities; how they might achieve their own goals along with those of others: these are matters she might think are best left to her colleagues in philosophy, psychology, or even religion. Questions about human flourishing are fundamentally ethical but the contemporary discipline of history seems allergic to tackling moral matters." Just who might this exquisite nonpareil be in Armitage's mind, towering majestically above a landscape filled with directionless, unselfconscious drones?

2   "History of the Present," https://www.kathleenbelew.com/courses-1 (accessed May 16, 2020).

3   Consider the "battle for history" that Foucault (1994: 656–7) discusses, explicitly as a "historian of the present," in "Anti-Rétro" (interviews with Pascal Bonitzer and Serge Toubiana).

4   See Geroulanos (2017: Ch. 18).

5   *Vierteljahreshefte für Zeitgeschichte* starting with issue 1 (1953); Moeller (2001); Weinke (2018) in "Bonn—Ludwigsburg—Jerusalem"; Rabinbach (2020: 369). My thanks to Jonas Knatz for this outline.

References

Armitage, D. (forthcoming), "In Defense of Presentism," in D. M. McMahon (ed.), *History and Human Flourishing*. Oxford: Oxford University Press.
Barzilay, A. (2019), "Michel Foucault's First-Philosophy: A Nietzschean End to Metaphysics in Postwar France, 1952–1984," Ph.D. diss., Yale University.

Bourdieu, P. (1988), *Homo Academicus*. Cambridge: Polity Press.

Canguilhem, G. (2005), "The Object of the History of Science," in G. Gutting (ed.), *Continental Philosophy of Science*. Oxford: Blackwell.

Canguilhem, G. (2008), *Knowledge of Life*. New York: Fordham University Press.

Canguilhem, G. (2012), *Writings on Medicine*. New York: Fordham University Press.

Cooper, F. (2005), *Colonialism in Question: Theory, Knowledge, History*. Berkeley, CA: University of California Press.

Derrida, J. (1982), *Margins of Philosophy*. Chicago, IL: University of Chicago Press.

Edelstein, D., S. Geroulanos, and N. Wheatley (2020), "Chronocenosis," in Edelstein, Geroulanos, and Wheatley (eds.), *Power and Time: Temporalities in Conflict and the Making of History*, 1–50, Chicago, IL: University of Chicago Press.

Editorial Note (1966), *Journal of Contemporary History* 1(1): iii–vi.

Editors (2011), "Introducing History of the Present," *History of the Present* 1(1): 1–4.

Foucault, M. (1977), *Discipline and Punish*. New York: Vintage.

Foucault, M. (1994), *Dits et écrits, Vol. 2: 1970–88*. Paris: Gallimard.

Foucault, M. (2002), *The Order of Things: An Archaeology of the Human Sciences*. London: Routledge.

Geroulanos, S. (2017), *Transparency in Postwar France*. Stanford, CA: Stanford University Press.

Getachew, A. (2019), *Worldmaking After Empire: The Rise and Fall of Self-Determination*. Princeton, NJ: Princeton University Press.

Hartog, F. (2015), *Regimes of Historicity*. Trans. S. Brown. New York: Columbia University Press.

Kleinberg, E. (2017), *Haunting History: For a Deconstructive Approach to the Past*. Stanford, CA: Stanford University Press.

Koselleck, R. (2004), *Futures Past: On the Semantics of Historical Time*. Trans. Keith Tribe. New York: Columbia University Press.

Leys, R., and M. Goldman (2010), "Navigating the Genealogies of Trauma, Guilt, and Affect: An Interview with Ruth Leys," *University of Toronto Quarterly* 79: 656–79.

Lorenz, C., and B. Bevernage (eds.) (2013), *Breaking Up Time: Negotiating the Borders Between Present, Past and Future*. Göttingen: Vandenhoeck & Ruprecht.

Marin, L. (1988), *The Portrait of the King*. Minneapolis, MN: University of Minnesota Press.

Mishra, P. (2017), *Age of Anger: A History of the Present*. New York: Farrar, Straus and Giroux.

Moeller, R. G. (2001), *War Stories*. Berkeley, CA: University of California Press.

Moyn, S. (2010), *The Last Utopia: Human Rights in History*. Cambridge, MA: Belknap Press.

Rabinbach, A. (2020), *Staging the Third Reich*. London: Routledge.

Scott, J. W. (2007), "History-Writing as Critique," in K. Jenkins, S. Morgan, and A. Munslow (eds.), *Manifestos for History*, 19–38, London: Routledge.

Steinmetz-Jenkins, D. (2020). "Beyond the End of History," *The Chronicle of Higher Education*, August 14, 2020.

Stocking, G. W. (1982), *Race, Culture, and Evolution*. Chicago, IL: University of Chicago Press.

Surkis, J. (forthcoming), "Engaging Intellectual History Otherwise," in S. Geroulanos and G. Sapiro (eds.), *The Routledge Handbook of Intellectual History and Sociology of Ideas*. London: Routledge.

Weinke, A. (2018), *Law, History, and Justice: Debating German State Crimes in the Long Twentieth Century*. New York: Berghahn.

Wilder, G. (2015). *Freedom Time: Negritude, Decolonization, and the Future of the World*. Durham, NC: Duke University Press.

CHAPTER EIGHT

Theses on theory and history

WILD ON COLLECTIVE (Ethan Kleinberg, Joan Wallach Scott, Gary Wilder)

We are the members of the Wild On Collective, authors of the "http://theoryrevolt.com/" "Theses on Theory and History," first published in May 2018 as an open access document at theoryrevolt. com. The "Theses" (also known as #TheoryRevolt) fostered a spirited conversation about the place of theory—any theory—in the discipline of history. The three of us are historians, though with different theoretical investments and different institutional locations. What drew us together was our impatience with the persistent refusal of disciplinary history to engage with long-standing critiques of its practice: critiques of its realist epistemology and empiricist methodology, its archival fetishism, its insistence on the primacy of chronological narrative, and its maintenance of reified boundaries between present and past. How had it happened, we wondered, that the critiques which had nourished our own thinking had somehow failed to transform disciplinary norms in significant ways? Why the need to repeat a certain kind of critique in generation after generation?

We decided that it was time to raise yet again the questions of what counts as historical evidence, argument, and truth in order to counter the discipline's narrowly circumscribed definitions. Since the last round of epistemological critique (roughly between the 1960s and 1990s) history, along with many of the human sciences, has become even more resistant to theoretical analysis and self-reflection. Whether due to a backlash against earlier theoretical challenges (or their perceived gains), neoliberal attacks on non-instrumental knowledge, academic downsizing, a depressed job market, mistaken perceptions of theory as intrinsically elite or elitist, or the tired canard that postmodern theory leads to the denial of truth, facts, and "reality", academia seems to be suffering a period of intellectual conservatism that is nourished by epistemological realism (and vice versa).

The local and global reception of the "Theses on Theory and History" has exceeded both our expectations and initial target (graduate students and younger academics in primarily North American institutions) but also reveals that the "Theses" have hit a nerve and provoked a response. At this moment, the "Theses" have been translated into Portuguese, German, Spanish, French, Polish, Italian, Russian, and Persian. There have been substantive blog posts and discussions on social media in Europe, the UK, the US, Australia, India, South Africa, Sri Lanka, Southeast Asia, Argentina, and Brazil. Given the enthusiastic response we have received so far, we see the "http://theoryrevolt.com/" "Theses on Theory and History" as an initial intervention. It is the first step in opening a broader debate about these issues about the practice of history. In this way we aim to create an international community of like-minded scholars, within and beyond the field of history, to share concerns and strategies, and to enact change in the discipline of history.

The time for #TheoryRevolt is now!

Prologue: Dedicated to Clio, Muse of History

Sing Clio, daughter of Zeus, Theory's rage
at the violations of your charge.
You, who told Hesiod,
"we know how to speak false things that seem true,
but we know when we will, to utter true things."

Now is the time to utter true things, for
Theory has been dishonored in your house,
displaced by empires of empiricism,
fetishism of archives, dictates of discipline,
enforcement of orthodoxy, and impotent story-telling.

Without Theory, History is naught but tales,
told by victors and moralists, signifying
nothing beyond themselves.

Without Theory, the operations of power
and sources of injustice remain mystified,
impenetrable to us mortals.

Our observations, when limited to description,
ill-equip us for the critical thought we so
desperately need, even to analyze those repositories
of memory that are your charge.

O Clio, we enlist your ear.
Listen, please, to our voices of rage.
With these theses on Theory and History we invite you
to sanctify our mission and to commend us
to the gods.

On the limits of disciplinary history

I.1 *Academic history has never managed to transcend its eighteenth-century origins as an empiricist enterprise.* By this we mean not David Hume's earlier skeptical approach but the scientist method intrinsically linked to positivism that Horkheimer called "modern empiricism," which was later adopted across the human sciences. Academic history remains dedicated to this method of gathering facts in order to produce interpretations by referring them to supposedly given contexts and organizing them into chronological narratives.

I.2 *Actually existing academic history promotes a disciplinary essentialism founded upon a methodological fetishism.* Treating reified appearances (i.e., immediately observable, preferably archival evidence) as embodying the real and containing the truth of social relations, it evaluates scholarship based on whether this empiricist method has been capably employed. The field tends to produce scholars rather than thinkers, and regards scholars in technocratic terms. Historians typically write for other professional historians, paying special attention to the disciplinary norms and gatekeepers upon which career advancement depends. This guild mentality fosters an ethos of specialized "experts," workmen who instrumentally employ their "expertise" as proof of membership and performance of status.

I.3 *The current obsession with "methodology" is premised on this "workman-like" approach; the odos or path to historical knowledge is assumed to be singular, and those who stray from it are considered lost.* This methodological emphasis narrows the disciplinary path of history, blinding researchers and readers to other possible routes to the past. In contrast, training in theory lays bare the logic, pitfalls, and advantages behind the choice of any one path.

I.4 *Lying behind this fetishism of method is an unquestioned allegiance to "ontological realism."* Central to this epistemology is a commitment to empirical data that serves as a false floor to hold up the assertion that past events are objectively available for discovery, description, and interpretation. Here the tautology is exposed: empiricist methodology enables the rule of this realism, while this realism guarantees the success of empiricist methodology.

I.5 *History, as a field, encourages a system of discipline or punish.* Those whose positions appear to be cutting-edge but hedge their bets and organize their thought around common convention are rewarded, while those who strike out for new territories are condemned. By "new territories" we mean alternative epistemological inquiries, orientations, or starting points, not new themes or topics. The disciplined are rewarded by the guild, while the innovators are punished. Nowhere is this disciplining process more apparent than in the review and publication process of the American Historical Association's flagship journal, the *American Historical Review* (AHR). The disciplining occurs via the practice of multiple anonymous reviewers policing their disciplinary turf and then congratulating themselves and their authors for their scientific objectivity and resultant meritocracy. The stultifying effect of the process leads to articles that may be broad in terms of geographic and even thematic reach but are stunningly homogeneous in terms of their theoretical and methodological approach. Employing large numbers of reviewers creates a veneer of democratic meritocracy, while affording even more power to editors, who are then able to select among the many opinions as to what should be allowed to pass. This inevitably leads authors to smooth out their arguments and pull back their claims in an effort to appease the widest possible audience and produce the minimum amount of offense. Only that which is already familiar typically finds its way into the pages of the journal. This and other disciplinary journals typically work to reproduce what counts as professional common sense, reaffirm guild solidarity, and reproduce boundaries between insiders and outsiders.

I.6 The editor of the AHR has recently announced a plan to "decolonize" the journal—to correct "decades of exclusionary practice, during which women, people of color, immigrants, and colonized and indigenous people were effectively silenced as producers of scholarship and subjects of historical study." It promises to do so by diversifying the board of editors, the authors of books reviewed, and the choice of reviewers. It also pledges to solicit articles from a more diverse group of scholars. These are welcome and overdue reforms. But he also notes that "procedures for evaluating article submissions" will not be revised because the existing "process of blind peer review" is already "highly democratic." By focusing primarily on the provinces and colonies of the reviews section, the editors thus concede that the primary articles will remain firmly under imperial rule. The editor does not acknowledge that decolonizing the journal must also include rethinking the scholarly norms and forms of knowledge that have enabled the kind of exclusions in which the AHR has long participated. By focusing exclusively on sociologically diverse authors and geographically diverse topics, empiricist methodology and realist epistemology will remain in place as the unquestioned disciplinary ground. Once again, existing hegemony is maintained by a nominal pledge to diversity which aims to co-opt rather than transform. *The field and the journal can only really be decolonized by radically reimagining the use and applicability of theory for history.*

I.7 *Given that historians analyze (the dynamic and changing character of) social formations, relations, experiences, and meanings, they cannot do without a solid grasp of critical theory* (whether it be semiotic, psychoanalytic, Marxist, hermeneutic, phenomenological, structuralist, post-structuralist, feminist, postcolonial, queer, etc.), as well as an understanding of the history of historical knowledge and the theory of history (theories underpinning historical analysis). Only then can we transcend the false opposition between history and theory by producing theoretically grounded history and historically grounded theory. Few history departments have any faculty dedicated to the theory of history or critical theory; instead, they rely on occasional courses from members with an interest in the field or those few figures outside of their departments to whom they send their students. This demotes "theory" as peripheral to the "real" work of history but also disciplines the students to think of theory as a supplementary exercise that is not integral to historical thinking and writing.

I.8 *History's normal (and normalizing) approach to doctoral training reveals (and reinforces) its anti-theoretical and unreflexive orientation.* Core components usually entail historiography courses and research seminars. The former typically focus on assembling a corpus of significant works in a specific subfield which students read for information (learning the master narratives), time–place–topic mastery (which will be tested in comprehensive exams), and technique (the more or less successful deployment of normative historical methodologies, which can be used or modified in students' own research). Doctoral research seminars typically charge incoming students with writing publishable essays based on primary source materials, as if "doing history" is a self-evident technical undertaking and students need simply to develop the methodological habit of gathering factual evidence to be contextualized and narrated. Although thematic and theoretical courses (of the gender—or fill in the blank—for historians model) are available, it is rare for doctoral students of history to be required to study the history of "history" as a form of knowledge, the epistemology of the human sciences, or critical theory.

I.9 *Disciplinary history usually brackets reflection on its own conditions of possibility*—i.e., on what counts as evidence, how methods may prefigure how such evidence may make arguments legible and valid, how such validity implies assumptions about social order and historical transformation; on the relation between social forms and forms of knowledge, accepted ways of relating and acceptable ways of knowing, normative orders and normalizing concepts; on the sociopolitical fields that inevitably shape and thus over-determine historians' intellectual, professional, and institutional orientations, priorities, and hierarchies. These norms of training and publishing reinforce disciplinary history's tendency to artificially separate data from theory, facts from concepts, research from thinking. This leads "theory" to be reified as a set of ready-made frameworks that can be "applied" to data.

I.10 *Theoretical frameworks and concepts that do not comport with disciplinary history's realist epistemology and empiricist methodology are usually consigned to—ghettoized within—"intellectual" history,* *which often relates ideas to society in ways that confirm rather than displace the conventional assumptions of the discipline.* In and of itself, intellectual history is no more likely to raise reflexive questions about historical epistemology and historiographic norms than other professional subfields. Intellectual historians of heterodox thinking (e.g., poststructuralism, psychoanalysis, Marxism) describe the ideas but rarely use those theories as starting points, methods, or frameworks for their own historical analysis.

I.11 *History's anti-theoretical preoccupation with empirical facts and realist argument nevertheless entails a set of uninterrogated theoretical assumptions* about time and place, intention and agency, proximity and causality, context and chronology. These work, however unwittingly, to reinforce the scholarly and political status quo.

On the resistance to theory

History's resistance to theory has taken many forms:

II.1 *An invidious distinction between a feminized philosophy and a masculinized history.* So, philosophy is mocked as a frivolous dance with "Fancy French theory," while history is praised for its solid hard work. Remember that image of the real historian slogging up the a hundred steps of the archives in Lyon (like so many penitent pilgrims before her) to search for facts. Philosophy is denounced as speculative (f), history revered as objective (m). The "noble dream" of a pure science (m) has never left the discipline: once moldy rye was offered to explain French revolutionary fervor; today historical "science" takes the form of DNA tests on ancient bones or the application of neuroscience to *mentalités.*

II.2 *The naturalizing of history* as something out there, waiting to be unearthed; the recovery of the dead as a sure way to know the living. History as the story that tells us, rather than the story we tell about ourselves.

II.3 *Thematizing i.* Theory as one more turn (a wrong one) in the ever-turning kaleidoscope of historical investigation. The lure of theory is taken to be an aberrant stage in the intellectual history of the discipline, happily outgrown, replaced by a return to more solidly grounded observation.

II.4 *Thematizing ii.* The objects of theoretical investigation are themselves thematized. So, for example, Foucault's radical epistemological investigations become just another empirical study of prisons or clinics or sexual practices. And "my" prison's differences from Foucault's become a demonstration of the error of his theoretical ways.

II.5 *Recuperation*: a variation on thematizing. A gestural inclusion that seems to welcome theory (usually offered in the preface or introduction or footnotes to an empirical study), only to ignore its implications in the work that follows. So deconstruction becomes a synonym for interpretation in conventional intellectual histories, Marxism is reduced to economic determinism or the application of "class" to local community studies, and "gender" replicates the sex/gender distinction or the fixity of the m/f opposition in the same way everywhere it is said to occur.

II.6 *The dismissal of theory i.* In this case structuralist or post-structuralist theory as dangerous relativism: by interrogating the relationship of language to reality, theory is said to compromise the necessary search for truths taken to be self-evident.

II.7 *The dismissal of theory ii.* The charge that theory—any theory—involves the distorting imposition of fixed ideological categories on self-evident facts. Like the endorsement by some literary scholars of "surface reading," this charge of distortion is contradicted by the unproblematic recourse of these scholars (historians and literary scholars alike) to so-called objective analytic categories: class, race, gender, and psychoanalytic diagnostics (Oedipus complex, family romance, etc., etc.).

II.8 *Disregard for the vagaries of language* and an insistence, instead, on the literal ("commonsense") meaning of words.

On theory and critical history

III.1 *Critical history is theorized history.* It does not treat "theory" as an isolated corpus of texts or body of knowledge. Nor does it treat theory as a separate, non-historical form of knowledge. Rather, it regards theory as a worldly practice (and historical artifact). The point is not for historians to become theorists; theory for theory's sake is as bankrupt as the idea that facts can "speak for themselves." The point is for disciplinary history to overcome its guild mentality (disciplinary essentialism) and empiricist methodology (methodological fetishism)—to interrogate its "commonsense" assumptions about evidence and reality, subjectivity and agency, context and causality, chronology and temporality. This would require serious engagement with critical theories of self, society, and history.

III.2 *Critical history does not apply theory to history or call for more theory to be integrated into historical works as if from the outside. Rather, it aims to produce theoretically informed history and historically grounded theory.* Critical history takes non-contiguous, non-proximate arrangements, processes, and forces seriously, be they social, symbolic, or psychic structures; fields and relations; or "causes" that may be separated from "effects" by continents or centuries. Critical history reflects on its own conditions of social and historical possibility. It specifies the theoretical assumptions, orientations, and implications of its claims. It elaborates the worldly stakes of its intervention.

III.3 *Critical history questions and historicizes the realist epistemology underlying both historical empiricism and philosophical rationalism.* It recognizes that inductive history is merely the flip-side of the deductive philosophy that professional history, from its inception, opposed. Each, however differently, separates being from knowing, world from thought, truth from history. Neither questions the underlying relation between social reality and the (socially produced, historically specific) frameworks, categories, methods, and epistemologies through which to understand that reality (whether inductively or deductively). Critical history points beyond the false opposition between empiricist induction and rationalist deduction, and between historicist description and transhistorical abstraction.

III.4 *Critical history recognizes all "facts" as always already mediated, categories as social, and concepts as historical; theory is worldly and concepts do worldly work.* So long as "facts" are equated with "truth," historians employ a logical contradiction, because both the inductive and deductive logic deployed imply a permanent unchanging concept of "truth" that is antithetical to the premises of even the most conservative notions of history: change over time. Training in theory and critical history allows historians to recognize such a contradiction. This then forces them to confront the way that what constitute the "facts" in an historical argument are bound up with the social conditions, the circumstances of the historian, and the range of acceptable questions asked of the past at any given moment in time.

III.5 *Critical history recognizes that every reference to context (as index of meaning) is itself an argument* about social relations and arrangements that cannot be presumed and should be elaborated. Context is never solely given nor self-evident; context always begs as many questions as it may seem to resolve.

III.6 *Critical historians are self-reflexive; they recognize that they are psychically, epistemologically, ethically, and politically implicated in their objects of study:*

   a. *psychically*, historians should acknowledge and try to work through, rather than simply act out, their unconscious investments in their material;

   b. *epistemologically*, there may be deep structural relations between the (socially produced) analytic concepts, frameworks, and methods used by historians and the social world being analyzed; every work of history implies or promotes a particular understanding of social relations and historical transformation;

   c. *ethically*, historians bear a responsibility toward—are in some way answerable to—the actors and ideas being analyzed, as well as their legacies and afterlives;

   d. *politically*, works of history are worldly acts that affirm or question commonsense understandings and existing arrangements, address social contradictions, and engage with ongoing struggles, implicitly or explicitly.

III.7 *Critical history is a history of the present* that links past to present dynamically and recognizes the persisting or repeating character of the past in the present and the non-necessary character of pasts present and presents past—whether through lines of genealogical descent, uncanny returns, haunting traces and spectral forces, or non-synchronous contradictions within an untimely now.

III.8 Critical history seeks not only to account for, and thereby denaturalize, actually existing arrangements. *It seeks to challenge the very logic of past and present, now and then, here and there, us and them,* upon which both disciplinary history and the actual social order largely depend.

III.9 *Critical history seeks to intervene in public debates and political struggles.* But rather than seek to collaborate with power as specialized experts, it questions the reduction of thinking to scholarship, scholars to specialization, and the very idea of the rule of experts.

III.10 *Critical history aims to understand the existing world in order to question the givens of our present so as to create openings for other possible worlds.*

Coda: The navel of the dream

If we think of the historian as akin to the interpreter of dreams, we see that those who look to make literal sense of the dream by presenting it in a chronological, realist, and self-evident manner are recognized and rewarded. But those whose inquiries lead to the obscure navel of the dream, the place where narratives and interpretation stop making conventional sense, are ignored or dismissed. The danger of a guild so highly disciplined is that the organization of meaning only allows for a narrow band of interpretation that is always aligned with what has come before, with what already "makes sense" (i.e., common sense). Structures of temporality, politics, or even identity that do not conform with convention are ruled out or never seen at all. *The historian equipped with a background in theory is attuned to the navel of the dream, to the places where history does and does not "make sense," and this is the opening to interpretative and political innovation.*

Acknowledgements

Theses on Theory and History is reprinted here as it originally occurred at theoryrevolt.com under a Creative Commons Attribution-NoDerivatives 4.0 International License.

CHAPTER NINE

Can historians be replaced by algorithms?

Jo Guldi

What kind of robot manufactures history?

The question was one that would annoy most humanists. "Why would a CEO want to understand text mining?" asked my friend. I shrugged, turned off by the implicit financial motivation of his question. But my friend pushed on. Ours was an era of data, he argued, where the documents of our time were the testimony of groups talking over Facebook. Historical training surely provided some angle of understanding about this data and its organization. Here was a version of the question that I could not resist.

Given a collection of textual data stamped with the time of its origin, how does the scholar move to describing a series of events, let alone ranking the most influential event documented in the collection? This is an important question, but not one to which digital history (DH) has a ready answer. The tradition of history has answers that begin in reading and intellectually organizing events over time. At the heart of this practice is the gentle art of comparison, by which the reader attempts to understand, event by event, which horizon was the one before which everything worked one way and after which everything was another.

In computer science, the pressure to automatically detect events has already motivated a race to create a tool to quantitatively extract evidence of change over time from a body of documents. Generally speaking, the scholars motivated by these questions work in disciplines outside of history, although sometimes they have collaborated with renowned historians to produce their work (Klingenstein, Hitchcock, and DeDeo 2014; Barron et al. 2018). In certain recent studies of this kind, it has become commonplace to measure history through an imaginary that we might call the "historian cyborg," an assortment of algorithms described as automatically detecting change over time. Actualized as a black-box algorithm contrived of a multiplicity of different measures of lexicon, grammar, and topic distribution, the cyborg is designed to "stand in" for an absent historian and measure how much the digitized documents in a particular database changed from one epoch to the next.

The historian cyborg in action

Consider one article (Risi et al. 2019) that appeared in a major scientific journal and purported to test whether computers could perform as well as historians at tracking which events would merit future attention. The study used data generated by contemporary information workers and later archivists dealing with U.S. State Department cables from the era of the Vietnam War. At the time, information workers had been asked to classify cables as meriting attention. A topic model of cables was matched with the historically assessed cables.

The archive of classified cables upon which the researchers worked offered rare materials, making possible a valuable experiment. Unlike the bulk of digitalized archives of newspapers, democratic debates, novels, and law reports—which catalog acts of speech, literature, or jurisprudence with dates suggestive of when they were created—the cable repository cataloged actual reportage of events and policies as observed from the war room of the State Department. The cables had previously been reviewed by two generations of information workers: both Vietnam War–era workers in the State Department who classified the cables, and post-war archive workers who ranked the significance of each cable in terms of its importance for posterity. The two systems offered two comparable lenses on history—one recorded as events transpired, and one extracted afterwards.

The existence of two systems tagging the data allowed researchers to contrive another species of "historian cyborg," which they dubbed a "Simulated Ideal Chronicler," referencing a thought experiment explained by Arthur Danto in his *Analytical Philosophy of History* (1965), where he describes the Ideal Chronicler as an imagined figure with absolute knowledge of all events as they pass. Essentially a compilation of algorithms, the "Simulated Ideal Chronicler," presented with the original patterns, delivered a raw significance score that matched the archival assessment reliably better than the tagging system of Vietnam War–era information workers. In the interpretation offered by the researchers, the experiment seemed to suggest the possibility of a cyborg that could automatically detect and classify significant historical events.

Or consider, perhaps, another recent case study (Underwood 2019) in which a machine-learning entity was "trained" on works of fiction from the early nineteenth century. The machine-learning algorithm is taught to "predict" female and male characters based on the adjectives, nouns, verbs, and other grammatical constructs frequently used around those characters. The expectation of the scholars was that an algorithm programmed with artificial intelligence (AI) trained on the 1840s would have an experience of disorientation if exposed to novels from the 1880s due to the extent to which gender expectations have changed. The AI, in other words, would have the bewildering experience of an elderly man exposed to the novels of George Gissing and talk of "new women" in the era of the department store. Historical change is a representation, in other words, of computationally represented "degree of bewilderment" as calculated by the rate of failure of the AI to correctly predict the gender of a character if exposed to the set of verbs, nouns, etc., that describe the character's actions.

Challenges to the historian cyborg

Many historians will be made uneasy by these case studies, although for different reasons. Classifying and understanding potential objections and refutations can help us to understand the merits, as well as the challenges, bound up with using quantitative tools to understand temporality in the past.

A first refutation: Against prediction, or the value of retrospection

A first possible refutation might run out of pure hostility to the principle of quantitative reasoning being applied to qualitative knowledge. How could a "cyborg" represent the projection of a personal experience of change in place of what another DH paper called an "ideal, unbiased historical observer" (Barron et al. 2018)? It is supposed to "predict" how much history changed from one decade to the next on the basis of how a suite of algorithms—a cyborg—"trained" on one decade "fails" to accurately predict gender when presented with another.

That something strange is going on here should also be signaled by the words "predict" in relation to historical time, as prediction is obviously *not* how historians formulate their modality of knowledge among themselves. The fantasy of constructing a non-human intelligence, common in certain AI and robotics communities, and the fantasy of predictive power over the future, common in economics and game studies, have in common their lack of resonance among most communities of humanists. Both fantasies are essentially foreign to practitioners who study the past.

At the same time, however, there is nothing explicitly wrong with the idea of comparison at the base of how both studies were set up. Studying the mismatch between norms of gender in one period and the next appeals to comparison that is at the heart of methods in the traditional humanities. When a historian assigns her class feminist utopian novels from 1880 and 1970, she is essentially urging them to think in terms of comparisons—lexical comparisons, concept comparisons, grammatical comparisons, and comparisons between lists of professions or body parts—many of which could be outsourced to a computer.

Yet we might add cautions about the retrospective performance of a classifying algorithm with help from Danto, who originated the thought experiment of the Ideal Chronicler. In Danto's work on analytic philosophy of history, the Chronicler is proposed as a fiction designed to illustrate the need for an analytical function in history associated with the ability to discern meaning about events in the distant past, which is precisely what the Chronicler is not capable of. "He knows whatever happens the moment it happens," writes Danto (1965: 149). The Chronicler's superpower—an omniscience of all events as they happen, even down to the ability to read minds—does not necessarily lead to him being able to supply an interpretation of the meaning or significance of the events, which can only, Danto (148–69) explains, be realized in retrospect. Because the Chronicler cannot see into the future, he cannot apprehend "concepts" that would become available to future writers who understood the same moment in retrospect (169). The point of the Chronicler, in other words, is that he is *not* a historian; an observer in real-time cannot possibly apply the analytic devices that will be relevant to future generations.

If anything, Danto explains the Chronicler in terms that suggest to the contemporary reader the power of large-scale databases, recording all events and even personal speech as they happen; the point is that the data is not history until it has been analyzed and rendered meaningful, with the flow of events, change, and long-term perspective in mind.

Danto thus suggests that the illumination of the past typical of *great* history requires a "lag," and that only *mediocre* history is possible within the present. The algorithms (and historians) of tomorrow will be able to understand the present better than those of today. But given our existence in the present, we might still nevertheless wish—in the absence of a time-traveling historian—for an Ideal Chronicler who could catalog events better than contemporaries, who do not possess the ability to read every document sent by the State Department in a single sitting.

Thus, even if we take on board Danto's idea that historical distance breeds conceptual innovations, we might still be intrigued by the possibility that a machine designed to sort events as they happen against a database of all historical opinions might arrive at something. Certainly, in naming their algorithm a "Simulated Ideal Chronicler," the researchers who designed the experiment demonstrate that they had such thoughts as well: the rich availability of historical data suggests that historical data is becoming actionable in a new way.

One element of the cyborg fantasy worth retaining is the use of the comparative method—where data scientists might scrape records of history in the past to look for possibly significant events in our own time. The comparative method is already at work whenever historians draw parallels, in op-eds, lectures, or interviews, between resistance against structural racism in the past and the consequences of structural racism in the present. The comparison of parallel events could be automated. Yet the comparative method presents challenges of its own, which historians would surely want to address before accepting the output of a historian cyborg. While historians may appreciate the Simulated Ideal Chronicler experiment, they are still likely to take issue with the description of the Chronicler's work as "prediction"—and with the fantasy of a "human-type intelligence" that accompanies that work. Those objections may be held fiercely, but in order to unpack them, we need to delve more deeply into the underlying principles represented by phrases of this kind. Let us dig further.

Second refutation: On the possible incomparability of different periods

A second possible objection of the work of automatic history begins with a line of questioning about accuracy. Suppose an AI were trained to recognize significant events using a chronology of the Vietnam War. How accurate might that AI's guesses about significance be when it encountered the events of the 2020s, when so much about world communications, identity, and political alignments had changed? An astute data scientist might wonder whether the historian cyborg, trained to predict significance on the basis of word distribution patterns in the era of the Cold War, could be trained to recognize the principle of "substitution" or "replacement," a fundamental principle of the history of concepts as developed in the work of Reinhart Koselleck.

In *Futures Past: On the Semantics of Historical Time*, Koselleck (2004: 41, 53–4) argues for "repetition" being a constituent part of the modern temporal experience, as linked with the notion of revolution theorized by Kant and Marx. Revolutions and, hence, revolutions as repetitions, are punctuated, according to Koselleck (2004: 84), by the introduction of new concepts that mark a rupture with the past—for example, the substitution of "democracy" for "republicanism."

For instance, imagine that gender expressions were equally binary in the two eras, but the terms of gender expression changed from a binary marked by masculine thinking vs. feminine feeling to a binary marked by masculine flowers vs. female fruits. Effectively, a series of cultural substitutions had taken place in which Cartesian symbols had been replaced by Linnean ones. Could an AI recognize such a transition?

The Digital Humanists Ted Underwood and David Bamman (2019) once trained an AI on gender roles in one decade of novels, and then recorded the rates of confusion when the AI was exposed to novels from a later time period. Measuring the "predictive" success of their algorithm in the decade in which it was originally trained and in the later time period, they concluded that the gender concepts of an earlier era had been "blurred." An AI that used word vectors, or a similar algorithm, to look for new words "substituted" in the same context once occupied by previous words might recognize blurring by a structured replacement. Computers have been trained to understand changes in the grammatical use, context, and frequency of words—for instance, understanding that the word "gay" changed its meaning from "happy" to "homosexual" in a political sense around 1960 (Kulkarni 2015). The difference of word context in one era and another can be both indexed and quantified.

A possible second objection to the cyborg historian—that cyborgs can't compare different time periods, lacking a sensitivity to changing context over time—is thus easily to dispense with as well. The objection here has no problem with the fact of computational reckoning about the past, only with the level of sensitivity and detail with which the computer understands different uses of words about the past. The second refutation suggests that more programming may be needed to ensure that change-point detection adequately picks up on these differences, but it doesn't suggest an overall rejection of the historian cyborg.

Third possible refutation: The attempt to unify one standard of intelligence within an AI

A third possible objection might take broader issue with the representation of scholarly inquiry about the past as best mirrored from the perspective of a single "intelligence." The AI here stands in for a discussion of the precise measurements that the team in question used to model the representation of gender in the early-nineteenth-century novel, be they grammatical, symbolic, lexical, geographical, or otherwise content-based.

Few digital humanities studies to date have offered a discussion of the many algorithms that might be used to measure change within these domains. Similarly, few DH scholars have engaged in discussion regarding the degree to which substituting different algorithms might produce different trend-lines, a theme that I have explored elsewhere (Guldi 2018).

The third refutation primarily targets as problematic the fact that the trend-line cannot be unpacked. The AI is represented as a "black box," is posited as representing scholarly "intelligence" about time, whose defining characteristic is that it adequately predicts gender in the early-nineteenth-century sample. The project in the case study has simply not been designed in such a way that unpacking the black box of the AI is a scholarly desideratum. The trend-line of the AI's intuitions about change is too over-reaching, too final, too hasty—not because there is anything problematic about measuring text or measuring text over time, but because historical change is a complex subject.

In contrast with the "black-box" algorithms of the cyborg historian, the other methods discussed in this essay cover the "white-box" approach to the measurement of time. "White-box" thinking has been explored in biology as a doctrine about making explicit the statistical components of an AI rather than compiling a set of algorithms that produce a desired result and offering the whole as a package (Yang et al. 2019). Applied to the digital humanities, white-box thinking implies that scholars should detail the theoretical components of change that they wish to examine (for instance, substitutions and repetitions), propose the statistical measures best suited to identifying those patterns.

A "white-box" approach means that historians in general, and digital practitioners in particular, need to begin not with the algorithms, but rather with a detailed review of methodological approaches to the study of change and temporality, including changes in Koselleckian concepts as well as collective memory, as in the work of Pierre Nora. Digital practitioners would need to work with care to translate questions of conceptual change or changing memories into statistically measurable problems of semiotics. Automatic detection of historical "difference" between two eras being compared would not be acceptable unless the quantities of change could be explicitly theorized, named, and counted. Important debates would be opened up about the preferred statistics of counting temporal difference, calculating influence, or comparing the relative size of change in a corpus of changing size and composition.

Assessing the critiques

Of the three critiques, all are plausible, but it is the third that is most incisive in terms of directing the future methods of digital history and the way that traditional historians engage with digitalized corpora. The principles of open articulation of principles and biases associated with white-box AI are transforming the digital humanities, and will necessarily be part of the exploration of the element of time. As digital humanists embrace white-box principles and borrow from historical theory, the measurement of historical change through text mining will become more perfect, and naïve fictions like the "historian cyborg" will tend to vanish.

In DH today, however, a majority of the tools for measuring or understanding historical change over time have been designed by non-practitioners of history. A "black-box" view is merely one example of the perplexing approaches that may be caused by a lack of specificity in the criteria of historical change that would be demanded by a professional.

This problem results, in part, from a lack of engagement by historians with the tools of measurement of time, a problem highlighted in *The History Manifesto* (2014), which I co-authored with David Armitage. That is, while historians (including myself) have used digital analysis to elucidate particular patterns in history, relatively few of the methods we use to do so were designed with the question of historical time in mind. We use topic modeling and word counts over time to illustrate a particular trajectory of words over time, but much of this work— including my own—has been naïve, treating years or decades, for convenience, as uniform containers of human experience and using computational comparisons of those containers as a way to pick up on the trajectories of influence and action.

My article "Critical Search" (Guldi 2018) describes what is essentially a failed early attempt at quantitative reading of texts, as I followed a path recommended by the career data scientists with whom my institution paired me—all intelligent individuals—and myself partook of the kind of data science pursued by the articles I describe here. The data scientists with whom I worked, like the data scientists published in the articles I cite constructively in this chapter, were following to the best of their ability the vogue of machine-learning at the time (and as it is still practiced in many places), which presumed that, in order to be finished, a data-science intervention essentially took the form of a single package, into which certain inputs (such as textual data and a preference for particular algorithms) were fed, and out of which would come definable outputs. Because the custom was to have one way in and one way out, my data-science colleagues piled algorithm on top of algorithm: first stemming and lemmatization, then word counts, then tf-idf to identify the importance of words, then topic modeling, then divergence measures of the topic models, sometimes followed by the slicing of the corpus, more topic modeling, and more divergence. By stacking algorithm atop algorithm, we worked as if we were trying to produce a homunculus historian who could replicate the historian's task.

While I liked some of the results, I remained dissatisfied with much that had transpired along the way. *What* did the topic model do, I wondered? Why this divergence algorithm and not another? I asked the data scientists to pull our machine apart, and as I examined the workings, I noted that choosing one divergence algorithm over another resulted in not a slight error, but a totally different reading of the material. My interest began to shift from the quantitative results in question to the methods of inquiry. "Critical Search" suggests that historians work with quantitative measures of text carefully, testing and comparing algorithms at every stage, using statistical measures or algorithms to characterize the larger quantities of change, and drawing out facts that can be illustrated with something as reliable as a word count over time. That experience pushed me toward a different method of writing about algorithms: one that foregrounds the many inputs into any topic model or statistical model, and how adjusting those algorithms—say from day to month to decade—substantially changes the output, helping the researcher to gain insight into the nature of the "fit" between counted words on the page and their abstract assessment.

Algorithms in historical work

In raising questions about the work of other digital historians, I certainly do not intend to disparage recent experiments in digital humanities, performed at a moment of rapid innovation, in which I have learned a great deal from all of the studies mentioned. Rather, I mean to underscore what I and others are beginning to learn from those early experiments.

Part of what we learn comes from the shape of the various doubts that have been raised—often informally around seminar tables—as input-/output-related black boxes fall into the hands of humanists and social scientists with doubts about prediction per se, and about the nature of black boxes. Some of these doubts are circumstantial, I argue, and have to do with the collective wisdom of liberal arts disciplines, which may find value in the illumination of long-term perspectives even while utilizing particular tools. Others of those doubts, I argue, have to do with the specific way in which quantitative tools have been applied, and they point toward the necessity of published work which unpacks the intermediate steps in a research process, demonstrating, for instance, how significant the choice of a particular algorithm or measure of time is for the success of the enterprise as a whole.

The cyborg is here to *lend* non-human intelligence, not to substitute for human intelligence. Arguments to the contrary partake of salesmanship and fantasies of automation. They have little role to play in serious research, which is still learning from experiments made three, six, nine, or fifty years before.

References

Barron, A. T. J., J. Huang, R. L. Spang, and S. DeDeo (2018), "Individuals, Institutions, and Innovation in the Debates of the French Revolution," *Proceedings of the National Academy of Sciences* 115(18): 4607–12.

Danto, A. C. (1965), *Analytical Philosophy of History*. Cambridge: Cambridge University Press.

Guldi, J. (2018), "Critical Search: A Procedure for Guided Reading in Large-Scale Textual Corpora," *Journal of Cultural Analytics*, https://doi.org/10.22148/16.030.

Guldi, J., and D. Armitage (2014), *The History Manifesto*. Cambridge: Cambridge University Press.

Klingenstein, S., T. Hitchcock, and S. DeDeo (2014), "The Civilizing Process in London's Old Bailey," *Proceedings of the National Academy of Sciences* 111(26): 9419–24.

Koselleck, R. (2004), *Futures Past: On the Semantics of Historical Time*. New York: Columbia University Press.

Kulkarni, V. (2015), "Statistically Significant Detection of Linguistic Change," *Proceedings of the 24th International Conference on World Wide Web, WWW 2015*, Florence, Italy, May 18–22, http://dx.doi.org/10.1145/2736277.2741627.

Nora, P. (1996–8), *Realms of Memory: The Construction of the French Past*, 3. vols. New York: Columbia University Press.

Risi, J., A. Sharma, R. Shah, M. Connelly, and D. J. Watts (2019), "Predicting History," *Nature Human Behaviour* 3: 906–12.

Underwood, T. (2019), *Distant Horizons: Digital Evidence and Literary Change*. Chicago, IL: University of Chicago Press.

Underwood, T., and D. Bamman (2019), "Instability in Gender," *The Sword and the Shell* (blog), January 9, 2019. Available online: https://tedunderwood.com/2016/01/09/the-instability-of-gender/ (accessed September 29, 2021).

Yang, J. H., S. N. Wright, M. Hamblin, D. McCloskey, M. A. Alcantar, L. Schrübbers, A. J. Lopatkin, S. Satish, A. Nili, B. O. Palsson, G. C. Walker, and J. J. Collins (2019), "A White-Box Machine Learning Approach for Revealing Antibiotic Mechanisms of Action," *Cell* 177(6): 1649–61.

PART TWO

History and the future

Historicities

CHAPTER TEN

Planetary futures, planetary history

Zoltán Boldizsár Simon

A new historical condition

As human societies face previously unthinkable futures, a new historical condition is taking shape. It emerges out of the technological advancements of the human world that intervene into, mingle with, and kick off natural processes in manifold ways.

Synthetic biology, geoengineering, nanotechnologies, and AI technologies attempt to steer what has previously been conceived of as the domain of natural order and a mystery we can barely fathom: life. Today, we engineer biological life, create non-biological, mechanical, and digital lifeforms, and thereby blur the former distinction between biological life and non-biological entities. And we engineer even ourselves, from medical enhancements (Gordijn and Chadwick 2008) to transhumanist imaginaries of technologically enhanced human bodies and minds escaping their biological human confines (More and Vita-More 2013; see also chapter 11 in this volume). What is more, both governmental and private enterprises plan to escape the Earth-bound human condition. While NASA's Journey to Mars project (2015: 33) talks about taking "steps toward establishing a sustainable human presence beyond Earth, not just to visit, but to stay," SpaceX CEO Elon Musk (2017) envisions humans becoming a multi-planetary species through the colonization of Mars.

At the same time, technological advancements paired with a logic of "techno-managerialism" (Crist 2019) fuel the many crises of today, being held responsible for the more dire future scenarios of human-induced climate change, biodiversity loss, and the sixth mass extinction of species (Leakey and Lewin 1996; Kolbert 2014). Tinkering with and entangling nature through technology is the main driver of altering planetary conditions to the extent that may compromise the continuation of the flourishing of human societies, at best, or of human life on the planet, at worst (Rockström et al. 2009).

Either way, utopian or dystopian, *human futures are inextricably bound with larger planetary futures.* They are constitutive of one another in mutual interactions instead of the planet being simply the frame or background of human activities. The recognition of the systemic entanglement of human and planetary futures is based on two fundamental and inseparable insights: the realization that the human being has become a primary drive behind ongoing transformations in the Earth System; and the very idea that the Earth is an integrated system. Earth System science (ESS), a knowledge formation that was formalized in the 1980s (Steffen et al. 2020), developed both insights into their most popular shapes—the ones we see today. It may be possible to look for earlier inspirations and/or alternatives, such as the Gaia framework (Lenton, Dutreuil, and Latour 2020), but ESS has arguably been the most instrumental and successful in grasping together physical and social processes into a single larger picture of the Earth as a complex interacting and integrated system.

For one thing, the notion of the Anthropocene (Crutzen and Stoermer 2000) started its career as an ESS effort to name the systemic collision of the human and the natural worlds by referring to anthropogenic changes in the Earth System as testified by stratigraphic evidence (Zalasiewicz et al. 2017). Yet it quickly became clear that the social components of the Anthropocene may not be as profoundly addressed by ESS as by scholars of the human world. No wonder that Eva Lövbrand and her co-authors (2015) asked the question "Who speaks for the future of Earth?" and argued for a more prominent role for social scientific knowledge in coping with planetary futures. A distribution of work may indeed yield important results, while there is an equally compelling extent to which the systemic entanglement of physical and social processes is actually no one's expertise in the modern disciplinary distribution of knowledge, which demands a new knowledge regime that is yet to be developed (Renn 2020; Simon 2020).

What does all this mean for historical understanding? The answer I attempt to sketch in this essay claims that *as the futures ahead gain a planetary character, our historical understanding cannot escape being planetary too.* For historical understanding is not merely a question of what to make out of the past. It is a question of what to make out of the past, the present, and the future as seen together. Or, to use the category of François Hartog (2015), it is a question of what to make out of our reigning "regime of historicity," the current configuration of the relation of past, present, and future. Drawing on Hartog, Dipesh Chakrabarty (2019: 1) thinks that "planetary or Anthropocenic regime of historicity" may be the term that best captures our current condition. In transferring Hartog's notion from the framework of referring to inner relations of temporal dimensions (past, present, future) to the framework of referring to time scales (the history of the planet, of life on the planet, of the globe), Chakrabarty suggests that ESS has already begun to write a new kind of history in a planetary regime of historicity.

Drawing on both Hartog and Chakrabarty, my thesis in this essay is that the planetary character of our regime of historicity is indeed compelling, but the fact that planetary history emerges as a correlate of our planetary futures demands two qualifications that simultaneously enlarge and confine planetarity. First, as linked with our current historical condition, we should not conceive of the planetary as being merely Anthropocene-related. The best way to think about planetary history is to conceive of it as a response to facing manifold planetary futures, including not explicitly Anthropocene-related ones too (at least not in the ESS meaning of the term), such as the aforementioned colonization of other planets. While this arguably expands what we mean by planetary, the second qualification rather narrows the category by stating that linking the planetary with the new historical condition does *not* mean that the planetary *is* the new historical condition itself. It is rather one of the central conceptual tenets of a renewed historical understanding through which we apprehend the world and ourselves historically in times of unprecedented change (Simon 2019).

The first of the above aspects is a matter of planetary futures, while the second one is a matter of planetary history that planetary futures demand. The pages that follow will explore both in more detail.

Planetary futures

What makes the previous modern regime of historicity distinct is "the predominance of the category of the future" (Hartog 2013: 34). Or, as Aleida Assmann (2020: 51) notes, in the modern time regime, "the future was freed up as a space of planning, foresight, and speculative transaction." But if the case is so, if the future already pervaded the modern idea of history, then the question arises: what's so new about our recent obsession with planetary futures?

The answer boils down to three interconnected constituents of modern Western future-orientation: first, the aim at betterment over the course of a historical process; second, the conception of betterment as a sociopolitical development toward the best attainable political constitution; and third, the notion of humanity implied by such scenarios as a sociocultural category. From Kant and Hegel to Comte, Marx, and beyond (even up to the implied future of recent discourses on universal human rights and the emancipatory politics of the Left), there is an immense disagreement about the specifics of how betterment plays out. Not to mention the even more profound disagreement about which future sociopolitical constitution amounts to betterment in the first place, and what makes humanity human. Yet, all disagreements aside, the futures of the modern regime of historicity are specifically human futures (cf. Jasanoff and Kim 2015).

Thinking with planetary futures takes issue with all three constituents of human futures. Let's briefly review how exactly, one by one. To begin with betterment over a historical process, in planetary futures the anticipated change is typically catastrophic, and the catastrophe is expected to be launched by an event instead of a historical process leading to it. For instance, we do not deliberately work toward reaching a tipping point in climate beyond which abrupt changes of the Earth System are expected to follow, and we do not consider this possibility in terms of progress and development. I explored this aspect elsewhere in more detail by describing recent ecological and technological futures as "inherently dystopian" (Simon 2019: 79–103). This is not to say that there are no longer futures around that some may consider utopian. It is only to say that, in the context of planetary futures that entangle human and physical systems and their futures, even the utopian is considered to be dystopian at its core due to the unfathomability of whatever comes after the abrupt change, and due to the prospect of losing the capacity to act on and steer planetary changes that were originally kicked off by human activity.

Second, being futures of entangled physical and social systems, planetary futures do not have a vision of the best sociopolitical constitution as their *telos*. With respect to the *telos*, inherently dystopian scenarios either do not postulate an endpoint at which planetary futures could be directed, or this endpoint is the catastrophe and not a purposeful one as was the case with modern visions of perfect societies. The overall relation of planetary futures to the best attainable sociopolitical constitution is a bit more complex, though, and far less definite. While there is a massive extent to which sociopolitical, cultural, and ethical concerns remain integral and pivotal to planetary futures given the human involvement, such concerns do not constitute the ultimate question of the future as they did in the case of modern human futures.

Planetary futures demand us to rethink politics instead of projecting our existing political stances into the future. Alongside efforts to re-tailor old conceptions such as cosmopolitanism to the new situation in order to uphold a positive vision as a critique of dystopianism (Delanty and Mota 2017), social theory, political science, and international relations are in no shortage of suggestions to address a planetary predicament. The catastrophic character of planetary futures and the urgency of the planetary predicament typically result in efforts aiming at a new "planet politics" to "assure the planet's survival" (Burke et al. 2016: 522), or in calls for Earth System governance tasked with "societal steering of human activities with regard to the long-term stability of geobiophysical systems" (Biermann 2014: 59). Such suggestions seem to be in line with scientists' calls for planetary stewardship "to become active stewards of our own life support system" (Steffen et al. 2011: 749). Together, they attest to the logic of management as *maintenance* in facing planetary futures instead of appealing to the modern logic of ideological action aimed at *betterment*. The merits and shortcomings of this shift are, of course, open to debate (to humanities sensibilities this likely comes out as yet another instance of techno-managerialism). What is important here is only to note the shift itself.

Third, in the ESS view of interacting physical and social systems, the human features as a species in a web of planetary life. This is the point at which the planetary predicament looms the largest and at which planetary futures of different ways of thinking come together. Conceiving of the human in a web of planetary life unites the ESS view with various lines of anti-anthropocentric humanities scholarship such as environmental humanities (Heise, Christensen, and Niemann 2017), with approaches to cross-species kinship and critical posthumanism (Haraway 2008; Braidotti 2016), and with technology-oriented planetary futures such as the transhumanist ones mentioned earlier. Despite their oftentimes conflicting views on other matters, these approaches share the imperative of going beyond an exclusively social and cultural understanding of the human.

None of this means that the specifically human futures of the modern regime of historicity and their three constituents are totally irrelevant today. Rather, it means that we must explore whether the questions and concerns of the modern regime can be readdressed within a new historical condition that demands new categories of thought, including that of the planetary. Some of the old concerns may find their way to a planetary frame, some may be integrated in an altered shape, while others may vanish. Exploring the fate of human futures as planetary futures is not a task that could be accomplished overnight. It will take tremendous time and effort as part of the larger task of enunciating the planetary regime of historicity that negotiates the old and the new.

Planetary history

Carrying out this larger task of situating new technological and Earth System concerns with the old concerns of the modern regime of historicity is precisely one that planetary futures demand from planetary history.

Do we already have such a history? Well, not in any established manner; but yes, we have one in the making. For one thing, remember Chakrabarty (2019) claiming that Earth System scientists are writing history within a new planetary regime of historicity. The fact that the endeavor is less visible (or even close to invisible) in professionalized historical studies tells a lot about the relevance of disciplinary knowledges in the emerging historical condition. If our regime of historicity is indeed changing, then it is an open question which knowledge formations will be part of it and in what ways. Surely, humanities and social scientific concerns need to find adequate expression in planetary history, equal to scientific concerns. But it is unlikely to happen along disciplinary lines, or at least this is what recent developments of the scientific field indicate, with ESS bringing together many approaches and former disciplines.

History as disciplinary knowledge might not play an exclusive or even a leading role in planetary history. Even though planetary history is most certainly a new kind of historical knowledge, the reigning disciplinary codes of professionalized history do not enable the development of such knowledge. Disciplinary history is challenged by planetary futures on three levels: those of epistemology, methodology, and worldview. All challenges derive from the aforementioned entanglement of physical and social systems. Like any other modern discipline, history may address certain elements of the entanglement, but it is not designed to address the entanglement itself.

First, whereas history as disciplinary epistemology is attuned to investigating the human world, the entanglement demands knowledge about a more-than-human world (Chakrabarty 2009; Domanska 2017; Tamm and Simon 2020). Second, even if a more-than-human history could be an epistemologically feasible enterprise, it would still lack the methodology to deal with evidence of physical systems. As Libby Robin (2013: 329) notes, in studying the deep past, "documents give way to different kinds of archives," to which geological methods offer better approaches than "the standard tools of the historian." But the natural sciences have developed methods to investigate the more recent human past, too—methods that are largely unfamiliar to disciplinary history. John McNeill (2016) recently argued that in order to be able to address the past in light of our recent concerns, history needs a methodological revolution to get rid of the fetish for textual evidence and embrace the various data that the natural sciences bring to the picture, from microbiology to genetics (on the latter, see de Groot in this volume).

Third, even if both epistemological and methodological challenges could successfully be addressed, planetary history necessitates a shift in the implied worldview to conceive of the human within a web of planetary life. Whether this would mean transporting historical studies into the larger family of non-anthropocentric posthumanities (Domanska 2010), or whether anthropocentrism is inescapable, is yet another open question. Either way, the shift is not possible without developing new concepts and categories through which we make sense of the world and ourselves.

"Planet," "planetary," and "planetarity" are central among the new categories that have already begun to resonate across the humanities and social scientific landscape, with varying degrees of attentiveness to scientific work. Theories of planetarity in literary studies (Spivak 2003;

Elias and Moraru 2015), for instance, at least in their early emergence in humanist discourse, have paid more attention to giving a new twist to previous ways of in-house theorizing than to the systemic collision of human and natural worlds. They have voiced ecological concerns and addressed relational interconnectedness typically without mentioning the work of ESS. Other segments of human and social scientific work on the "planetary" respond to the impulse of the sciences by having a more explicit recourse to the work of the sciences as the provider of impulse (Burke et al. 2016; Chakrabarty 2019; Mbembe 2019; Chuang 2020; Clark and Szerszynski 2020). Although the latter efforts greatly diverge with respect to the extent of anchoring their views in traditional human and social scientific concerns, they represent more fruitful approaches that may lead to a new knowledge regime. The recognition in the human and social sciences that ESS and knowledge about emerging technologies are indispensable for adequately addressing the overall predicament (Simon 2020; Thomas 2020)—together with the acknowledgement that scientific work brought the predicament to the common agenda in the first place—is where knowledge production of a planetary character can begin. And this, needless to say, applies to planetary history, too, regardless of whether it comes from historians, sociologists, Earth System scientists, or collaborative efforts.

Conclusion

To bring together all diverging lines, let me offer the following description (meaning less than a definition): planetary history is a way to situate our knowledges of the past, present, and future of the planet as a system and our knowledges of life on the planet. Life on the planet obviously includes human life, in which the human is understood both as a species in a web of planetary life, and as a sociopolitical and cultural being fraught with inequalities and differentiations. How to bring all this—humans, social fissures, life, species, non-humans, Earth System—into a meaningful relation to each other? Whereas an innate humanities theory of planetarity such as that of Spivak (2003: 72) proposes "the planet to overwrite the globe," Chakrabarty (2019) thinks of the planet as the humanities equivalent of the scientific notion of the Earth System. Unlike the category of the global, which entails a history that features the human (in a sociocultural understanding) at its center, the planetary entails a history of life. The respective key terms of global and planetary thinking attest to this fundamental difference, with the human-centered idea of sustainability informing global thought and the life-centered idea of habitability underlying planetary thought (Chakrabarty 2019: 17–23). Instead of overwriting the global with the planetary, this rather means that "we are all living, whether we acknowledge it or not, at the cusp of the global and the planetary" (Chakrabarty 2019: 23).

Inasmuch as the planetary intends to capture the collision of physical and social processes from a humanities point of view, the task of planetary history is to relate the global and its differentiated human world to the extra-human dimensions that the category of the planetary entails on a level where the human acts as a species. This, however, may not be the end of the story. We can do better than looking at the new from old humanities viewpoints; we can develop a wholly new viewpoint. Planetary history can potentially be an experimental pool for nurturing new knowledges that spring out of the encounter of old and new (in which, perhaps, even the planetary turns out to be a bit narrow, as Tamm wonders in the next chapter).

In the long run, we cannot content ourselves with categories that separately apply to human and natural sciences. Developing a humanities holism along the already-existing scientific holism of ESS is hardly a desirable ultimate aim. It condemns us to a sort of methodological atomism that intends to build a picture of the whole through investigating its social and physical parts, as seen in the light of their own respective categories. If we really want to upgrade our understanding of the past, present, and future of a system of entangled social and physical processes, we need to nurture knowledges equipped with a vocabulary of categories applying to the whole and not only to the respective social or physical elements. This, I think, would set us on a course of learning to inhabit a planetary regime of historicity through planetary history as self-knowledge, which, in turn, would be the most instrumental in coping with the very planetary futures we are facing.

References

Assmann, A. (2020), *Is Time Out of Joint? On the Rise and Fall of the Modern Time Regime*. Trans. S. Clift. Ithaca, NY: Cornell University Press and Cornell University Library.

Biermann, F. (2014), "The Anthropocene: A Governance Perspective," *Anthropocene Review* 1(1): 57–61.

Braidotti, R. (2016), "Posthuman Critical Theory," in D. Banerji and M. Paranjape (eds.), *Critical Posthumanism and Planetary Futures*, 13–32, New Delhi: Springer.

Burke, A., S. Fishel, A. Mitchell, S. Dalby, D. J. Levine (2016), "Planet Politics: A Manifesto from the End of IR," *Millennium: Journal of International Studies* 44(3): 499–523.

Chakrabarty, D. (2009), "The Climate of History: Four Theses," *Critical Inquiry* 35(2): 197–222.

Chakrabarty, D. (2019), "The Planet: An Emergent Humanist Category," *Critical Inquiry* 46(1): 1–31.

Chuang, C.-M. (2020), "Politics of Orbits: Will We Meet Halfway?" *e-flux* #117. Available online: https://www.e-flux.com/journal/114/366096/politics-of-orbits-will-we-meet-halfway/ (accessed August 31, 2021).

Clark, N., and B. Szerszynski (2020) *Planetary Social Thought: The Anthropocene Challenge to the Social Sciences.* Cambridge: Polity Press.

Crist, E. (2019), *Abundant Earth: Toward and Ecological Civilization.* Chicago, IL: University of Chicago Press.

Crutzen, P. J., and E. F. Stoermer (2000), "The 'Anthropocene'," *Global Change Newsletter* 41: 17–18.

Delanty, G., and A. Mota (2017), "Governing the Anthropocene: Agency, Governance, Knowledge," *European Journal of Social Theory* 20(1): 9–38.

Domanska, E. (2010), "Beyond Anthropocentrism in Historical Studies," *Historein* 10: 118–30.

Domanska, E. (2017), "Animal History," *History and Theory* 56(2): 267–87.

Elias, A. J., and C. Moraru (2015), "Introduction: The Planetary Condition," in A. J. Elias and C. Moraru (eds.), *The Planetary Turn: Relationality and Geoaesthetics in the Twenty-First Century*, xi–xxxvii. Evanston: Northwestern University Press.

Gordijn, B., and R. Chadwick (eds.) (2008), *Medical Enhancement and Posthumanity.* Berlin/Heidelberg: Springer.

Haraway, D. J. (2008), *When Species Meet.* Minneapolis, MN: University of Minnesota Press.

Hartog, F. (2013), "The Modern *Régime* of Historicity in Face of Two World Wars," in C. Lorenz and B. Bevernage (eds.), *Breaking up Time: Negotiating the Borders between Present, Past and Future*, 124–33, Göttingen: Vandenhoeck & Ruprecht.

Hartog, F. (2015), *Regimes of Historicity: Presentism and Experiences of Time.* Trans. S. Brown. New York: Columbia University Press.

Heise, U. K., J. Christensen, and M. Neimann (eds.) (2017), *The Routledge Companion to the Environmental Humanities.* London and New York: Routledge.

Jasanoff, S., and S.-H. Kim (eds.) (2015), *Dreamscapes of Modernity: Sociotechnical Imaginaries and the Fabrication of Power.* Chicago, IL: University of Chicago Press.

Kolbert, E. (2014), *The Sixth Extinction: An Unnatural History.* London: Bloomsbury.

Leakey, R., and R. Lewin (1996), *The Sixth Extinction: Patterns of Life and the Future of Humankind.* New York: Anchor Books.

Lenton, T. M., S. Dutreuil, and B. Latour (2020), "Life on Earth is Hard to Spot," *Anthropocene Review*, online first, doi: 10.1177/2053019620918939.

Lövbrand, E., et al. (2015), "Who Speaks for the Future of Earth? How Critical Social Science Can Extend the Conversation on the Anthropocene," *Global Environmental Change* 32: 211–18.

Mbembe, A. (2019), "Bodies as Borders," *From the European South* 4: 5–18.

McNeill, J. (2016), "Historians, Superhistory, and Climate Change," in A. Jarrick, J. Myrdal, and M. W. Bondesson (eds.), *Methods in World History: A Critical Approach*, 19–43, Lund: Nordic Academic Press.

More, M., and N. Vita-More (2013) (eds.), *The Transhumanist Reader: Classical and Contemporary Essays on the Science, Technology, and Philosophy of the Human Future*. Malden: Wiley-Blackwell.

Musk, E. (2017), "Making Humans a Multi-Planetary Species," *New Space* 5(2): 46–61.

NASA (2015), *NASA's Journey to Mars: Pioneering Next Steps in Space Exploration*. Available online: https://www.nasa.gov/sites/default/files/atoms/files/journey-to-mars-next-steps-20151008_508.pdf (accessed August 31, 2021).

Renn, J. (2020), *The Evolution of Knowledge: Rethinking Science for the Anthropocene*. Princeton, NJ: Princeton University Press.

Rockström, J., et al. (2009), "Planetary Boundaries: Exploring the Safe Operating Space for Humanity," *Ecology and Society* 14(2): art. 32.

Robin, L. (2013), "Histories for Changing Times: Entering the Anthropocene?" *Australian Historical Studies* 44(3): 329–40.

Simon, Z. B. (2019), *History in Times of Unprecedented Change: A Theory for the 21st Century*. London: Bloomsbury.

Simon, Z. B. (2020), *The Epochal Event: Transformations in the Entangled Human, Technological, and Natural Worlds*. Cham: Palgrave.

Spivak, G. C. (2003), *Death of a Discipline*. New York: Columbia University Press.

Steffen, W., et al. (2011), "The Anthropocene: From Global Change to Planetary Stewardship," *AMBIO* 40: 739–61.

Steffen, W., K. Richardson, J. Rockström, H. J. Schellnhuber, O. P. Dube, S. Dutreuil, T. M. Lenton, and J. Lubchenco (2020), "The Emergence and Evolution of Earth System Science," *Nature Reviews Earth & Environment* 1: 54–63.

Tamm, M. and Z. B. Simon (2020), "More-than-Human History: Philosophy of History at the Time of the Anthropocene," in J.-M. Kuukkanen (ed.), *Philosophy of History: Twenty-first-century Perspectives*, 198–215, London: Bloomsbury.

Thomas, J. A. (2020), "The Anthropocene Earth System and Three Human Stories," in J. A. Thomas and J. Zalasiewicz, *Strata and Three Stories. RRC Perspectives: Transformations in Environment and Society* 2020/3, 41–67. Available online: http://www.environmentandsociety.org/perspectives/2020/3/strata-and-three-stories (accessed August 31, 2021).

Zalasiewicz, J., et al. (2017), "The Working Group on the Anthropocene: Summary of Evidence and Interim Recommendations," *Anthropocene* 19: 55–60.

CHAPTER ELEVEN

Future-oriented history

Marek Tamm

This chapter is an attempt to think about history and historical understanding *from the future*. My excuse for choosing such a big and speculative topic for a very short essay is mostly tactical—it is written as a sort of prelude, to sketch out main themes, put forward key concepts, and see if and how readers would react to them. The main argument I propose for discussion is that our contemporary regime of historicity is producing *new modalities of the future* that have, retroactively, an *important impact on our historical thinking*. Put differently, my interest is in discussing how to make sense of the past in a world where the future is not what it used to be.[1]

Following Frank Ankersmit, I claim that in recent decades the center of gravity of the present has shifted (again) from the past to the future (Ankersmit 2013: 10). In other words, our point of temporal orientation is not in the past anymore, but in the future. This future, however, is not the same as in modernity, but radically different. This creates a need for a new research program that I propose to call *future-oriented history*. This term is coined in the spirit of Hans Jonas, who in the 1970s advocated a future-oriented ethics (*Zukunftsethik*), a hypothetical moral position in the future in order to look back on the present. "It is only in its lightning flash from the future—in the recognition of its planetary scope and profound implications for mankind—that it is possible to discover the ethical principles that our newfound powers call for," Jonas (1979: 7–8) declared in his *Imperative*

of Responsibility: In Search of an Ethics for the Technological Age.[2]
In the same vein, I would argue that it is only from the future that
we can discover the epistemological principles for a new historical
understanding, appropriate at the time of the Anthropocene and
increased technological powers.[3]

Presentism and the new modalities of the future

The most prevalent *Zeitdiagnose* of the contemporary Western world
is that of presentism (for a discussion, see Tamm and Olivier 2019). We
are told by various authors that we live in a new regime of historicity
characterized by dominance of the category of the present. François
Hartog was probably the first to argue that today's experience of time
has become increasingly present-oriented, "the present has taken hold to
such an extent that one can really talk of an omnipresent present" (2015:
8). He has rapidly found many followers, and the epithets to characterize
our new present keep accumulating: "perpetual present" (Baschet 2004),
"perennial present" (Harootunian 2007), "permanent present" (Stiegler
2011), "broad present" (Gumbrecht 2014), etc. According to Hartog
and many others, the main feature of this presentist regime of historicity
is the vanishing of the future—the dominant category of the previous,
modern regime of historicity. "So futurism has sunk below the horizon
and presentism has taken its place," Hartog (2015: 113) concludes,
seconded by Hans Ulrich Gumbrecht (2014: 31): "By no means, in the
early twenty-first century, does the future present itself as a horizon of
open possibilities for action." In brief, we are invited to accept that there
is a serious "crisis of the future," if not the very "collapse of the future"
(Torpey 2008).

While I do espouse the idea that our dominant regime of historicity
is presentism, this does not mean, in my understanding, that the future
is disappearing from our horizon, devoured by the ever-broadening
present. Rather, I would argue, supported by Jérôme Baschet (2018),
that we are witnessing the emergence of *new modalities of the future*,
characteristic to the presentist regime of historicity. By "modalities of
the future," I mean the variety of possible but not necessary futures
figured simultaneously in different societal and cultural practices. In his
book *Undoing the Tyranny of the Present: Emerging Temporalities and
Novel Futures*, Baschet contends that instead of the withering of the
future, we should speak about a burgeoning of new futures under the

regime of presentism (for a discussion, see Tamm 2020). The future and the present are inseparably connected in presentism, the one depending on the other: "the future being predetermined by the present, while the present can only sustain itself by annexing the future" (Baschet 2018: 114). No matter how paradoxical it may sound, the presentist regime of historicity should not be defined through the category of the present, but through the new modalities of the future it generates. However, it is important to emphasize that the presentist modalities of the future differ significantly from the modernist ones. There is no way back to optimistic and progressive visions of the future, widespread in the futurist regime of historicity; in our new historical condition, we have to cope with new modes of the future.

In the modern regime of historicity, all futures were exclusively *human futures*, while in our regime of historicity the future modalities extend beyond the human (see also chapter 10 in this volume). There is certainly a rich variety of futures available in the contemporary Western world, but I would argue that at a very general level, we can speak about two main modalities: the *posthuman future* and the *transhuman future*. The first mode of the future refers to a *more-than-human world*, the world that *exceeds the human*, whereas the second mode of the future points toward a *better-than-human world*, the world that *enhances the human*. This double future scenario has been well captured by Steve Fuller (2013: 2):

> for the past half-century, humanity's self-understanding has been pulled in two opposing directions: the first, promoted by both ecology and evolutionary theory, is towards our greater reembedding in the natural environment; the second, which ultimately aspires to a digital incarnation of humanity, aims for the enhancement, if not outright replacement, of the bodies of our birth.

Put differently, I would claim that the modern temporal configuration is challenged by a new vision of the human condition, both from an ecological and a technological perspective. In our age of the Anthropocene, human and non-human agency are no longer distinguished, we are transcorporeal subjects enmeshed in the Earth's biophysical processes and entangled in technological developments. This situation calls for a dissolution of the human historical subject as we know it, because the future promises not to bring along simply a "change *in the condition* of a subject; instead, it means a change *of* the subject" (Simon 2019a: 11).

When we take seriously the post- and transhumanist visions according to which "the future ceases to be made of the same matter as the past; it becomes radically *other*, not-ours" (Danowski and Viveiros de Castro 2016: 26), this will pose an important challenge to our historical thinking, forcing us to work "at the limits of historical understanding" (Chakrabarty 2009: 221).[4]

In the remaining pages, my aim is to discuss very briefly how these new modalities of the future come to bear on today's notion of history and, more generally, to explore how thinking about the future beyond its status as a temporal category can bring the renewed concept of *futurity* back into historical understanding.

Posthuman future

Posthumanism is not a clear and distinct idea; rather, as noted by Cary Wolfe (2010: xi), it "generates different even irreconcilable definitions." I understand here by posthumanism the efforts to decenter the human and to reconfigure the relationship between humans and non-humans. Posthumanism rejects that humans are the only species capable of producing knowledge and causing changes. All humans, Timothy Morton (2013: 22) argues, "are now aware that they have entered a new phase of history in which nonhumans are no longer excluded or merely decorative features of their social, psychic, and philosophical space." Posthumanism is based on a new idea of subjectivity, a transversal alliance involving both human and non-human agents. "This means that the posthuman subject relates at the same time to the Earth—land, water, plants, animals, bacteria—and to technological agents—plastic, wires, cells, codes, algorithms" (Braidotti 2019: 46).

Posthumanism is not automatically generating posthuman visions of the future, especially within the tradition of the so-called critical posthumanism. Rosi Braidotti (2019: 1–2) states unequivocally that "the posthuman is not so much a dystopian vision of the future, but a defining trait of our historical context." However, posthumanism is clearly aspiring toward a more-than-human future, to a species-wise blurring of the human boundaries. The new awareness of the Anthropocene is confronting us with the question "what does it mean to be human when this means to be part of a global force that changes everything—even the future of an entire planet" (Ellis 2018: 15). The posthumanist vision of the future is characterized by the intensification of the interrelationship that defines the co-constitution of human with other life forms and forces of the planet. In some cases, it has also brought along a "larger turn to apocalyptic language," a series of new tropes in environmental discourse: "end of nature," "world without us," "Earth after us," the "revenge of Gaia," etc. (Northcott 2015: 105). *We will have never been,* is in a nutshell the most pessimistic vision of the posthuman future (Danowski and Viveiros de Castro 2016: 26).

Seen from a posthuman future, our current notion of history needs a major revision (for more details, see Tamm and Simon 2020a). First, we need to rethink the idea of history along multispecies lines, to develop an epistemological platform for a *multispecies history* which escapes the confines of studying the human world. It is primarily in the light of the more-than-human future that we can recognize that "history ... is the record of many trajectories of world making, human and not human" (Tsing 2015: 168) or that "there has never been any purely human moment in world history" (Nance 2015: 5). Ewa Domanska argues compellingly that posthuman perspective "might lead to radical reconfiguration of the field, even to abandoning history as a specific approach to the past because it is too reductive to grasp the complexity of interspecific relations and the decrease of epistemic authority of the human in (historical) knowledge-building" (Domanska 2017: 282).

Second, we need to rethink the notion of history beyond our usual anthropocentric scales, to develop something that we could call a *multiscalar history*. Posthuman future "opens up a new space for thinking about the connections between long-term geological or planetary timescapes and human or earthly time-frames" (Kelly 2019: 3). Sverker Sörlin (2018: 90) has asked aptly: "How do genes and micro-organisms 'from below' or geophysical teleconnections 'from above' become integrated parts of the kind of complex narratives of change, and the attempts to explain change, that we call 'the writing of history'?" To be able to address this issue, we have to develop new types of historical scaling techniques and a new pluralistic understanding of temporality that is able to encompass a wide range of tempos, intervals, and periodicities. Historical timescales regulate what can count as an event or what kind of actors come into play, the shifts in scales necessarily revise our understanding of historical causality and agency. "This heterogeneity of timescales and temporalities calls for completely new forms of historiography," Eva Horn and Hannes Bergthaller (2020: 162) conclude convincingly.

Transhuman future

I understand transhumanism to mean various visions for transcending the human condition by means of technology and the advancements of science (from biotechnology to nanotechnology and AI). When posthumanism can be seen as a break from humanism, transhumanism is an "intensification of humanism" (Ranisch and Sorgner 2014: 8) inasmuch as it aims for "the indefinite promotion of the qualities that have historically distinguished humans from other creatures" (Fuller and Lipinska 2014: 1). Transhumanism is motivated by the idea of human enhancement unfolding in various procedures: from genetic and morphological to pharmacological and cyborg enhancement (Sorgner 2014: 30). The transhuman future is, thus, a vision about "the human self-liberation from the shortcomings of carbon-based humanity" which will culminate in a better-than-human cyber existence (Tirosh-Samuelson and Hurlbut: 2016: 9).

Transhumanism advocates, at least in some of its branches, the expansion of life to the universe—the colonization of the cosmos. Max Tegmark (2017: 261) captures these hopes well in his book *Life 3.0*: "Our dreams and aspirations need not be limited to century-long life spans marred by disease, poverty and confusion. Rather, aided by technology, life has the potential to flourish for billions of years, not merely here in our Solar System, but also throughout a cosmos far more grand and inspiring than our ancestors imagined." While Tegmark and most of the other transhumanists rely in this on the emergence of artificial general intelligence (AGI), there are also other visionaries, like Elon Musk, who are working actively in the space industry to "make life multiplanetary" and to turn "humans into a multiplanetary species" (Musk 2017, 2018).

Most often, the transhumanist visions of the future contain an irreversible turning point—called an "intelligence explosion" (coined in 1965 by I. J. Good) or "technological singularity" (coined by Vernor Vinge in 1993)—the result of the exponential process of technological progress. This turning point is the moment where the exponential curve of technological evolution reaches the point where unprecedented and unpredictable changes take place in the blink of an eye. Ray Kurzweil, the main advocate of the Singularity theory, defines this moment in the following terms: "It's a future period during which the pace of technological change will be so rapid, its impact so deep, that human life will be irreversibly transformed" (Kurzweil 2005: 9). If we follow Kurzweil and other transhumanists, then history as we know it will be entirely different after the Singularity. This moment is hardly graspable for the human mind, but Kurzweil finds the following important to add: "Understanding the Singularity will alter our perspective on the significance of our past and the ramifications for our future" (ibid.).

What are the main epistemological consequences of a transhumanist future for historical understanding? I would argue that, first, we would need to give up a historicist notion of continuous, developmental, and processual history. Building on the work of Zoltán Boldizsár Simon (2019b), I believe that we need to elaborate on the concept of *evental history*, a new notion of history as a sequence of interruptions instead of a continuity (see also Kelly 2018). "Evental history" should be understood as a broad concept that covers all forms of historical non-continuity, including, but not reduced to, abrupt, disconnective, and explosive transformations. While processual history creates an illusion of a linear and causal stream of historical time which excludes all unpredictable and disruptive elements, in evental history it is crucial to conceptualize the course of history as a series of unpredictable and unprecedented changes. But changes conceived in evental history also concern changes in the world of human–technology–nature entanglement "which bring about a previously inexistent subject in a non-continuous manner, through unprecedented changes" (Simon 2019b: 80).

Secondly, the transhumanist future might have in hold, in a longer perspective, something that we could call *multiplanetary* or *cosmic history*. The "multiplanetary imaginary" of human beings who are no longer subject to Earth, but able to create social life on other planets, is becoming the main motif of the transhumanist vision of the future (Tutton 2018). If we take seriously the scenario that humanity will become a spacefaring and multiplanetary species, then it would be justified to argue that the planetary history, promoted recently by Dipesh Chakrabarty (2019a, 2019b) and others, is not the terminal station of historical understanding. Transhumanist future might suggest something beyond that, namely the emergence of a multiplanetary history, as life and technology expand into the entire universe.

Conclusions

In stating that "new future means new history," Zoltán Boldizsár Simon (2018: 199) has succinctly captured the main argument behind this chapter. Indeed, I believe that the shifting of the vantage point from the present into the future in order to make sense of history is a very important and valuable step. This is a starting point for a *future-oriented history* that I consider an important new perspective in theory of history. The future perspective will invest history with a new responsibility, historical understanding should be recast so as to take into account the more-than-human and better-than-human modalities of the future.

Future-oriented history is not meant to supersede the existing historical understanding, but to open up potentially new ways of exploring history that are inconceivable within the confines of an exclusively human-focused modern notion of history. Future-oriented history imagines a future in which the past has significance but which produces, at the same time, a past in which the future has significance.

In his characteristically melancholy way, Frank Ankersmit wrote some years ago that "we do not live in the *aftermath* of a previous catastrophe, such as the Holocaust, but in the *foremath* of a coming one, if you allow me to introduce this neologism into the English language" (Ankersmit 2013: 9). I'm happy to pick up this neologism and add it to the conceptual toolbox of the future-oriented history, next to *multiscalar, multispecies, evental history*, and perhaps even *multiplanetary history*. Indeed, historical understanding is not formed in the aftermath of past experiences, but even more so, in the foremath of new modalities of the presentist future.

Notes

1 For a more detailed discussion, see Simon and Tamm (2021).
2 This passage is from the preface to the original work in German and it is absent from the English translation of the book (Jonas 1984). Quoted here from Horn (2018: 204).
3 This project of "future-oriented history" is close to Ewa Domanska's (2014) earlier call for an "anticipatory history." It also has similarities with Lucian Hölscher's (2019) idea of "future pasts," i.e., anticipations of a past as it could be seen at some future point in time.
4 For more on this, see Tamm and Simon (2020b).

References

Ankersmit, F. (2013), "Aftermaths and 'Foremaths': History and Humans," in M. Turda (ed.), *Crafting Humans: From Genesis to Eugenics and Beyond*, 9–37, Göttingen: V&R unipress//Taipei: National Taiwan University Press.
Baschet, J. (2004), "History Facing the Perpetual Present: The Past-Future Relationships," in C. Barros and L. J. McCrank (eds.), *History Under Debate: International Reflection on the Discipline*, 133–58, Binghamton, NY: The Haworth Press.
Baschet, J. (2018), *Défaire la tyrannie du présent: Temporalités émergentes et futurs inédits*. Paris: La Découverte.

Braidotti, R. (2019), *Posthuman Knowledge*. Cambridge: Polity Press.
Chakrabarty, D. (2009), "The Climate of History: Four Theses," *Critical Inquiry* 35(2): 197–222.
Chakrabarty, D. (2019a), *The Crises of Civilization: Exploring Global and Planetary Histories*. New Delhi: Oxford University Press.
Chakrabarty, D. (2019b), "The Planet: An Emergent Humanist Category," *Critical Inquiry* 46: 1–31.
Danowski, D., and E. Viveiros de Castro (2016), *The Ends of the World*. Cambridge: Polity Press.
Domanska, E. (2014), "Retroactive Ancestral Constitution, New Animism and Alter-Native Modernities," *Storia della Storiografia* 65(1): 61–75.
Domanska, E. (2017), "Animal History," *History and Theory* 56(2): 267–87.
Ellis, E. C. (2018), *Anthropocene: A Very Short Introduction*. Oxford: Oxford University Press.
Fuller, S. (2013), *Preparing for Life in Humanity 2.0*. Basingstoke: Palgrave Macmillan.
Fuller, S., and V. Lipinska (2014), *The Proactionary Imperative: A Foundation for Transhumanism*. Basingstoke: Palgrave Macmillan.
Gumbrecht, H. U. (2014), *Our Broad Present: Time and Contemporary Culture*. New York: Columbia University Press.
Harootunian, H. (2007), "Remembering the Historical Present," *Critical Inquiry* 33: 471–94.
Hartog, F. (2015), *Regimes of Historicity: Presentism and Experiences of Time*. Trans. S. Brown. New York: Columbia University Press.
Hölscher, L. (2019), "Future Pasts: About a Form of Thought in Modern Society," *Sustainability Science* 14: 899–904.
Horn, E. (2018), *The Future as Catastrophe: Imagining Disaster in the Modern Age*. Trans. V. Pakis. New York: Columbia University Press.
Horn, E., and H. Bergthaller (2020), *The Anthropocene (Key Issues for the Humanities)*. London and New York: Routledge.
Jonas, H. (1979), *Das Prinzip Verantwortung: Versuch einer Ethik für die technologische Zivilisation*. Frankfurt: Insel.
Jonas, H. (1984), *The Imperative of Responsibility: In Search of an Ethics for the Technological Age*. Trans. H. Jonas and D. Herr. Chicago, IL: University of Chicago Press.
Kelly, D. (2019), *Politics and the Anthropocene*. Cambridge: Polity Press.
Kelly, M. J. (2018), "Introduction: Evental History and the Humanities," in M. J. Kelly and A. Rose (eds.), *Theories of History: History Read across the Humanities*, 1–15, London: Bloomsbury.
Kurzweil, R. (2005), *The Singularity Is Near: When Humans Transcend Biology*. New York: Viking.
Morton, T. (2013), *Hyperobjects: Philosophy and Ecology after the End of the World*. Minneapolis, MN, and London: University of Minnesota Press.
Musk, E. (2017), "Making Humans a Multi-Planetary Species," *New Space* 5: 46–61.
Musk, E. (2018), "Making Life Multiplanetary," *New Space* 6: 2–11.
Nance, S. (2015), "Introduction," in S. Nance (ed.), *The Historical Animal*, 1–16, Syracuse and New York: Syracuse University Press.

Northcott, M. (2015), "Eschatology in the Anthropocene: From the *chronos* of Deep Time to the *kairos* of the Age of Humans," in C. Hamilton, C. Bonneuil, and F. Gemenne (eds.), *The Anthropocene and the Global Environmental Crisis: Rethinking Modernity in a New Epoch*, 100–11, New York and London: Routledge.

Ranisch, R., and S. L. Sorgner (2014), "Introducing Post- and Transhumanism," in R. Ranisch and S. L. Sorgner (eds.), *Post- and Transhumanism: An Introduction*, 7–27, Frankfurt am Main: Peter Lang.

Simon, Z. B. (2018), "History Begins in the Future: On Historical Sensibility in the Age of Technology," in S. Helgesson and J. Svenungsson (eds.), *The Ethos of History: Time and Responsibility*, 192–209, Oxford and New York: Berghahn.

Simon, Z. B. (2019a), *History in Times of Unprecedented Change: A Theory for the 21st Century*. London: Bloomsbury.

Simon, Z. B. (2019b), "The Transformation of Historical Time: Processual and Evental Temporalities," in M. Tamm and L. Olivier (eds.), *Rethinking Historical Time: New Approaches to Presentism*, 71–84, London: Bloomsbury.

Simon, Z. B., and M. Tamm (2021), "Historical Futures," *History and Theory* 60(1): 3–22.

Sorgner, S. L. (2014), "Pedigrees," in R. Ranisch and S. L. Sorgner (eds.), *Post- and Transhumanism: An Introduction*, 29–47, Frankfurt am Main: Peter Lang.

Sörlin, S. (2018), "Environmental History: Comment," in M. Tamm and P. Burke (eds.), *Debating New Approaches to History*, 86–91, London: Bloomsbury.

Stiegler, B. (2011), *Technics and Time: Cinematic Time and the Question of Malaise*. Trans. S. Barker. Stanford, CA: Stanford University Press.

Tamm, M. (2020), "How to Reinvent the Future?" *History and Theory* 59(3): 448–58.

Tamm, M., and L. Olivier (eds.) (2019), *Rethinking Historical Time: New Approaches to Presentism*. London: Bloomsbury.

Tamm, M., and Z. B. Simon (2020a), "More-than-Human History: Philosophy of History at the Time of the Anthropocene," in J.-M. Kuukkanen (ed.), *Philosophy of History: Twenty-First-Century Perspectives*, 198–215, London: Bloomsbury.

Tamm, M., and Z. B. Simon (2020b), "Historical Thinking and the Human: Introduction," *Journal of the Philosophy of History* 14(3): 285–309.

Tegmark, M. (2017), *Life 3.0: Being Human in the Age of Artificial Intelligence*. New York: Alfred A. Knopf.

Tirosh-Samuelson, H., and J. B. Hurlbut (2016), "Introduction: Technology, Utopianism and Eschatology," in J. B. Hurlbut and H. Tirosh-Samuelson (eds.), *Perfecting Human Futures: Transhuman Visions and Technological Imaginations*, 1–32, Wiesbaden: Springer.

Torpey, J. (2008), "An Avalanche of History: The 'Collapse of the Future' and the Rise of Reparations Politics," in M. Berg and B. Schäfer (eds.), *Historical Justice in International Perspective*, 21–38, Cambridge: Cambridge University Press.

Tsing, A. L. (2015), *The Mushroom at the End of the World. On the Possibility of Life in Capitalist Ruins*. Oxford and Princeton, NJ: Princeton University Press.

Tutton, R. (2018), "Multiplanetary Imaginaries and Utopia: The Case of Mars One," *Science, Technology & Human Values* 43(3): 518–39.

Wolfe, C. (2010), *What is Posthumanism?* Minneapolis, MN, and London: University of Minnesota Press.

CHAPTER TWELVE

What future for the future? Utopian lessons from a global pandemic

Patrícia Vieira

COVID-19: A foreseeable pandemic

When news about the first cases of COVID-19 in China started to appear in the Western media, when we started to hear about the confinement of millions of people in Wuhan and the surrounding provinces, of families locked at home, of hospitals overflowing with patients, and of countless medical staff dying from a new disease, the feeling I had was that we were living through a Hollywood blockbuster. This impression deepened as the pandemic spread to other parts of Asia, to South Korea, to Japan, to the international passengers of numerous cruise ships, and then to Europe and the Americas. And it became even more palpable when Italy, Spain, France, the United Kingdom, several US states, Brazil, Peru, South Africa, and so many other countries closed schools, non-essential stores and other services, and ordered their populations to stay home for weeks and, in some cases, months on end. As friends and acquaintances quarantined after traveling or simply because they had been in touch with someone affected by the virus, as the number of infected people and of COVID-19 victims increased, and as a generalized fear took hold of almost the entire world population, my sense of déjà vu only increased.

It turns out I really had watched this kind of movie before. *Contagion* (2011), a thriller directed by Steven Soderbergh, tells the story of a pandemic that originates in Hong Kong. The inability to contain the virus through contact tracing and quarantine of those infected leads to its rapid dissemination throughout the planet. As the dead pile up and the economy collapses, widespread social unrest and violence ensue. In the film, the virus is transmitted through infected droplets that enter the human respiratory tract, as well as through contact with surfaces that had previously been touched by infected people. Sound familiar?

The vast majority of specialists in public health were well aware of the fact that a pandemic similar to COVID-19 was a likely scenario. The SARS epidemic in 2003, the 2009 H1N1 influenza outbreak, and the MERS syndrome from 2012 all pointed in that direction. Bill Gates's TED talk from 2015 in which he warned that the world was not prepared to deal with epidemics with transmission mechanisms and symptoms similar to those of the common flu has, meanwhile, been widely shared. Celebrated by some for its prophetic description of what was to come, and in other cases fanning the flames of conspiracy theories convinced of an evil cabal orchestrated by the world's billionaires, Gates's TED talk reveals something simple: we were clearly not seeing the writing on the wall, or, worse still, we were ignoring it at our own risk.

Overlapping crises

Pandemics such as COVID-19 are, in this sense, similar to the crises of capitalism. Everybody knows that they periodically flare up with lesser or greater intensity. However, when they do emerge, most people act as though they are an unexpected phenomenon, something that appeared completely out of the blue. The current pandemic irrupted twelve years after the massive 2008 economic meltdown. Roughly a century ago, in 1918, the world was gripped by the so-called Spanish flu outbreak, which killed about 50 million people, eleven years before the momentous economic collapse of 1929. Marx ([1852] 1978) famously wrote that history repeats itself, first as tragedy and then as farce. In this case, though, history always seems to repeat itself as tragedy, as if each of these occurrences—economic and public health crises—were something absolutely new. And yet we have a clear pattern of regularly occurring calamities. This predictability is routinely ignored by politicians and by civil society, so that nations are utterly unprepared when these events strike. Far from trying to avoid these crises, authorities act surprised and respond with reactive instead of preventive measures when they inevitably surface. If we are unable to heed the lessons of the past, we cannot carve a path toward a desirable future, and instead resignedly lie in wait, only to concoct yet another half-baked response to the next emergency.

The economic and public health crises that cyclically plague our societies and disturb their normal functioning—and we would do well to ask ourselves what "normality" is when we are always at the risk of another crisis, always on the brink of collapse; imminent crises are the new normal and, therefore, the state of exception becomes the rule, as Giorgio Agamben (1998) has rightly pointed out; from crisis to crisis, we live in permanent fear and anxiety becomes the defining trait of our existence—come about in the context of yet another crisis, namely the environmental crisis. Environmental degradation has been intensifying since at least the Industrial Revolution with the large-scale use of fossil fuels, and has proceeded at a fast pace alongside the rapid growth of the world's population made possible by breakthroughs in medicine and the green revolution in agriculture. The human population was about 500 million in the seventeenth century, and we now have almost eight billion people on the planet. Between the 1970s and today, the world population has more than doubled and consumption has skyrocketed, a situation that has significantly worsened environmental problems.

It is well known that the contamination of the air, of the soils, of waterways, and of the oceans as a result of massive industrialization and the use of increasingly large parts of the Earth's surface to meet human food and consumption needs have had a devastating impact of the planet. Global warming, ocean acidification, the rampant destruction of rainforests, and the sixth mass extinction of non-human living beings are all proof of the fact that we are undergoing an unprecedented crisis in the life of our species. Just like other animals and plants that expand beyond the carrying capacity of their ecosystems and thus compromise their own survival, *Homo sapiens* risks rendering the Earth uninhabitable for human beings, not to mention all the other forms of existence irreparably damaged by human action.

To sum up, we are currently in the grip of a public health crisis that emerged in the wake of the 2008 economic and social crises. These irrupted while another, long-duration crisis has been unfolding, i.e., the environmental crisis. What are the points at which these three crises converge? In Western medieval times, people believed that society and individual human beings reflected what was going on in nature and that the microcosm mirrored the macrocosm. If we follow this line of thinking, we realize that the planet is increasingly sick (environmental crisis), that our social and political body—the Hobbesian Leviathan—is sick (with the cyclical crises of capitalism), and that people are sick (with the cyclical onset of pandemics such as COVID-19). How can we think about the future when we are submerged in overlapping crises? And what can these crises teach us about the very possibility of a future for our species?

First, one should note that these crises are not simply taking place concurrently. Rather, they feed off and intensify one another. For example, COVID-19 has affected lower-income people much more aggressively than middle- and high-income social groups, since the former often need to work outside their homes and therefore do not have the luxury to stay in lockdown. Furthermore, lack of access to quality healthcare has exacerbated the effects of the disease in underprivileged communities. The economic impact of the pandemic also disproportionately fell upon poorer segments of the population, on minorities, those working in the informal economy, or those without job security. In short, the public health crisis is worsened by economic vulnerability and, in turn, exacerbates already-existing social and economic inequalities.

Some of the causes of the environmental crisis have contributed to the onset of the pandemic. For instance, the mass production of animals—that is to say, the logic of capitalism applied to the production of meat and other animal products—is one of the possible drivers of the virus, which may have passed on to humans from domestic animals contaminated in animal farms. Forest destruction and the encroachment of people and domestic animals on the natural habitats of wild animals is also often identified as being among the main causes of the frequent zoonotic pandemics plaguing humans. And the congregation of large numbers of human beings in crowded, sprawling megalopolises such as Wuhan, Paris, Madrid, and New York, all epicenters of COVID-19, has greatly contributed to the rapid spread of the disease. In other words, the environmental and the public health crises are tightly linked.

COVID-19 is clearly not a natural revenge against human destruction of the biosphere or, worse still, a divine punishment for human hubris, as some extremist religious groups would have us believe. *Homo sapiens* has suffered from pandemics at least since the development of agricultural societies that required the establishment of sizeable human communities in one location, first in villages and then in cities. Let us recall, for example, the Black Death that killed millions of people in Eurasia in the fourteenth century. But, while pandemics have been part of human history for millennia, the combination of global environmental disaster, capitalist economic meltdowns, and public health emergencies is a sign of our times. What kind of a future can we hope for when the present appears to be so bleak?

Another world is possible

We would do well to remember that the feeling of living through an unprecedented moment is not new. The idea that ours is an extraordinary epoch, that our society is undergoing exceptional events, and that the end of human history is near goes back to the roots of Western thought. Eschatological thinking is part and parcel of the Judeo-Christian culture that has left an indelible mark on the DNA of the West. Be it with the advent of a millenarian kingdom of peace and prosperity for all or with an apocalypse that will bring destruction and death to all of humanity, Westerners have been convinced for centuries that the end of the world is nigh. The difference between previous eschatological thought and the present moment is that, in the past, the end of the world as we know it required the intervention of a divine entity that heralded the annihilation of a corrupt society. Only in the twentieth century have humans acquired the ability of becoming eschatological agents—that is to say, of being able to exterminate or radically change the lives of all other human beings and of the planet itself—through nuclear technology, genetic manipulation, and the profound transformation of the biosphere. This is the culmination of a process of secularization: humanity now has a role formerly played by god(s), namely to create and/or destroy life itself. Previous generations could count on divine wisdom to make the right judgment about the eschaton. Since the beginning of the nuclear age, that momentous decision is in the hands of humanity (see Vieira 2020).

Let us return to the three crises we have identified: the environmental, socio-economic, and public health crises. The etymology of the word "crisis" goes back to Ancient Greek, and it was already then linked to a context of disease. It meant a turning point in an illness, a change that indicated a path toward either recovery or death. The word derived from a verb that meant "to separate, decide or judge." If we take this etymology into consideration, we realize that *Homo sapiens* is truly in a moment of crisis: we humans are at a turning point in our history as a species, having the possibility to self-destruct. COVID-19 made it very clear that a basic common denominator unites humanity: we are all members of the same species and, therefore, we are all vulnerable to the same pathogens, as well as to economic privation, pollution, climate change, and so on. In this time of crisis, we need to judge or evaluate our situation and make a collective decision about the future.

It is a matter, then, of thinking about the possibility of the future in the context of the multiple crises we face. During the COVID-induced lockdown, it became clear that radical changes in the current way of life are well within our reach: traffic almost stopped; flights were grounded; people stayed home with their families or roommates; there was a drastic decrease in air and water pollution, and so on. This does not mean that all transformations brought about by the pandemic were positive. The inability to socialize with friends and with some family members left many of struggling with loneliness and other mental health problems. And home confinement led to a sharp increase in violence against those who are more vulnerable (women, girls, children, the elderly), who were permanently sharing a space with their aggressors. These and other examples show that COVID-19 was certainly not beneficial. What was positive about the crisis was that it opened up a whole horizon of possibilities. It showed us that another world is possible, a notion that has been the hallmark of utopian thought even since Thomas More ([1516] 2002) created the word "utopia" in his homonymous book more than five hundred years ago.

The COVID-19 outbreak unveiled utopian possibilities at a time that has been predominantly marked by dystopia. From at least the beginning of the twentieth century, and especially in the last few decades, a dystopian outlook has been the decisive feature of our times.[1] The devastation wrought by colonialism, imperialism, and neo-colonialism, the oppression caused by authoritarian political regimes, growing economic inequalities, the environmental, economic, and public health crises mentioned above, and the very real possibility of *Homo sapiens'* demise have all contributed to our dystopian zeitgeist. We are far from the optimism of the Enlightenment, according to which technical, social, and political progress would go hand in hand. Dystopia tells us that there is no alternative to the status quo and that a better future is impossible, or, to put it differently, that there is no future for the future. Dystopian thought spells the end of the famous "principle of hope" that, according to Ernst Bloch (1986), is the basis for utopia.

If dystopias express, from the inception of the genre, a renunciation of our techno-scientific modernity, that rejection often transforms into a repudiation of *Homo sapiens*, who brought about modern life and its attendant evils. Such an assessment of humankind goes hand in hand with contemporary reflections on the Anthropocene, a geological era marked by human beings' lasting impact on the planet. As Dipesh Chakrabarty (2009) argues, the distinction between human and natural history, as well as humanist accounts of modernity and globalization, collapses when we regard humans as a geological force. The unprecedented rate of anthropogenic changes to the Earth have led some thinkers to consider that the disappearance of *Homo sapiens* might be a positive development, if not for humans, then for the Earth and all other living beings. From being regarded as an unintended, dystopian outcome of modernity-gone-wrong, human extinction has come to acquire utopian undertones.

The various crises we face have a twofold effect upon our collective consciousness. On the one hand, and following a long line of dystopian thought, they show us that *Homo sapiens* is on the brink of an existential abyss from which there is no coming back. On the other hand, they reveal humankind's ability to effect swift and decisive changes in its way of life. The crises prompt us to learn from the past and to reflect upon the shape of a more desirable future, and thus enable our return to utopia. To be sure, this notion of utopia does not entail a well-defined blueprint for a better future, a plan that we need to follow through at all costs. Rather, utopia is here understood as the possibility of a future that would not simply be a repetition of the present, of a future that would not be more of the same—that is to say, a future as such.[2] Perhaps we should not even call such a future a utopia, given the ideological baggage of the word. We could simply call it future, *tout court*. In the final paragraphs of this article, I would like to sketch some of the possibilities inherent in this thinking of the future that the crises have triggered.

What future for *Homo sapiens*?

As a guide to my reflection on a possible future for our species, I will use three novels by Canadian writer Margaret Atwood: *Oryx and Crake* (2003), *The Year of the Flood* (2009), and *MaddAddam* (2013). I read Atwood's so-called MaddAddam trilogy shortly before the outbreak of COVID-19, which contributed to the feeling I mentioned above of living in a fictional world when news of the pandemic broke in the media. The novels narrate the final years before and the time immediately after a so-called "waterless flood" that killed almost all human beings on the planet. Before the "flood," the world was dominated by hyper-capitalism and most of humanity survived in overcrowded and extremely polluted cities, while a privileged few scientists and business people lived in highly protected, well-appointed condos. Genetic manipulation had run wild and countless hybrid species proliferated. It is in this apocalyptic scenario that a rogue scientist creates a virus—the equivalent to the biblical flood that cleansed the Earth of a fallen Creation—and embeds it in a sexual enhancement pill. Only a few humans survive the illness, together with a group of hominids who had been genetically engineered by the same scientist to survive the virus and to thrive on a significantly warmer planet.

I have analyzed Atwood's trilogy at length elsewhere (Vieira forthcoming). For the purposes of this chapter, I would like to point out that her texts exacerbate some of the socioeconomic, scientific, and environmental trends already at work in our societies, including the excesses of unbridled capitalism, a cavalier approach to the dangers of genetic manipulation, and widespread environmental devastation. The author does not consider these texts to be science fiction and prefers instead to use the term "speculative fiction." She argues that her narratives invent "nothing we haven't already invented or started to invent" (Atwood 2005: 322). Instead, they expand upon a "what if" question: "What if we continue down the road we're already on? How slippery is the slope? What are our saving graces? Who's got the will to stop us?" (323). The novels are therefore a thought experiment that nudges us out of complacency and leads us to ask: what if a deadly virus were to hit human beings? What if we drastically changed our way of living? What if we were forced to halt our destructive relationship to the natural world? Atwood's novels are some among a plethora of possible responses to these questions. They prompt us to reflect on the historical trajectory of *Homo sapiens* and to consider different possibilities for the future of our species.

The COVID-19 pandemic, in conjunction with the cyclical socioeconomic crises of capitalism and the *longue durée* environmental crisis, invites us to follow Atwood's lead and undertake a thought experiment akin to the one she suggests in her novels. I will finish this chapter with ten proposals for the future, ten "what if" questions or utopian ideas to counter the crises that feed the dystopian mood of the present. These propositions are utopian only in the sense that they are different from present-day reality, but they are completely feasible in the here and now. Several already circulate within our societies in the context of ongoing discussions about the future of our human future. The first five are broader notions, while the last ones are more concrete suggestions that open up a possible future for *Homo sapiens*:

1   What if ecology—the logic or logos of our home, which is the Earth—overrode economy, understood as the capitalist, for-profit ordering of bodies and matter on the planet?

2   What if we placed technology at the service of living beings, human and non-human, and not at the service of the economy?

3   What if we reframed the current arithmetical notion of economic and populational growth, based upon expansion and increase, and considered growth as an unfolding of promises inherent in humans and non-humans, including the growth of well-being, of creativity, and so on?

4   What if we abandoned the imperialistic logic of expansion that has already devastated vast regions of the globe and now promotes the colonization of Mars and other planets as a solution to the environmental crisis?

5   What if we learned to share the Earth and live in a balanced relationship with other beings?

6   What if we stopped the mass production of animals to be exterminated for human consumption?

7   What if our societies adequately funded public services, including healthcare and social security, and supported the transition to renewable energies, instead of bolstering banks and large companies and subsidizing the fossil fuel industry?

8   What if we changed the way we live and work, so that people would not spend hours in traffic and more than half of their days in an office, with their homes empty?

9   What if we had gender parity both at work and in housework and more support for family planning?

10   What if we better distributed wealth in our societies and drastically reduced working hours, so that each person could spend more time at leisure and with their loved ones?

Acknowledgements

A version of this chapter was published in *Esboços: Histórias em Contextos Globais*. I thank the journal for their permission to include in this volume a different version of the text. Research for this article was funded by a Grant from the Portuguese Foundation for Science and Technology (FCT), Project IF/00606/2015.

Notes

1   Most utopia studies scholars agree that the twentieth century marked a shift from a predominantly utopian outlook to a dystopian one. Keith Booker (1994: 15) writes that "much of the history of recent utopian thought can be read as a gradual shift from utopian to dystopian emphases." For Krishan Kumar (2013: 19), "it is mainly in the twentieth century that dystopia truly comes into its own." Lyman Tower Sargent (2013: 10) argues that "dystopia has been the dominant form of utopianism since around World War I" and goes on to add that "the twentieth century has quite correctly been called the dystopian century, and the twenty-first century does not look much better."

2   I am drawing here on Jacques Derrida's distinction throughout his work between the French *future* as a repetition of the present and *avenir*, which stands for an open-ended, unpredictable future of possibilities.

References

Agamben, G. (1998), *Homo Sacer: Sovereign Power and Bare Life*. Trans. D. Heller-Roazen. Stanford, CA: Stanford University Press.

Atwood, M. (2004), *Oryx and Crake*. New York: Anchor Books.

Atwood, M. (2005), *Curious Pursuits: Occasional Writing, 1970–2005*. London: Virago.

Atwood, M. (2010), *The Year of the Flood*. New York: Anchor Books.

Atwood, M. (2013), *MaddAddam*. New York: Nan A. Talese/Doubleday.

Bloch, E. (1986), *The Principle of Hope*, 3 vols. Trans. Neville Paice, S. Paice, and P. Knight. Cambridge, MA: MIT Press.

Booker, K. (1994), *The Dystopian Impulse in Modern Literature: Fiction as Social Criticism*. Westport, CT: Greenwood Press.

Chakrabarty, D. (2009), "The Climate of History: Four Theses," *Critical Inquiry* 35: 197–222.

Contagion (2011), [Film] Dir. S. Soderbergh, USA: Warner Bros. Pictures.

Gates, B. (2015), *The Next Outbreak? We're Not Ready, TED Talk*. Available online: https://www.ted.com/talks/bill_gates_the_next_outbreak_we_re_not_ready?language=en (accessed September 30, 2021).

Kumar, K. (2013), "Utopia's Shadow," in F. Vieira (ed.), *Dystopia(n) Matters: On the Page, on Screen, on Stage*, 19–22, Newcastle upon Tyne: Cambridge Scholars Publishing.

Marx, K. ([1852] 1978), "The Eighteenth Brumaire of Louis Bonaparte," in R. C. Tucker (ed.), *The Marx-Engels Reader*, 594–617, New York: W. W. Norton and Co.

More, T. ([1516] 2002), *Utopia*. Edited by G. M. Logan and R. M. Adams. Cambridge: Cambridge University Press.

Sargent, L. T. (2013), "Do Dystopias Matter?" in F. Vieira (ed.), *Dystopia(n) Matters: On the Page, on Screen, on Stage*, 10–13, Newcastle upon Tyne: Cambridge Scholars Publishing.

Vieira, P. (2020). "Utopia and Dystopia in the Age of the Anthropocene," *Esboços: Histórias em Contextos Globais* 27(46): 350–65.

Vieira, P. (forthcoming) "Utopia," in F. Vieira, J. Wagner-Lawlor and P. Marks (eds.), *Palgrave Handbook of Utopian and Dystopian Literatures*, London: Palgrave Macmillan.

Histories

CHAPTER THIRTEEN

The future as a domain of historical inquiry

David J. Staley

I wish to claim the future as a domain of historical inquiry. One important story in the history of twentieth-century historiography was the expansion of the historical method into new areas of inquiry: the history of women, of emotions, of the environment. Nothing, it seems, was off limits to the interests of historians. The expansion of historiography meant the extension of the historical method into domains beyond politics. The future is our next historiographic frontier, our move into this domain similar to the ways in which some historians have entered into the subjunctive spaces of the counterfactual.

Figure 13.1 maps different ontological domains using a matrix based on the axes actual vs. inactual and present vs. absent. The world we inhabit at the moment—reality—might be described as a domain that is ontologically present and actual (the upper-left quadrant of the matrix). The past, in contrast, might be understood as a domain that is (or was) at one time actual but is now absent to our direct senses. This domain occupies the upper right of our matrix. The lower left of the matrix is that ontological domain that is present but non-actual. This unusual domain includes fictional characters—Sherlock Holmes exists as an entity in our imaginations, and thus is present to our senses, but is non-actual—and certain mathematical entities, such as the square root of – 1, which is a non-actual entity that is nevertheless present, and useful in making certain kinds of mathematical calculations.

actual

reality | the past

present ———————————————————————————————— *absent*

√ - 1 | counterfactual history

fictional characters | the future

inactual

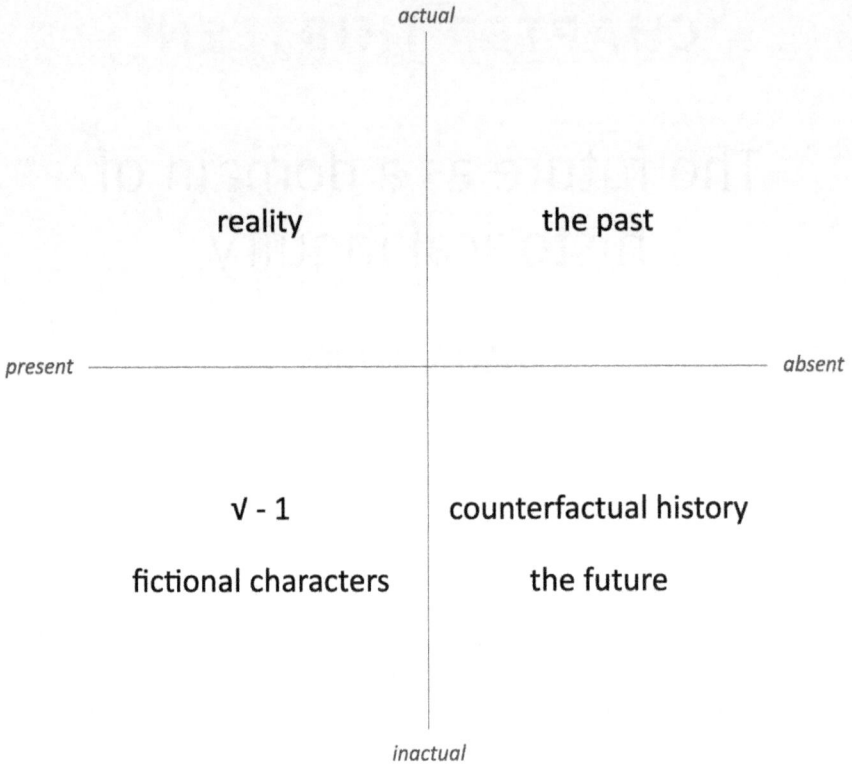

FIGURE 13.1 Ontologically actual/inactual/present/absent domains.

It is the lower right of the matrix that is the particular area of concern for this essay. Unlike the domain of the past—which is ontologically actual yet absent—the conceptual terrain of the counterfactual is ontologically inactual. The future is a conceptual area that shares characteristics with the counterfactual. What I present here is a strategy for so claiming the domain of the future—this ontologically absent and inactual domain—as an object of historiographic study.

Thus, an inquiry into the future must begin with questions of ontology. Or rather, I want to recast the debate about determinism versus free will in regard to the future as a debate about the ontological status of the future. Does the future exist? If so, what is the nature of its existence? The answer one gives and how that answer is arrived at says much about the nature of the inquiry. If we are to treat the future as a domain of historical inquiry, then we must first consider its dimensions and properties. The particular properties of the future make it amenable to study via the historical method.

The ontology of the future

A feature of the Enlightenment/Scientific Revolution was a belief that the future was an ontologically actual domain. So confident were some Europeans in the actuality of the future that Pierre-Simon Laplace (1951: 4) could proclaim that

> We ought then to regard the present state of the universe as the effect of its anterior state and as the cause of the one which is to follow. Given for one instant an intelligence which could comprehend all the forces by which nature is animated and the respective situation of the beings who compose it—an intelligence sufficiently vast to submit these data to analysis—it would embrace in the same formula the movements of the greatest bodies of the universe and those of the lightest atom; for it, nothing would be uncertain and the future, as the past, would be present to its eyes.

By asserting that there are fundamental laws underlying the operation of the universe, and that a human mind could apprehend all of the information required, the future can be predicted. In this formulation, Laplace assumes the future already exists. It is the assumption underlying any prediction: that the future is a domain that is ontologically actual, that there is a space called the future filled with events that are already in place, waiting to be experienced. It considers the future like the past: being ontologically actual, but not present. Thus, when astronomers tell us when and where the next solar eclipse is going to be, this supposes that at least that portion of the future already exists. Bill Gates's book *The Road Ahead* (1995) had Gates standing alongside a paved road. The visual rhetoric being that the future is already in existence—it is even paved!—and that Gates has seen this (or, alternatively, Gates will make/pave the future for us. More on this point later.) The future exists somewhere, although it may be impervious to our methods of detection, thus a prediction or a forecast is either right or wrong, measured against what will actually unfold. If the solar eclipse occurs a week after the predicted day and time, then that is the fault of the astronomer and her methods—it is the prediction that is incorrect, not the future.

Indeed, predictions often prove to be wrong, especially in the realm of human affairs. These predictions are so frequently wrong that it would be reasonable to ask if it is even possible to make accurate predictions. Economics is often held up as the most rigorous and predictive of the social sciences, but the forecasting record of economics has not been especially sound. Ruchir Sharma (2017) writes that:

> The forecasting misses of 2017 reflect mistakes humans have been making since we started thinking about the future. Every forecaster knows that economies rise and fall constantly, oscillating around a long-term trend line. Yet forecasts typically extrapolate current trends on a straight line, so the vision of tomorrow closely resembles today, often implausibly so. A year ago forecasters thought 2017 would look like 2016; instead the world economy had its best year since the financial crisis of 2008. The weakness of straight-line forecasts explains why the consensus of leading economists has consistently missed big turns. They have not predicted a single United States recession since the Federal Reserve began keeping such records a half-century ago, and missed many revivals, including the unusually broad global expansion of 2017.

What should these failures signal to us? That our methods of prediction are flawed and need to be made even more rigorous? That these failures signal that economics is not really a predictive science at all? This is not because the methods are not rigorous: it is because these methods are based on a flawed ontological assumption. Seeing the future as a straight line from the past (or any shaped line) assumes that the future already exists. The reason forecasts are so often wrong is because forecasters are trying to peg down an entity that in fact does not yet exist. What is required, then, is not more scientific prediction, but rather a method that looks more like narrative history.

Sharma (2017) says that "In early 2017, forecasters took rising poll numbers for nationalists, extrapolated them into the future and imagined formerly fringe right-wingers gaining influence and setting off a Eurozone crisis. Instead, the center held, and sheer relief helped propel the surprise economic recovery." In my view, there is another explanation for this "failure": a prediction assumes a pre-existing future against which we judge the accuracy of predictions. But if the future were not already in existence, then we would need to assess statements about the future according to some other criteria. I would counter that the world described in the above sentence was not an incorrect prediction but rather an entirely plausible scenario of what might have happened—and may still happen. A scenario is a statement about the future established on very different logical, epistemological, and ontological foundations.

A scenario assumes that the future does not already exist, but is instead a space of possibility. And, as I have written elsewhere (Staley 2007), scenarios are produced through a process that looks very much like the historical method.

Even in the face of these repeated failures, there remains the hope and the expectation that the future can nevertheless be predicted. Big data and data analytics, especially, has opened up this possibility. The assumption is that our previous attempts to predict the future have suffered from insufficient data (not a lack of theoretical rigor). If we only had more data, we could uncover patterns in those data that would reveal behavioral regularities. (This is the premise of Asimov's Foundation trilogy, and the fictional science of psychohistory.) A decade ago, Albert-Laszlo Barabasi (2010: 10) wrote (perhaps anticipating our current Cambridge Analytica moment):

> Today just about everything we do leaves digital breadcrumbs in some database. While we choose not to think about it, the truth is that our life, with minute resolution, can be pieced together from these mushrooming databases … Computer scientists, physicists, mathematicians, sociologists, psychologists and economists [pore] over [these databases] with the help of powerful computers and a wide array of novel technologies. Their conclusions are breathtaking: they provide convincing evidence that most of our actions are driven by laws, patterns, and mechanisms that in reproducibility and predictive power rival those encountered in the natural sciences.

Rebecca Costa (2017: 2, 10–11) breathlessly exclaims that we are (according to the title of her recent book) "on the verge" of such predictive certainty. "Recent breakthroughs in technology," she writes,

> such as the proliferation of predictive analytics, Big Data, and sensor and satellite technologies—have made it possible to anticipate future outcomes with unprecedented accuracy … Technology [has] made it possible to string together millions of variables, in real time, revealing cause-and-effect relationships we never knew existed … With the Information Age came data. With data, analytics. With analytics, foreknowledge. And with foreknowledge, foresight. As our prowess for prognostication spread, we stumbled upon an

unexpected truth—one with tectonic implications: there is far less randomness to the future than we thought. More of it is predictable than not.

Data analytics uncovers patterns of behavior that follow predictable laws such that the future path of the system must be predetermined. As long as one can demonstrate that the future is ontologically actual, it must be predictable.

The future as a complex adaptive system

I do not believe the future is pre-existing, that it is ontologically actual. In truth, that statement requires a bit more nuance: there are some features of the future that do exist. The solar eclipse is one example: we can state with some certainty that this feature of the future is ontologically real. A solar eclipse is the product of the actions of a relatively simple system. Indeed, the behavior of simple systems is more amenable to prediction. The challenge is, of course, that there are relatively few simple systems. Indeed, most of the systems we are interested in are complex adaptive systems, which are inherently unpredictable. When making a prediction, however, we tend to treat the subject of our inquiry *as if it were* a simple system and proceed accordingly.

Usually, whenever anyone says they are interested in the future, what they mean to say is they want to know the configuration or state of some complex system at point *n* in the future. I have had occasion to consult with a client who is interested in "the future of crime." What this CEO was saying in effect is that there is a complex system called "crime" that has a certain configuration today. In the future, that system will have a different configuration, and he is curious to know what that configuration might be. I was very clear with him that the state of that system cannot be known with certainty: the best we can hope to achieve is to identify possible states the system might take. Complex adaptive systems exhibit emergent behavior, are sensitive to initial conditions, and thus do not behave in the manner that Laplace would have expected. The future state of a complex system is "to be determined."

Because some of its aspects are ontologically real and others—most of them?—are not, we might say that the future exists in a quantum-like state. That is, much of the future exists as potential. As evidence of its quantum nature, the future can be influenced in a way that the past cannot. George

Soros's (2003: 2–3) idea of "reflexivity"—a feedback process between our understanding of a situation and the situation itself, including the notion that our actions alter the very situation we are trying to understand— suggests that the future is not actual but potential, and that it is, in fact, malleable, capable of being shaped or influenced by actions we take (or don't take). Also, as mentioned earlier, another way of reading *The Road Ahead* would be to say that Bill Gates was not predicting an already-existing future but was, instead, creating the road that he himself would pave. Finally, consider Nick Montfort (2017: xi–xii) claiming that he "seek[s] to show that it is possible to imagine the future systematically and in sufficient detail, that one can share the imagination of the future with others, and that it is possible to work to develop specific innovations that are components of such a future." "By doing so," he continues, "people, communities, and organizations can influence what lies ahead of all of us … The future as I discuss it is more like an unwritten book. We can't just think about how to view it—we need to write it. The future is not something to be predicted," he concludes, "but to be made." The future is void, substance, and potential all at once.

Counterfactuals and the future

I hold that historical counterfactuals are evidence of the quantum nature of the future. Historians exploring counterfactuals are saying, in effect, that particular systems—the rise of the Nazis, the drift toward the Great War—were complex adaptive systems: deterministic, perhaps, but not predetermined. Those systems could have unfolded in any number of directions, taken any number of configurations. Those of us anticipating the future are in a similar position as the counterfactual historian placing herself at a moment in the past and looking "ahead" toward a future that has yet to occur. Without employing preknowledge of what actually occurred, the counterfactual historian imagines how events might have plausibly unfolded. If there was no such thing as counterfactuals—if there was only one inevitable path—then we might assume the same about the future: there is only one inevitable path forward. But if counterfactuals reveal potential alternative configurations of historic systems, then we might also claim the future as an analogous state of alternatives.

In a similar manner to the way they have explored the subjunctive, counterfactual domains of the past, historians can explore the domain of the future. Historians who explore counterfactual domains have devised a set of protocols that ensure methodological rigor and prove useful when inquiring into the subjunctive domain of the future. Counterfactual historians—like all historians—ask questions, seek evidence, draw reasonable inferences from that evidence. The same thought process can inform an inquiry into the future. Catherine Gallagher (2018: 2) makes the counterfactual statement "If John F. Kennedy had not been assassinated in 1963 and had lived to be a two-term president, the war in Vietnam would have been over by 1968." She says:

> the sentence is not attempting to call the assassination into question or to imply that we should look into it more deeply; it is simply asserting that but for the assassination, history would likely have taken a different path. Insisting on this definition of "historical counterfactual" at the outset should not only clarify the topic but also emphasize that the works under discussion are hinged onto the actual historical record, usually at a juncture that is widely recognized to have been both crucial and underdetermined.

Philip Tetlock and Geoffrey Parker (2006: 27) assert that engaging in counterfactual history is to identify these "'critical junctures,' those events perceived as turning points in the early stages" of some historical inquiry. Indeed, "disputes over historical causality often revolve around disagreements over how to separate those moments when alternative outcomes seem evenly balanced ... from those when trends seem so self-reinforcing that they feel unstoppable" (Tetlock and Parker 2006: 20). Those "underdetermined junctures" that surround us today—not just in the past—are a key feature of our reality and are a principal reason that the future is ontologically non-actual.

Counterfactual thinking is a part of everyone's cognitive toolkit. That is, it is not just historians who occasionally dabble in counterfactual reasoning. Indeed, we might identify "everyday counterfactuals." Ruth Byrne (2005: 3) says that we perceive "fault lines of reality" all around us. She cites an "everyday" example:

> Paul was 47 years old, the father of three and a successful banker. His wife has been ill at home for several months. On the day of the accident, Paul left his office at the regular time. He sometimes left early to take care of home chores at his wife's request, but this was not necessary on that day. Paul did not drive home by his regular route. The day was exceptionally clear and Paul told his friends at the office that he would drive along the shore to enjoy the view. The

accident occurred at a major intersection. The light turned amber as Paul approached. Witnesses noted that he braked hard to stop at the crossing, although he could easily have gone through. His family recognized this as a common occurrence in Paul's driving. As he began to cross after the light changed, a truck charged through the intersection at top speed, and rammed Paul's car from the left. Paul was killed instantly. It was later ascertained that the truck was driven by a teenage boy, who was under the influence of drugs.

When asked "if only," people tend to answer "if only Paul had driven home by his regular route." When the account is altered slightly to say that Paul left his office earlier than usual, a second group answered the "if only" question by saying "if only Paul had left at his regular time." Byrne concludes that

> Some aspects of reality seem more "mutable"—that is, more readily changed in a mental simulation of events—than others. Different people tend to change the same sorts of things when they think about how things might have been different. These regularities indicate that there are "joints" in reality, junctures that attract everyone's attention. There are points at which reality is "slippable."

I take the slippability and mutability of reality—these joints and fault lines—to be evidence that the procession of time is not inevitable: that time consists instead of these junctures, these multiple "if, then" moments where events could proceed in one direction or just as easily in another direction. Assumed in Byrne's formulation is the notion that there are just as many points in reality that are less slippable or malleable. "If only there were no automobiles" or "If only there were no traffic lights" appear to be less slippable features of reality. Similarly, we know that there are 76 million "Baby Boomers" today and that that population is approaching its mid-seventies. Rather than describing this as inevitable, we might instead say this is a feature of reality that is less slippable or malleable than other features.

Rather than make predictions about the future, we might instead behave like a counterfactual historian by identifying the slippable joints of our present reality, prying open those fissures, and then projecting the many possible directions the future might travel. That is, in this formulation, our statements about the future are not predictions about an ontologically real domain but imaginative projections into a quantum-like domain. What we create are proposals about the future, in the terms of Frank Ankersmit (2001: 81). Historical representations are proposals: we understand that what we are representing is not the same thing as that which is absent, and is always subject to new interpretations or new evidence. Historians might consider developing "proposals about the future" that are useful for thinking about the future until new evidence or new interpretations emerge. Or we might think of "historical representations of the future" as being like prototypes. A prototype is not the final product (the future projection is not the future itself), but it is something that we can nevertheless use to think about, plan, and learn about the future.

Imagination

To rigorously think about the future, we must employ our imaginations, and historians employ their imaginations as a central feature of our method. We construct a version of the past in the mind's eye, a mental image that we later write out. In our imaginations, we are picturing that which was once actually present. But, given the paucity of direct evidence, we also "fill in gaps" in that picture any time we draw an inference from direct evidence. That is, we imaginatively project that which must have once been present but is now absent from even our indirect observation. "What the Greeks call 'phantasies,'" said Quintilian, "we rightly term 'sights,' through which the images of absent things are so represented in the mind" (cited in Brann 1991: 21). That could well describe what historians are doing; indeed, one could recast history as the discipline that rigorously imagines absence.

The counterfactual historian is imagining something beyond absence: something that is also inactual. The counterfactual historian has migrated to this other domain, bringing along the cognitive tools of the historian to inquire into a domain that is both absent and inactual. Futures studies—emulating the approach of the historian—could therefore be recast as the rigorous imagination of absence.

References

Ankersmit, F. R. (2001), *Historical Representation*. Stanford, CA: Stanford University Press.
Barabasi, A.-L. (2010), *Bursts: The Hidden Pattern Behind Everything We Do*. New York: Dutton.

Brann, E. T. H. (1991), *The World of the Imagination: Sum and Substance*. Savage, MD: Rowman and Littlefield.

Byrne, R. M. J. (2005), *The Rational Imagination: How People Create Alternatives to Reality*: Cambridge, MA: The MIT Press.

Costa, R. D. (2017), *On The Verge*. New York: Rosetta Books.

Gallagher, C. (2018), *Telling It Like It Wasn't: The Counterfactual Imagination in History and Fiction*. Chicago, IL: University of Chicago Press.

Gates, B. (1995), *The Road Ahead*. New York: Viking Press.

Laplace, P.-S. (1951), *A Philosophical Essay on Probabilities*. New York: Dover Publications.

Montfort, N. (2017), *The Future*. Cambridge, MA: The MIT Press.

Sharma, R. (2017), "When Forecasters Get It Wrong: Always," *New York Times*, December 30, 2017, https://www.nytimes.com/2017/12/30/opinion/sunday/when-forecasters-get-it-wrong-always.html (accessed September 13, 2021).

Soros, G. (2003), *The Alchemy of Finance*. Hoboken, NJ: John Wiley and Sons.

Staley, D. J. (2007), *History and Future: Using Historical Thinking to Imagine the Future*. Lanham, MD: Lexington Books.

Tetlock, P., and G. Parker (2006), "Counterfactual Thought Experiments: Why We Can't Live Without Them & How We Must Learn to Live With Them," in P. Tetlock, R. N. Lebow, and G. Parker (eds.), *Unmaking the West: "What-if?" Scenarios That Rewrite World History*, 14–46, Ann Arbor, MI: University of Michigan Press.

CHAPTER FOURTEEN

Periodization of the future

Cornelius Holtorf

It may be said that one important goal of historical scholarship in society is to foster a historical consciousness that places past, present, and future processes into a joint perspective, appreciating not only specific differences but also long-term trajectories of development. A subtle awareness of change over time can inform how we all, as human beings alive today, perceive the unique conditions in our present and thus how we act and make the future (Rüsen 2004). Accordingly, historians are well versed in studying and representing conditions and processes of the past. This is all the more important when debates in contemporary society seem all too short-sighted and one-dimensional. However, when it comes to the future, historical expertise, and not least the historians' willingness to offer long-term perspectives, quickly comes to a halt. Although there are studies of past futures (e.g., Hölscher 1999), our own future largely remains an unexplored territory that has escaped all but the most minimal attention and conceptualization by historically minded scholars. In particular, there is a general lack of detailed periodization and differentiation of the many ages of history that still lie ahead of us. This is strange, because past and future are directly connected in the period we know best: the present.

Historians and the future

Robin G. Collingwood ([1946] 1994: 54) famously stated that "the historian's business is to know the past, not to know the future, and whenever historians claim to be able to determine the future in advance of its happening, we may know with certainty that something has gone wrong with their fundamental conception of history." This kind of dismissal of the future as a legitimate object of study for historians appears to be as widespread as it is misguided and unwarranted. A rather narrow view of the historians' working methods lurks behind it, as, again, expressed by Collingwood ([1927] 2009: 247–8):

> We cannot know the future, just because the future has not happened and therefore cannot leave its traces in the present. The historian who tries to forecast the future is like a tracker anxiously peering at a muddy road in order to descry the footsteps of the next person who is going to pass that way.

Collingwood ignores that, as a matter of fact, the past is not happening now either. Exactly as the name suggests, it is past. The present contains fragments of both past and future deserving to be studied, analyzed, and interpreted in equal measure. David Staley (2007: 58) believes, therefore, that historical thinking can be applied to help gain knowledge of the future:

> We gain access to the future through a similar means by which we gain access to the past: indirectly, through an examination of evidence. … Like evidence of the past, evidence of the future makes some future state or condition evident. If we wish to inquire into the future, we have little choice but to examine objects and processes that exist in the present, for all evidence—of both past and future—resides in the present.

There are many differences between studying the future and writing history, but there are also many similarities (Männikkö 2017). Past and future are equally material and elusive, real and imagined. They are not polar opposites but tightly connected. Indeed, at the heart of the notion of history lies the idea of change over time, which implies a future that is not only different from a past but (at least in its modern version) also evolving from it: "history—the very possibility of history—begins with the formulation of a vision of the future, that is, with the postulation of a future different from the present and the past" (Simon 2018: 198). And yet: historians have hardly begun to pay attention to what is still to come in human history. They largely left the topic to engineers, architects, biologists, archivists, artists, and authors, among others (Benford 1999; Graves-Brown 2020).

As far as the discipline of history is concerned, the future might be said to be in a pre-discursive phase: historians have not yet come to apply their full arsenal of tools to the vast (one hopes) realms of time ahead of us. They occasionally measure temporal distance in an informal way related to direct descendants (their children and grandchildren, as others do, too; Rydén 2019). They can construct economic or political cycles of the past that extend decades ahead (market cycles, political cycles; e.g., Pop 2019). They are more than willing to debate open-ended global periods of future development on Earth under rather one-dimensional labels (Anthropocene, Capitalocene, Chthulucene; see Quenet 2017). Historians may also work for cultural institutions whose specific genealogies are well known to them but whose futures are placed in a realm of timelessness, as they are quite simply expected to remain in place "as long as possible" (e.g., archives and museums, world heritage sites; Rydén 2019). Only in their spare time may scholars of the past enjoy predictions about the future, e.g., when indulging in the field of psychohistory, which allows them to foresee behavior in populations of the Galactic Empire, as portrayed in Isaac Asimov's "Foundation" series of science-fiction stories (Psychohistory 2019).

It was not always like this. In the pre-scientific age, medieval religious accounts of human history featured revelations of an apocalypse with a clear sequence of future events: in one version, after the imminent rapture and end of the world, it was said that the dead would be resurrected and Christians tested by Satan while preparing for the second coming of Christ, which would occur on Judgment Day and, in turn, start the Millennium, a thousand years of peace.

Classical Marxism, too, provided a theory of developmental history that extended long into the future, offering some clear expectations of what lay ahead in different periods:

Period	Phase	Characteristics
Until the revolution	Capitalism	Dictatorship of the bourgeoisie, accumulation of capital
Post-revolutionary transitional period	Socialism	Dictatorship of the proletariat, nationalized means of production
Eventual emergence	Communism	Classless society, socialized means of production

With a different political background, Oswald Spengler conceived of an organic kind of world history within which various cultures and civilizations followed historical lifecycles of about one millennium in length. In his view (from 1918), the West was fast declining and had entered its final phase, whereas the Russian civilization was developing quickly and would gain in strength during the coming centuries until it, too, would eventually be expected to come to an end.

One century after Spengler, the lack of rigid analysis and identification of distinct futures by contemporary historians can appear in positive terms: a future that, unlike the past, is empty, open, and has not yet been colonized by modernity and modernist thinkers and conquerors (Adam and Groves 2007: 13–15). The future may thus be one of the few remaining sanctuaries of communities otherwise at constant risk of falling victim to intellectual and political occupation in the name of historical (and possibly also historians') progress. But other sectors in society do not show the same restraint and go on to plan for years and centuries ahead.

Planning for the future

According to a recent survey of time horizons adopted for planning and monitoring purposes by Swedish state authorities, it is not unusual for them to consider a future of *c.* thirty to forty years ahead (Hansson et al. 2016: 59–60). This perspective is used, for example, in depreciating traffic infrastructure, determining landslide risks, urban planning for the construction of housing, emergency risk preparation, and planning for the dismantling of nuclear power stations. In some sectors, even a hundred-year perspective is taken routinely. This includes biodiversity conservation, responses to climate change, forest management, and the provision of infrastructure such as buildings, dams, and municipal sewage systems. Some products in the building industry (e.g., insulation, roof tiles, bricks) have warranties of seventy–one hundred years.

As these examples illustrate, anticipation and planning, although intellectually taking a colonial attitude toward the future, can provide important benefits for future generations. They help us to establish for the next generation(s) an environment within which, based on all we know, we can expect them to thrive. In planning thirty, forty, or a hundred years ahead, several sectors in contemporary society are dividing up the coming decades into distinct phases that relate to the specific tasks they are charged with. It is not unreasonable to assume that historians' skills at critically analyzing, creatively structuring, and comprehensively synthesizing information about human societies could be helpful in creating an overarching perspective of the future that could integrate and assist the anticipations of various individual sectors.

It seems odd that the historical disciplines largely opt to refrain from looking ahead to the future of human development when so many others do, especially at a time when the world's joint agenda is focused on achieving sustainable development goals to build a better future for us all. I therefore take the view that it is timely for historians (and members of all historical disciplines) to get to grips with the future. Let us start by together advancing a discussion about periodizing the future, anticipating what may lie ahead both historically and for professional historians.

Among the most significant reasons why current planning is not carried out for periods longer than forty, or sometimes a hundred years, are existing knowledge gaps about natural conditions, technical developments, and patterns of human behavior (Hansson et al. 2016: 60–1). But even for periods of less than forty years, planners are continuously revising their anticipations as data and evaluations change—much like data and evaluations of the past forty years keep on changing, too. It is likely that future generations will continue to revise their judgments about the future ahead of them. But this does not make the task of periodizing the future futile; revision is only to be expected as knowledge and experiences increase.

Future people will keep making sense of their own presents (including their own futures) in ways that will not necessarily correspond with what we assume will happen, much like past people made sense of their own presents (including their own pasts) in ways that do not necessarily correspond with what we, thanks to historians, assume to have happened. All representations of past and future are provisional and are subject to later revisions: "If futuring is to be rejected because the statements and representations of futurists are frequently inaccurate, then we may as well reject history as a method of thought as well" (Staley 2007: 150, but see also 66–7).

Periodizing past or future is not about revealing any previously hidden patterns of human development. The aim is something rather different: constructing informed perspectives of distinct past and future periods aims at placing past, present, and future processes into a joint perspective, serving the formation of a historical consciousness that in various ways can inform human understanding and decision-making in the present (Rüsen 2004).

Concerning the periodization of the future and its benefits, it is particularly informative to take a look at one particular sector in contemporary society where long-term planning and making assessments as much as a hundred thousand years in advance (or even more) is already current practice: the sector responsible for building repositories of nuclear waste. Although its time scale lies far beyond the realms normally frequented by historians, it has been attracting attention from archaeologists for some time (Joyce 2020; Holtorf and Högberg 2021).

There are certain legal obligations, but there is also a global consensus throughout the nuclear waste sector that records, knowledge, and memory concerning repositories of nuclear waste should be preserved as long as possible. In order to facilitate relevant work today, several distinct phases are used in the ongoing international deliberations, which have come a long way (Schröder 2019: 47–51), as captured by the following table.

Period	Phase	Characteristics
Current regime (10–20 years ahead)	Very short term	Staff stability, cycles of organizational change, periodic safety reviews
Until repository closure (c. 100 years)	Short term	Pre-operational and operational phases of the repository, waste still accessible without major effort, records archived
From closure until end of oversight (a few hundred years)	Medium term	Post-operational phase, oversight continues, preservation of records, knowledge, and memory
Post-oversight (up to hundreds of thousands of years)	Long term	Possibility to recover records, knowledge, and memory after loss

The distinct future phases of repositories of nuclear waste constitute a periodization of the future, as first suggested by David Staley (2007: 72–3, 80–2). They give a structure to the future that helps define future environments and create coherent relationships between various events projected to happen. Contrary to Staley's expectations, these phases feature a number of relevant processes and anticipated events, as illustrated in Figure 14.1.

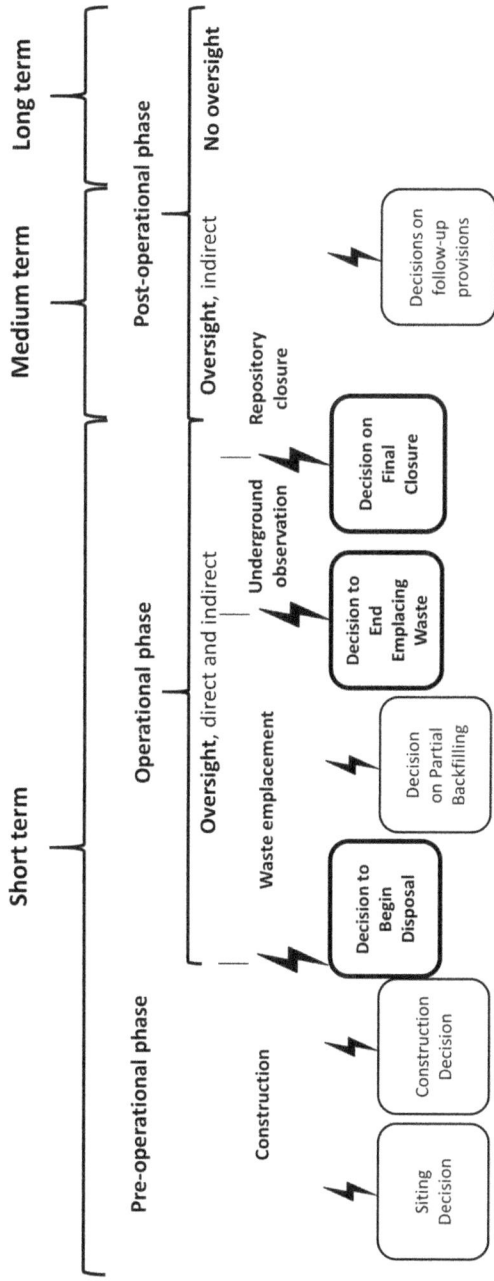

FIGURE 14.1 Anticipated future processes and events relating to nuclear waste repositories, divided into various periods and phases of the future (adapted from Schröder 2019: 47, redrawn by Martin Van der Linden).

The events and processes related to building repositories of nuclear waste, as well as the events and processes related to the various other sectors planning thirty, forty, or a hundred years ahead, are anticipated to happen in the future. They are available as reference points for historians periodizing the future and writing future histories.

Toward writing histories of the future

In addition to such available reference points relating to planning, how much can historians confidentially know will happen in the future? Even though exact dates and predictions of very specific events may not always be obtainable, many future events are uncontroversial as such, and are known to happen at some point, especially when they occur at relatively large scales and are linked to natural laws (Graves-Brown 2020). This includes astronomical occurrences such as another meteor colliding with the Earth, Vega taking over as the North Star (presumably in the year 13727 CE), and eventually the Earth and the Moon ceasing to exist when they fall into the Sun, in *c.* 7.59 billion years' time. In the somewhat shorter term, we can expect with some certainty the occurrence of natural disasters, including major earthquakes and volcanic eruptions in areas of tectonic instability (sometimes resulting in tsunamis), global pandemics, floods, and hurricanes.

Moreover, we can also know certain societal events of the future that are the outcome of human agency. For example, we know that Hong Kong and Macau enjoy their remaining relative autonomy from China until 2047 and 2049, respectively, when current arrangements with relevant stakeholders will expire and one period in their political histories will come to an end. Historians could also divide the future of humanity into a pre- and post-period in relation to the availability of malaria protection for all, or the eradication of extreme poverty and adult illiteracy, all of which are not exactly predictable but may be attainable in our lifetime (Our World in Data n.d.).

What is more, some members of future generations are already alive today and can be interviewed. Even those who are not alive yet may later become directly inspired or otherwise affected by the goals, visions, and judgments of individuals living today. These living individuals can be asked today about their perspectives on the future, including their expectations and aspirations. Their statements carry significance as "oral futures" that express how human beings perceive what will come, what may come or what should come, much in the same way as other people's memories are significant as oral histories that express how they perceive what was in the past, may have been, or should have been (Staley 2007: 59).

Next, just as there are tangible remains from all periods of the past which archaeologists are capable of studying as historical sources, there are also many materials around today which will last for centuries or longer. It is thus possible to conduct an archaeology of the future. Indeed, nuclear waste repositories are such archaeological sites of the future, containing much material that will be preserved for thousands of years (Holtorf and Högberg 2021). In terms of durability, tests conducted in the context of creating permanent markers for a nuclear waste repository in the United States suggested that varieties of rock (especially basalt), concrete, stainless steel, ceramics, and polymers may best resist physical destruction over time and could last for millennia (John Hart and Associates 2000).

Different objects made of durable materials, events whose occurrences are foreseeable, and a variety of conditions or processes that will start at certain points in the future do not have to be treated as isolated from each other or as separated from larger historical processes that we are discussing today. They should be integrated into a future perspective that encompasses a number of discernible trends and mega-trends which will frame social developments on Earth for the next few decades or longer. Relevant ongoing processes that link past, present, and future include demographic trends such as absolute numbers and proportions of human population in different world regions, distributed between cities and countryside, by age and by health. They also include anticipated climate change and its relation to economic development around the world. In addition, among many other discernible developments, technological trends of computational power and the availability of DNA sequencing are steadily increasing (Steffen 2011; Our World in Data n.d.).

Surely, if anyone is able to evaluate these kinds of trends, weigh them in relation to each other, and propose meaningful future periods that help us make sense of complex processes connecting past, present, and future, it is a historian. There are welcome indications that the interest among historians in the future is growing, not least in the present volume, where a separate chapter (chapter 13 by David Staley) discusses the future as a domain of historical inquiry.

Acknowledgements

Over the years, Anders Högberg and Sarah May have been contributing significantly to my thinking about the future. For specific comments and suggestions to previous drafts of this paper, I am grateful to Paul Graves-Brown, Christian Holtorf, Adrian Pop, and Zoltán Simon in particular.

References

Adam, B., and C. Groves (2007), *Future Matters. Action. Knowledge. Ethics.* Leiden and Boston: Brill.

Benford, G. (1999), *Deep Time. How Humanity Communicates Across Millennia.* New York: Avons.

Collingwood, R. G. ([1946] 1994), *The Idea of History.* Oxford and New York: Oxford University Press.

Collingwood, R. G. ([1927] 2009), "Oswald Spengler and the Theory of Historical Cycles," in A. Budd (ed.), *The Modern Historiography Reader. Western Sources*, 245–50, London and New York: Routledge.

Graves-Brown, P. (2020), Warranty. Blog entry available online: http://slightlymuddy.com/kuriosum/?p=637 (accessed February 21, 2020).

Hansson, S. O., K. Lilieqvist, K. E. Björnberg, and M. V. Johansson (2016), "Time Horizons and Discount Rates in Swedish Environmental Policy: Who Decides and on What Grounds?" *Futures* 76: 55–66.

Hölscher, L. (1999), *Die Entdeckung der Zukunft.* Frankfurt: Fischer.

Holtorf, C., and A. Högberg (2021). "What Lies Ahead? Nuclear Waste as Cultural Heritage of the Future" in C. Holtorf and A. Högberg (eds.), *Cultural Heritage and the Future*, 144–58, London and New York: Routledge.

John Hart and Associates (2000), "Permanent Markers Materials Analysis. Contractor Report," Waste Isolation Pilot Plant: Carlsbad, New Mexico, USA. Available online: https://wipp.energy.gov/library/cca/CCA_1996_References/Chapter%207/CREL2701.PDF (accessed December 31, 2019).

Joyce, R. A. (2020), *The Future of Nuclear Waste: What Art and Archaeology Can Tell Us about Securing the World's Most Hazardous Material.* Oxford and New York: Oxford University Press.

Männikkö, M. (2017), "Studying the Future and Writing History," in S. Heinonen, O. Kuusi, and H. Salminen (eds.), *How Do We Explore Our Futures? Methods of Futures Research*, 28–39, Helsinki: Finnish Society for Futures Studies.

Our World in Data (n.d.), online resource available at: https://ourworldindata.org (accessed August 31, 2021).

Pop, A. (2019), "Long Cycles and Anticipation," in R. Poli (ed.), *Handbook of Anticipation*, 1–29, Cham: Springer, http://doi.org/10.1007/978-3-319-31737-3_85-2.

Psychohistory (2019), Psychohistory (fictional). *Wikipedia*, available online: https://en.wikipedia.org/wiki/Psychohistory_(fictional) (accessed December 29, 2019).

Quenet, G. (2017) "The Anthropocene and the Time of Historians," *Annales. Histoire, Sciences Sociales* 72(2): 267–99. Available online: https://www.cairn-int.info/article-E_ANNA_722_0267--the-anthropocene-and-the-time-of.htm (accessed September 30, 2021).

Rüsen, J. (2004), "Historical Consciousness: Narrative Structure, Moral Function, and Ontogenetic Development," in P. Seixas (ed.), *Theorizing Historical Consciousness*, 63–85, Toronto: University of Toronto Press.

Rydén, R. (2019), "Archivists and Time: Conceptions of Time and Long-Term Information Preservation among Archivists," *Journal of Contemporary Archival Studies* 6(1), art. 6. Available online: https://elischolar.library.yale.edu/jcas/vol6/iss1/6 (accessed December 31, 2019).

Schröder, J. (2019), *Preservation of Records, Knowledge and Memory (RK&M) Across Generations: Final Report of the RK&M Initiative*. Paris: OECD, Nuclear Energy Agency. Available online: https://www.oecd-nea.org/rwm/pubs/2019/7421-RKM-Final.pdf (accessed December 31, 2019).

Simon, Z. B. (2018), "History Begins in the Future. On Historical Sensibility in the Age of Technology," in S. Helgesson and J. Svenungsson (eds.), *The Ethos of History: Time and Responsibility*, 192–209, Oxford and New York: Berghahn.

Staley, D. J. (2007), *History and Future. Using Historical Thinking to Imagine the Future*. Plymouth: Lexington.

Steffen, A. (2011), *Worldchanging. A User 's Guide for the 21st Century*, rev. edn. New York: Abrams.

CHAPTER FIFTEEN

History and technology futures: Where history and technology assessment come together

Silke Zimmer-Merkle

Throughout the centuries, many controversies have taken place about the practical use of history and the various approaches for promoting it. In recent years, this debate has once more gained momentum (for instance, Pihlainen 2018; Berger 2019). As the theoretical debate intensified, practical examples of historical intervention in the public domain became more common. Mostly, however, these examples originate in the fields of political history or general history and aim at historical engagement in broad society. In this essay, I want to put forward an example of historical engagement that originates not from general history, but from a specific field of historical research: the history of technology. In the case I want to exemplify here, the audience is a certain societal actor—namely, technology assessment (TA)—and not society as a whole. In my particular example, the field where the two practices—historical research and the study of emerging technologies—come together is the field of technology futures and their history. To elucidate my approach, I will point out what technology futures are and why they can be interesting for both the history of technology and TA. Expanding a little on the practice of TA, I will give a personal account of what this particular kind of engaged history could look like.[1] I will close with a short excursus on the theoretical base of my approach.

What are technology futures?

Futures in general are imaginings people have in mind about a time to come. In sociotechnical constellations, particularly if technology plays a major role, we speak of technology futures. So, technology futures are visions of what a sociotechnical world could possibly look like in the future. They can stem from fictional sources (like science-fiction stories), originate from research and development processes (like technological promises), or be expressions of old dreams of mankind (e.g., flying—and its technical realization).

Whether they are labeled as "imaginaries" (Jasanoff and Kim 2015), "visions" (Grin and Grunwald 2000), "expectations" (Van Lente and Rip 1998), or "futures" (Lösch et al. 2019; Grunwald 2020), multiple fields of research have attended to their study, especially in the last twenty years. As diverse as these approaches might be, they all agree on the insight that these futures are influential and effective—*wirkmächtig*—in our daily lives. They are often widely shared, while being part of the unspoken and the tacit in discourse. They are long-time imaginings of varying levels of concreteness. In present disputes, technology futures build—mostly unnoticed—bridges between past visions (that we might not even be aware of anymore) and present imaginaries of possible future worlds. As futures of the past, they are—not least since Koselleck (2004)—in the scope of historians (Hölscher 2017; Radkau 2017; Popplow 2020; particularly Simon and Tamm 2021).

As already mentioned, the diverse approaches for dealing with technology futures (under this term or a different one) agree that they are influential and effective in the present. Assuming that the future is not determined, we are usually able to freely shape the world yet to come, in constant tension with being constrained by social, cultural, and political factors. Nevertheless, technology futures influence our thinking and decision-making—more often than not without being aware of the exact nature of such influence. In debates concerning "the" future and decision-making processes in particular, they can affect the present in biasing our assumptions and premises as well as, eventually, our debates and decisions. Technology futures are collectively shared and part of collective and communicative memory. They create the horizon of expectation, as Koselleck (2004) describes it.

Thus, technology futures are mostly implicit and appear hidden in the discourse on new and emerging technologies. Frequently, they appear as part of the unspoken, the unsaid, and are not necessarily articulated. As their roots lie in the past, a historical approach, particularly that of the history of technology, may prove useful in mapping and understanding them.

Technology futures and TA

A field where awareness and knowledge of performative technology futures is of particular importance is technology assessment. TA is a multidisciplinary practice that investigates technological developments, aims at understanding and anticipating current and future sociotechnical change as triggered by technological or scientific developments, and studies the impact of such changes on society (see Grunwald 2018). It is explicitly (and most likely in contrast to some varieties of futurology) not about doing games with crystal balls. Quite the opposite: it is very much about understanding the present. TA usually asks questions that inquire into the actors of a sociotechnical novelty, what their arguments are, what they do and do not speak about, what the technological state of the art is, what the "known unknowns" are, and how we can reduce the number of "unknown unknowns."[2]

In asking these kinds of questions, the endeavor of TA is not as much about the future as about the present time, and, as I want to stress here, about the past. One crucial aspect of TA's daily routine is becoming informed about imaginaries and visions—technology futures, as introduced above—that are connected to emerging sociotechnical novelties. Typically, this activity is called "vision assessment" in TA. The visions and technology futures TA deals with, though, do not emerge out of the blue; they generally have a relevant history and they are not at all exceptional. Nevertheless, as explained above, imaginations of the future that people may have in mind are likely to influence decisions that will shape the future. Hence, these imaginations of possible technology futures need historicization.

The history of technology has asked questions on technologies and their emergence for many years, but—unfortunately, as I have argued elsewhere in a co-authored paper (Zimmer-Merkle and Fleischer 2017)—history and TA only very seldom refer to each other. In general, TA practitioners understand that the subjects they deal with have a noteworthy history while often being unaware of the historicity of their topics. If history is taken into account in TA practice, it (usually) happens in the form of inadequate/insufficient "practical pasts" (more on this later), but for understanding past futures a more complex "historical past" approach is required. Armin Grunwald's hermeneutic TA approach—referring to disciplines TA has so far often ignored—shows that TA practitioners, too, have realized this (Grunwald 2020).

To exemplify what technology futures actually are and how they can be interesting for both history and TA, I will provide an example from my own work with them. Automated driving has been widely debated throughout recent years, in broad society as well as in TA contexts. Conscious and unconscious technology futures of automated driving—long-term visions of self-driving vehicles as well as recent visualizations of sociotechnical promises—play an equally significant role. To a large extent, these technology futures are the same as those that were brought forward in the discussion about traffic telematics some twenty/thirty years ago. Back then, though, they were already historical, as imaginations of self-driving cars date back at least to the 1930s. Visualizations of cars without a driver, often operated by a guide wire, formed part of the collective imagination long before microelectronics made traffic telematics appear a desirable solution for traffic congestion and environment issues.

Over the twentieth century, visualizations and imaginaries about driverless cars have been recalled several times and fostered different kinds of knowledge about the future, from dreams and expectations to (socio-)technical promises. Today, when such past imaginations experience a revival in the debate about automated and "autonomous" driving, the use and the relevance of the past and its influence on the present becomes crucial to address in the future-oriented practice of TA. And this is where historical theory comes in.

Practical and historical pasts

As the possibility of the use of history is regularly contested, it may be worthwhile to attempt to contextualize—and perhaps to challenge—the approach of an engaged history as described here. Not so long ago, Hayden White entered the debate on the use of the past and history, with a revival of Michael Oakeshott's distinction between "historical past" and "practical past." Having always been a fierce although never hostile critic of academic modes of historiography, in his late work he seems rather gloomy about the capabilities of the knowledge produced by academic historians. He claims that "historical knowledge is of no use at all for the solution of practical problems in the present," because "the more precise, accurate, and authoritative the accounts by historians of the historical past, the less relevance it can be said to have as an analogue of any situation in the present" (White 2012: 127).

In the original distinction of Oakeshott (1999: 36), the "historical past" is what results from historians' critical inquiries: being based upon sources, a "historical past" is what "answers to questions about the past formulated by an historian"; it is "the conclusion of a critical enquiry of a certain sort; it is to be found nowhere but in a history book." Oakeshott already recognized that complex histories as written by historians are not appropriate for use in practical life. Contrary to this, the "practical past" is decidedly not the product of historians' work, but "a 'living' past which may be said to 'teach by example', or more generally to afford us a current vocabulary of self-understanding and self-expression" (Oakeshott 1999: 21).

White, updating this perspective for today's historiography, sees in practical pasts a starting point for a somewhat novel kind of engagement with history (2012: 129 and passim). White shows that practical pasts are (still) alive and kicking in societies, unlike the historical pasts of professional historians. With such a move, White seems to abandon every hope for academic history, sending historians into seclusion to the ivory tower, closing the door behind them. For me as well as—mostly likely—for most historians, this does not appear a satisfactory solution. As we learned from Reinhart Koselleck (2004) the *historia magistra vitae* topos did not dissolve without reason, and learning from the past takes different shapes nowadays. White (2012: 133) argues that art could do that job today—and whether one buys into this suggestion or not, it is possible to develop White's invocation of art further (instead of giving up on history) in accordance with the approach described in this essay. In doing so, it may even become clear that a way out for academic historiography could lie in niche solutions and in a historical past written with certain audiences in mind.

Engaging with history is not a bicolored endeavor. It is not as simple as one either doing it or not. There are innumerable shades between the poles Oakeshott once described. The original concept may be suitable for classifying some of the kinds of history and historical engagement around. However, it is not complex enough to capture the full spectrum of possibilities. Just as there is no one-size-fits-all kind of history, there is no one-size-fits-all kind of engagement with the present for historians. There are manifold approaches, attuned to specific audiences.

Conclusion: Reaching the right audience

How we can address certain audiences, what we can do to reach them, and why we will probably not be successful 100 percent even if we try our hardest, are far-reaching topics. There are piles of literature on interdisciplinary collaboration and—probably equally relevant in this context—science communication studies (e.g., Dascal et al. 2020; Humm and Schrögel 2020). Although the latter works usually focus on communication with audiences outside academia, the divide between the two cultures of science and the humanities and the increasing specialization within disciplines and fields of study have made thoughtful communication across divisions indispensable.

For the purpose of conclusion, we stay with technology futures that have many and very different stakeholders. They are very often used to push forward certain ideas and present them as unavoidable. Similarly, they are oftentimes used to close or end debates. There are, however, many contradictory futures out there, and mapping them also means keeping debates open and orienting everyday life through these different narratives. To frame this in the aforementioned Oakeshott/White terms, some of these technology futures are part of practical pasts.

TA may study current futures and what they could mean for our present practices of shaping the future, but it will only notice part of the big picture if it does not take the historical dimension of futures into account. Academic history can take a firm stand here. In my practice of an "engaged history," as I called it above, opening up to other fields of study and to the aforementioned crossings of knowledge divisions is a valuable effort. Having a "historical past"-eye on these futures, contextualizing them, showing their contingency and the underlying structures of power, can enable a richer understanding of the past as well as of the present that will shape the future.

Notes

1   The term "engaged history" in this essay is used in a similar, but not identical, sense to that understood in "Engaged Historian," as in the volume edited by Berger (2019).
2   Referring—in risk assessment—to knowledge gaps whose existence is unacquainted or unexpected, the phrase became famous for its specious use by Donald Rumsfeld, United States Secretary of Defense, in a 2002 press conference.

References

Berger, S. (2019) (ed.), *The Engaged Historian. Perspectives on the Intersections of Politics, Activism and the Historical Profession*. New York: Berghahn Books.

Dascal, M., A. Leßmöllmann, and T. Gloning (eds.) (2020), *Science Communication*. Berlin and New York: De Gruyter Mouton.

Grin, J., and Grunwald, A. (eds.) (2000), *Vision Assessment: Shaping Technology in 21st Century Society: Towards a Repertoire for Technology Assessment*. Berlin, Heidelberg, New York, Barcelona, Hongkong, London, Milan, Paris, Singapore, Tokyo: Springer.

Grunwald, A. (2018), *Technology Assessment in Practice and Theory*. Abingdon, New York: Routledge.

Grunwald, A. (2020), "The Objects of Technology Assessment. Hermeneutic Extension of Consequentialist Reasoning," *Journal of Responsible Innovation* 7(1): 96–112.

Hölscher, L. (2017) (ed.), *Die Zukunft des 20. Jahrhunderts: Dimensionen einer historischen Zukunftsforschung*. Frankfurt am Main: Campus.

Humm, C., and P. Schrögel (2020), "Science for All? Practical Recommendations on Reaching Underserved Audiences," *Frontiers in Communication* 5(42): 1–13, https://doi.org/10.3389/fcomm.2020.00042.

Jasanoff, S., and S.-H. Kim (eds.) (2015), *Dreamscapes of Modernity: Sociotechnical Imaginaries and the Fabrication of Power*. Chicago, IL, and London: University of Chicago Press.

Koselleck, R. (2004), *Futures Past: On the Semantics of Historical Time*. New York: Columbia University Press.

Lösch, A., A. Grunwald, M. Meister, and I. Schulz-Schaeffer (2019), *Socio-Technical Futures Shaping the Present: Empirical Examples and Analytical Challenges*. Wiesbaden: Springer.

Oakeshott, M. (1999), "Present, Future and Past," in *On History and Other Essays*, 1–48, Indianapolis, IN: Liberty Fund.

Pihlainen, K. (2018) (ed.), *Futures for the Past*. London and New York: Routledge.

Popplow, M. (2020), "Zur Erforschung von Technikzukünften aus technikhistorischer Perspektive," in P. Dobroć and A. Rothenhäusler (eds.), *2000 Revisited—Visionen der Welt von morgen im Gestern und Heute*, 41–58, Karlsruhe: KIT Scientific Publishing, http://dx.doi.org/10.5445/KSP/1000117728.

Radkau, J. (2017), *Geschichte der Zukunft: Prognosen, Visionen, Irrungen in Deutschland von 1945 bis heute*. München: Carl Hanser.

Simon, Z. B., and M. Tamm (2021), "Historical Futures," *History and Theory* 60(1): 3–22.

Van Lente, H., and A. Rip (1998), "Expectations in Technological Developments: An Example of Prospective Structures to be Filled in by Agency," in C. Disco and B. v. d. Meulen (eds.), *Getting New Technologies Together: Studies in Making Sociotechnical Order*, 203–31, Berlin: De Gruyter.

White, H. (2012), "Politics, History, and the Practical Past," *Storia della storiografia: rivista internazionale* 61(1): 127–33.

Zimmer-Merkle, S., and T. Fleischer (2017), "Eclectic, Random, Intuitive? Technology Assessment, RRI, and Their Use of History," *Journal of Responsible Innovation* 4(2): 217–33.

CHAPTER SIXTEEN

Tomorrow is the Question: Modernity and the need for strong narratives about the future—and the past

Franz-Josef Arlinghaus

"Somebody says 'make America great again'.[1] But when has America ever been great?" The question raised during the funeral of George Floyd by his niece Brooke Williams[2] was weeks later taken up in a town hall meeting in Philadelphia by Pastor Carl Day. Day, directly addressing the presidential candidate of the Republican Party in the room, asked: "*[W]hen* was that great? Cause that pushes us back to a time we could not identify with such greatness." Day then said that there has been no change in the situation of the Black community during recent decades, while the candidate claimed that during his time in office people of color had never done better until the coronavirus came, and that they will do better in 2021, and in the future too.[3]

This is but one instance to show how important the relationship between past, present, and future is, even in everyday life, and how strongly it is debated at times. This controversy also shows that the question about *how* yesterday, today, and tomorrow are related to each other is basically the question of change over time and what the present has to do with it (Day accused past administrations, just as well as the actual one, that they failed to deliver change, the candidate claimed that during his time in office there was change, and that there will be more change in the future).

This raises a question that may sound familiar to readers of Reinhart Koselleck (2004): Is the future (still) perceived as open, or was this idea just an episode that dominated "classical modernity" only during some decades in the twentieth century? And what does "open" mean, anyway? Does the past still matter when a lot of people are convinced that the whole planet is in danger? Astonishing enough, different as the perspectives of politics between Brooke Williams, Carl Day, and the candidates are, their attitudes toward time seem to be similar.

In this essay, I want to make five suggestions in this regard. First, I try to show that even at the beginning of the twenty-first century, like in modernity as a whole, the future is still perceived as open. Second, I will argue that this openness is specified by looking to the past. Third, the narratives that emerge by linking past and future conceptualize time as a *process*, in which the present occupies a privileged position. Drawing on Koselleck's ideas, the fourth point (leading back to point one) is that these narratives, different and even contradictory as they are, have in common that they are an answer to the need to hedge in the openness of the future. Here I rely on the argument of Zoltán Simon (2019a) regarding modern history's function of domesticating novelty. While some chapters of this volume—just like recent Koselleck interpretations or Simon's argument on narrative domestication as a shortcoming of historical understanding today—focus on the extent to which historical understanding as we know it was challenged, my chapter emphasizes the other side of the coin: the continuing relevance of modern history and historical understanding. This leads to my fifth and last point: counterintuitive as it seems, turning points, breaks, and ruptures have been an integrated part of processual history since the beginning of modern historiography in the eighteenth century. What is more, stories that draw on history and aim to display breaks, new epochs even, also contribute decisively to taming the openness of the future.

History of the future

The future has its own history, as is very well known. Other epochs dealt with "tomorrow" differently than our age. Considering medieval time perceptions seems to be essential to formulating the question of the problems (and solutions) surrounding modern ideas about the past, present, and future. Concepts of time in the Christian Middle Ages are based on solid information on how the world started, who started it, how it will end, and even what will come afterwards. To fear that humanity is endangered by an ecological or military disaster in, say, 2070, *if the present* does not deal with the problem *now*, would not make too much sense in medieval Christian thought, since a) there is an end to this world anyway and the present cannot do much about it; and b) people, like Martin Luther, for instance, typically believed that the end was very near. 2070? Not really a concern.

The certainty that this world is only a kind of "interplay" prior to the eternal life with the Lord in heaven (or the Devil in hell) had an immediate impact on everyday activities and relations to the future. This does not mean people did not prepare for "tomorrow" and its contingencies (see Bernhardt 2016); on the contrary: even a far-reaching future beyond individual life was taken into account, and not even death was the "end of story." The last wills of kings, courtiers, and simple folk alike left money for church services and prayers with the aim of shortening their years in purgatory. The foundations established to provide the money are, by earthly standards, designed for eternity, and some of them still exist today (Borgolte 2018).

Although planning for decades, even centuries ahead was common in the Middle Ages, "whenever medieval text talk about 'futura', they always talk about 'future events', but never about future as a space of time," as Lucian Hölscher (1999: 20) argued. The repeated prayers and masses one provided are events, just like death and resurrection. Moreover, what we do *not* see here is an unfolding of time as a "development" or "process" of any kind.

From event to event: Medieval historiography

Medieval historiographical and life-writing texts display occurrences like pearls put in line on a blanket, without connecting the thread. The "Deeds of Emperor Frederick," written by bishop Otto of Freising, reports mainly on the activities of Frederick I, Barbarossa. While Otto's philosophical view on history is that of constant changes in this world (*mutatio rerum*), he attributes these to the fact that all things in this world are composed of different entities. This is especially true for the human being, who is, more than anything else on Earth, a combination of units opposed to each other (*ex opositis compactus*). Given the constancy of changes and their very fast flow, one can hardly lay hand on time, he argues (Ehlers 2013: 89ff.). According to Otto, "since the passage of time follows this swift course of forms, time passes so rapidly that its present moment can scarcely, if ever, be perceived" (Schmale 1965: 140; Mierow and Emery 1994: 39). Time is given no "space" where things can develop, it has no "agency." Rather, time itself falls under the rule of the ever-faster change of the forms of things themselves, incorporating "fluxus" by virtue of their composed nature. (Little wonder that worldly time is the opposite of eternity, and the mundane world of opposing things is the opposite of heavenly harmony.) The medieval view of time is not only derived from the Bible; instead, it is rooted in a specific view on the world (Descola 2005).

To give but one example of the way this affects Otto's writing, consider how "Gesta" reports on Frederick's campaign to Rome in order to become emperor. After crossing the Alps, the knights almost constantly had to fight adversaries, both on the way to Rome and in Rome itself. It comes as no surprise that Otto typically attributes success in the military campaign to the wit or courage of the title character of the book, Frederick. However, withdrawals of the army are explained by unfavorable polluted air, the unbearable heat, or the like (Schmale 1965: 12–43). Altogether, the campaign took about a year, and while Otto gives reasons why certain events turn out the way they did, the year "abroad" as a considerable time span as such is not much taken into consideration. He could have mentioned the exhaustion after a month-long journey, a decrease (or increase?) of armed forces during that year, and the like, but that is not how this learned man wants to write history.

One is tempted to attribute Otto's view on time to his position of being a high medieval bishop, who may have been more interested in the coming world than the earthly one. However, a quick glance at late medieval laymen underlines that even merchants do not deal with time in a different way.

Burkhard Zinck was only eleven years old when, in 1407, he was sent a thousand kilometers away from his family in Memmingen to his uncle, a priest, in Rebnica (Slovenia), to get educated. Following the death of both his uncle and his parents, he remained on his own, a young traveling scholar who, despite earning some money as a private tutor, had to beg for bread to survive. Later in life, following a few setbacks, Zinck eventually settled in Augsburg, worked his way up and died as a wealthy merchant around 1475. All this can be read today in the chronical of his adoptive home, Augsburg, written by Zinck himself. In the text, Zinck combines the history of the city with his personal "autobiography" (Moeglin 1997; Arlinghaus 2020: 97ff.). But there is no "and during these years I saved enough money to buy a house" or the like. Rather, one event occurs after the other, introduced by an *item*, without assuming a development that prepared for the following occurrence, without any time-consuming transitions.

These observations are in line with Gabrielle Spiegel's analysis of the characteristics of medieval concepts of temporality. Spiegel (2016: 26) singles out three points: "(a) a strict series of events, paratactically presented without causal connection between the events that make up the *series temporum*; (b) a cyclical view of history, … ; and (c) a far-reaching typological construction of events … in which antecedent events become prophecies of later ones, which represent their fulfillment but which are not connected to the earlier events in any direct, causal manner." In the end, as Spiegel continues, "the overall effect of such organization is to produce a non-developmental episodic narrative informed by a theme that is continually re-expressed in separate events."

To sum up: In the Middle Ages, the future has no "space" (Hölscher), and time is not linked to "developments" (Spiegel); it is not conceptualized as a process.

Modern historical writing to take away

In a 2011 article in *Süddeutsche Zeitung*, Michael Hüther commented on the consequences of the 2009 financial crisis in Europe. Reading Hüther, the director of the German Economic Institute, an influential think tank financed by big German companies, one would expect suggestions concerning state, company, and European Union strategies in facing the crisis. Instead, Hürther (2011) points at history: "Over centuries, the cultural union of Europe grew together. Romanesque and Gothic art, … Baroque and the Enlightenment are European phenomena. At the same time, it was always Europe, where 'Reason' was expressed always in new forms—be it Ancient philosophy, medieval scholasticism, … the Enlightenment or modern science." After mentioning some political events, the emergence of the nation-state, and so forth, Hüther argues for the necessity of forming a European nucleus around Germany and France as part of a greater geographical space of integration.

This is not the occasion to question the open Eurocentrism and the optimism of the text. More important is that the chief concern of Hüther, who received education both in economics and history, is the future: the future of Europe. To retain the core strength of Europe, Hüther argues that the center of the continent has to work together. According to the well-known story, *throughout the centuries*, Europe *developed* a special set of achievements. Despite differences between medieval and modern forms of reason or law, which Hüther is certainly aware of, he sees century-long processes at work. *If* the continent manages to stick to those achievements *today*, *then* tomorrow's problems can be dealt with. The future is not simply open, but also portrayed as manageable via conditional clauses that point to the present. The basis for this narrative is time conceived as a process; and this concept is so "natural" that there is no need to address this explicitly.

In my view, a cornerstone for the success of interpretations such as the above one, regardless of all criticism, lies in the way they link past, present, and future. In the midst of a severe debt crisis, Hüther insists that Europe has developed strong tools over centuries which, *if* applied today, will solve tomorrow's problems. However, he does not tell a story of *developments* that led to the financial catastrophe. Precisely because he points to general values that are not linked to the event, the crisis remains an unexpected rupture. Through the back door, Hüther underscores the unexpected fracturing of the global economic system caused by the 2008 bankruptcy of Lehman Brothers Holdings Inc., precisely because he drew on the supposed general achievements of Europe instead of portraying the crises as part of a process.

A and B futures

Optimism is not the soundtrack of "The Global 2000 Report to the President," published in 1980. The famous memorandum, commissioned by US President Carter during his Environmental Message to the Congress on May 23, 1977, compiled a vast amount of data by leading scientists. Presuming a 2 percent fossil fuel combustion growth per year, the study predicted "a 2°–3°C rise in temperatures in the middle latitudes of the earth" and an "increase of 5°–10°C in polar temperatures" which could "eventually lead to the melting of the Greenland and Antarctic ice caps and a gradual rise in sea level, forcing abandonment of many coastal cities" by the middle of the twenty-first century. The old predictions sound very much up to date, even today. However, out of the roughly thirty pages of the summary only one page (!) addresses possible changes in climate and only a third of that page deals with the growth of atmospheric carbon dioxide as the main driver of global warming. Instead of climate change, the report gives priority to population growth, food production, and the management of resources, especially farmable land and water (Barney 1980: 37). In essence, the major concern of the report was how to fill the refrigerator in the face of an ever-growing family, and not how to deal with the overspill of the wastebin and its consequences.

While the report's priorities seem somewhat outdated, the red thread of the narrative is not. The first sentence below the headline "Major Findings" reads: "If present trends continue, the world in 2000 will be more crowded, ... less stable ecologically, and more vulnerable to disruption than the world we live in now" (Barney 1980: 1). Today's environmental analysis surely emphasizes other threats. However, the world of tomorrow will be much worse or even impossible to live in "if present trends continue," as research on climate change and the proliferation of nuclear arms rightly keep on warning us about.

Whether the future of Europe will be bright because of its brilliant century-long past or whether the future of the world will look gloomy because of decade-long environmental misdeeds is not the question I want to answer. My focus lies on the shared concept of time these narratives are based on. Both the optimistic and the pessimistic "stories" present us with *how* "tomorrow" will look, if ... Both futures come with such an "if," meaning that the present is confronted with two alternatives and today's decisions will pave the way to future A or future B. Instead of multiple futures, most narratives—although not all—talk about only two. Their expectations are based on strong assumptions about the past. This is especially true for the debate on climate change today, which, more than the discussion on population growth in the 1960s and 1970s, regularly refers to long, and often very long, time spans (see Chakrabarty 2018).

The success of such narratives, the reason why they receive so much attention and why they are always produced anew, lies, in my view, in the need to channel the future. A radically open future is the *horror vacui* of modernity, it seems, and the sciences and the humanities fill this void with strong narratives that provide us with a compass for navigating through time. Now, this does not mean that climate change or population growth are just narratives. However, the very real concerns they express do not simply address the problem they draw the attention to. In doing so, they also provide the modern mind with an urgently needed response to a future that is perceived as radically open and thus difficult to cope with.

Processes and breaks

"Processes that lead to a certain outcome" seem to be the red thread of the modern concepts of history; and this, it seems, is the story needed to counterbalance the open future (Simon 2019a: 17–27). But what about turning points, ruptures, and breaks? Simon (2019b: 80), distinguishes "between a processual and an evental understanding of historical time," the latter one informing immense ruptures and bringing about previously non-existent worlds in the outburst of momentous events. While Simon suggests that this view is linked to a quite recent perception of the present world that now supposedly is undergoing—and will undergo—unforeseen changes, this paper proposes that the unforeseen has been part of processual history right from its start in around 1800.

As for a start, please remember Hüther's article, which, on the one hand, surely tames the future in a time of crisis by suggesting that we have the capacity to get over it. Yet, on the other hand, Hüther's article does not play down the level of damage the 2009 financial crises wrought on the world. On the contrary! While it tries to minimize the fear of the consequences that might follow, it does not try to relativize the exceptionality of the world economy's troubles.

More recently, the COVID-19 pandemic has led a number of authors—journalists, doctors, and historians alike—to compare the disease with the cholera epidemic of the nineteenth century or, more often, to the 1347–51 European plague. The historian Volker Reinhardt (2021) sees striking similarities between COVID-19 and the fourteenth-century pest. Reinhardt (2021: 1) underlines that both diseases were completely unknown, that nobody knew anything about them, and that they changed society, culture, and religious practices dramatically. To be fair, Reinhardt's book also highlights the many differences between the situation today and "back then" (advances in medicine, differences in mortality rates, etc.), although it claims that the difference between the extent of changes they brought about remains an open question.

Aligning the famous plague of the Middle Ages with modern events—and modern ruptures—is nothing new. After the First World War, J. W. Thompson (2020: 565) pointed to the fourteenth-century disease because "historians and students ... have been searching if possibly they might discover a precedent in the past for the present order (or rather disorder) of things." Searching history for parallels to the "disorders" of the present has a long tradition and is certainly not limited to pandemics. The motive for this surely is, as Thompson's phrase indicates, to smoothen the turmoil society is confronted with in the present or the future. Nevertheless, in doing so, ruptures and breaks are highlighted. The analogies that are looked at are *first* of all analogies of the unexpected new that brings unforeseeable consequences. Smoothening such events by saying "we already survived other unpredicted ruptures" comes second.

Emphasizing that something unexpected, unforeseeable happened (and may happen again) is, it seems to me, the second red thread of historical narratives. The two threads—narrating processes or narrating analogies—are linked together because the openness of past, present, and future is not plausible without it being conceptualized as a consequence of possible developments *and* possible ruptures alike. And the two red threats are linked together insofar as both offer a way to deal with uncertainty, although in different ways. The new, the unexpected is and has been part of historical understanding and writing since the development of modern historiography. Hence the fact that the proclamation of different epochs during the *Sattelzeit* went hand in hand with the "discovery" of an open future and is itself a new thought. In contrast to the Six World Ages, in which the Middle Ages periodized time, the concept of epochs, in my view, combines developments that lead to breaks that open unforeseeable worlds.

To conclude

In this chapter, I argued that while "make America great again" and "Friday's for future" point in opposing directions in terms of politics, they are very much alike with respect to their shared concepts of time and their combination of past, present, and future. This also applies to optimistic and pessimistic views on the future, which, in general, share the same basic narrative: that the future has to be "modeled" on decisions taken today, that narratives about the past inform decisions about the future. Modern utopias and dystopias offer a solution to the same problem: they provide *strong narratives* that "channel" the radical openness of time in all three directions (past, present, and future). In doing so, they provide the present with an enormous power not only over times to come, but also over the past.

However, modern historiography since its early days has written about breaks, about new epochs, even, and establishing analogies is its favorite way of doing so. "Analogy" does not mean that history repeats itself, but, so the story goes, ruptures do. In a way, they become less intimidating, because something similar already occurred "back then." Nevertheless, the event as such is exposed as a rupture, and if "the present" is in the middle of a rupture or an epochal shift, phrases like "we do not know how the world will look tomorrow, after the event" are often heard. No comfort here.

In the course of argumentation, I made three points: first, within a fractioned society, history is becoming increasingly important, inside and outside academia. Second, from a medieval perspective, and in line with Simon (2019a), I discussed how modern historical time considered as a process tames the future. Third, with a processual understanding of time during the *Sattelzeit* comes the break, the rupture, the epoch, even, and what follows is not the outcome of a development. There is some taming here, too, by pointing to analogies in history. However, even analogies underline that unexpected ruptures have taken place and will take place again, without foreseeable consequences.

Notes

1   The title of this chapter, "Tomorrow is the Question," is borrowed form Ornette Coleman's music record.
2   Speech of Brooke Williams, in "Live: Funeral for George Floyd Held in Houston | NBC News," YouTube video, 2:11 minutes. Available online: https://www.youtube.com/watch?v=mufpOyoFrrg (accessed September 30, 2021).
3   "Trump on ABC News Town Hall: Trump Responds to Questions on US's Racial Inequalities," YouTube video. Available online: https://www.youtube.com/watch?v=wop7fEvcAf8 (accessed September 30, 2021).

References

Arlinghaus, F.-J. (2020), "Relationierungen: Das vergleichende Selbst in autobiographischen Texten von Hermann dem Juden, Burkhard Zink und Didier Eribon," in F.-J. Arlinghaus, W. Erhalt, L. Gumpert, and S. Siemianowski (eds.), *Sich selbst vergleichen. Zur Relationalität autobiographischen Schreibens vom 12. Jahrhundert bis zur Gegenwart*, 53–115, Bielefeld transcript.

Barney, G. O. (eds.) (1980), *The Global 2000 Report to the President: Entering the Twenty-First Century*, Washington.

Bernhardt, M., S. Brakensiek, and B. Scheller (eds.) (2016), *Ermöglichen und Verhindern: Vom Umgang mit Kontingenz*. Campus: Frankfurt.

Borgolte, M. (2018), *Weltgeschichte als Stiftungsgeschichte: Von 3000 v.u.Z. bis 1500 u.Z.* Darmstadt: WBG.

Chakrabarty, D. (2018), "Anthropocene Time," *History and Theory* 58(1): 5–32.

Descola, P. (2005), *Par-delà nature et culture*. Paris: Gallimard.

Ehlers, J. (2013), *Otto von Freising: Ein Intellektueller im Mittelalter*. München: C.H.Beck.

Hölscher, L. (1999), *Die Entdeckung der Zukunft*. Frankfurt: Fischer.

Hüther, M. (2011), "Forum: Europa neu denken. Schuldenkrise und Euro-Zweifel gefährden die Union. Rettung können nur unterschiedliche Integrationsräume bringen," *Süddeutsche Zeitung* 173 (2011.07.29): 16.

Koselleck, R. (2004), *Futures Past: On the Semantics of Historical Time*. Trans. Keith Tribe. New York: Columbia University Press.

Mierow, C. C., and R. Emery (eds.) (1994), *Otto of Freising and his Continuator, Rahewin: The Deeds of Frederick Babarossa*. Toronto: University of Toronto Press.

Moeglin, J.-M. (1997), "Les élites urbaines et l'histoire de leur ville en Allemagne (XIVᵉ–XVᵉ Siécles)," in *Les élites urbaines au moyen âge: Actes du XXVII e Congrès de la Société des historiens médiévistes de l'enseignement supérieur public*, 351–83, École Française de Rome.

Reinhardt, V. (2021), *Die Macht der Seuche. Wie die Große Pest die Welt veränderte 1347–1353*. München: C.H.Beck.

Schmale, F.-J. (eds.) (1965), *Otto von Freising, Gesta Frederici seu rectius cronica/ Die Taten Friedrichs oder richtiger Cronica*. Darmstadt: WBG.

Simon, Z. B. (2019a), *History in Times of Unprecedented Change: A Theory for the 21st Century*. London: Bloomsbury.

Simon, Z. B. (2019b), "The Transformation of Historical Time: Processual and Evental Temporalities," in M. Tamm and L. Olivier (eds.), *Rethinking Historical Time: New Approaches to Presentism*, 71–84, London: Bloomsbury.

Spiegel, G. (2016), "Structures of Time in Medieval History," *Medieval History Journal* 19(1): 21–33.

Thompson, J. W. (2020), "Westfall, The Aftermath of the Black Death and the Aftermath of the Great War," *American Journal of Sociology* 26: 565–72.

PART THREE

Relations to the past

Historicities

CHAPTER SEVENTEEN

Probing the limits of a metaphor: On the stratigraphic model in history and geology

Chris Lorenz

In my contribution, I analyze an important and influential way in which an increasing number of historians and historical theorists have conceived the problem of historical time over the last twenty years. Helge Jordheim has aptly baptized this way of thinking the "stratigraphic model of time"—derived from stratigraphy, a subdiscipline of geology (Jordheim 2017). According to this model, which was made famous by Reinhart Koselleck (2000), historians can best conceive of historical times in terms of layers of time or temporal strata—*Zeitschichten* in German—analogous to the way in which geologists conceive of the crust of the Earth in terms of geological strata. So the stratigraphic model basically consists of a metaphor that maps specific characteristics of the study of Earth history on the study of human history. Next to Jordheim, other interpreters have debated and promoted the stratigraphic model that has recently acquired an extra relevance in the light of the debate about the Anthropocene, although this debate is rarely mentioned (Pomian 1984: 323–47; Zammito 2004; Olsen 2012; Bouton 2016; Esposito 2017; Hoffman and Franzel 2019; Lorenz 2019; Hellerma 2020).

The advantage of the stratigraphic model for history is usually located in at least two characteristics. First, it is supposed to capture and represent the fundamental *plurality* of historical times—in contrast to the modern idea that history consists of *one* unidirectional flow of time. Koselleck famously argued that Enlightenment philosophers were responsible for transforming the notion of history from a plurality of "histories," i.e., stories about the past, into history as progress and process—although Rohbeck (2020: 159–77) fundamentally questions Koselleck's arguments concerning progress. Second, the stratigraphic model is supposed to catch and represent the *"simultaneity of the unsimultaneous"*—that is, the simultaneous presence of layers of time that have different origins in chronological time. According to Jordheim (2011), it aims to synthesize synchrony and diachrony.

In my chapter, I question the suggested deep analogy between layers of time in geology and history in general, and the supposed cognitive "surplus value" of the geological metaphor for our understanding of historical times, in particular. First, I start with the nineteenth-century classical, linear model of periodization and show which problems inherent in this model Koselleck meant to solve with his stratigraphic model. Second, I present two critical arguments against Koselleck's stratigraphic model. The first is a general one and boils down to the thesis that this model is based on a fundamentally flawed image of geology—a flaw that, surprisingly, has gone unnoticed by the booming Koselleck industry. The second is particular and boils down to the thesis that the stratigraphic model is playing no role in the debate concerning the Anthropocene whatsoever—although this is the *only* debate in which present-day historians are trying to connect to a discussion in geology. My two critical arguments combined suggest that there are good grounds to conclude that Koselleck's idea concerning *Zeitschichten* in history is little more than a seductive metaphor.

The problems of linear time and Koselleck's proposed solution: *Zeitschichten* instead of *Zeitgeist*

The stratigraphic model was meant as a solution to the problem of the modern way of periodizing the historical past. Since the beginning of the nineteenth century, European historians had increasingly conceived of historical time as one continuous sequence of distinct periods that succeeded each other on the same linear time line. "To the modern European mind ... the past appears as a succession of blocks of time," as Jürgen Osterhammel (2006: 48) observed.

The division of historical time into the ancient, medieval, and modern periods acquired a paradigmatic status in the course of the nineteenth century, and history was basically represented by historians as the progressive "march to modernity." Each period derived its internal coherence from its own "spirit of time" (*Zeitgeist*) and was divided from its neighbors by clear "epoch-making" events, otherwise known as caesura. Epoch-making events ideally had an unambiguous chronological date, like the fall of Rome in 476, the discovery of the Americas in 1492, the French Revolution in 1789, and the fall of the Berlin Wall in 1989. It is not accidental that when later historians increasingly started to doubt the existence of a *Zeitgeist* and of *one* chronological timeline for all domains of history, they also started to develop an aversion to explicit periodizing (Osterhammel 2006; Bevernage and Lorenz 2013).

These doubts fed into the stratigraphic model in history that pictures historical times not diachronically as successive periods but in terms of multiple "layers" which move synchronically at different speeds. After 1945, this model started to compete with the "successive" model of periodization, which also took place within Marxism, as Immanuel Wallerstein's "world-system" theory (1974) nicely exemplifies. Fernand Braudel became the global godfather of this new way of writing history, but Reinhart Koselleck was the first to formulate the model of geological strata explicitly. He claimed that the stratigraphic model of time enabled historians to transcend the dichotomous way in which historians used to conceive time: either as linear and irreversible time or as circular and reversible time. Both ways of conceiving historical time are insufficient and one-sided according to Koselleck (2000: 19–20): because "every historical sequence contains both linear and recurrent elements," history is characterized by the experience of both the particularity (*Einzigartigkeit*) of events and their "repetitive structures" (*Wiederholungsstrukturen*). The latter can even be seen as the condition of the possibility of the former, just as is the case with events in geology (Rudwick 2014). And although "repetitive structures" in human history are usually directly or indirectly connected to human intentions—in contrast to those in Earth history, in which *all* "repetitive structures" "transcend" the human will—this difference for Koselleck (2000: 25) does not make the use of the geological metaphor in human history questionable.

On the contrary, Koselleck claims that, like Earth history, human history consists of different layers of time, with different moments of origin and different speeds of change that nevertheless operate simultaneously. The past, therefore, is a composite of multiple and simultaneously "effective" layers of time (Koselleck 2000: 13)—just as in geology. In Koselleck's eyes, the geological model is even the perfect means to understand "the simultaneity of the non-simultaneous" (*Gleichzeitigkeit des Ungleichzeitigen*). The stratigraphic model and "the simultaneity of the non-simultaneous" in his view are basically the same thing:

> Layers of time refer, as their geological example, to several levels of time that are of differing duration and of differentiable origin, which are nonetheless present and effectual at the same time. Also the simultaneity of the unsimultaneous, which is one of the most telling historical phenomena, can be brought under a common denominator by "layers of time". (Koselleck 2000: 9)

To gain a better understanding of Koselleck's use of the geological metaphor and the implied claims, we must first clarify the problem(s) he wanted to solve with its help. As we've seen, his first objective was to transcend the onesidedness of conceiving historical time as either linear or cyclical, and the respective ways of breaking up time—meaning of transcending linear and cyclical periodizations. This presupposes that Koselleck rejects the modern linear periodization of history—and so far, Jordheim's (2012) thesis that Koselleck's adoption of layers of time is directed "against periodization" appears to be correct.

The second objective of Koselleck (2000: 238) was to incorporate the different "speeds of change" of the "structures of repetition"—meaning incorporating the "acceleration" (*Beschleunigung*) or "deceleration" (*Verzögerung*) of layers of time, where he apparently conceives of the layers of time as the dynamic "buildingblocks" of history, and history as its container. Because all imagining of temporal notions is expressed in spatial terms, acceleration and deceleration translate into the spatial thickness of specific layers of time, although Koselleck (2000: 9) does not make this spatial implication explicit himself (see Hoffman and Franzel 2019: xiv). Take the example of a lava flow: all other things being equal, the speed of a lava flow translates into the thickness of the resulting basalt layer. Or take the example of a deposition of sand or chalk on a sea bottom: all other things being equal, the speed of deposition translates into the thickness of the resulting sandstone or limestone layer. As these examples already seem to indicate, in the view of Koselleck (2000: 167), history as a whole does not accelerate or decelerate—only specific layers of time do. So, Koselleck's second objective presupposes that layers of time do not all move with the same speed—and thus are not equally "thick" (Koselleck 2000: 13, 238; see Figure 17.1, however). Historical time as a collection of time layers thus appears to be conceived by Koselleck in terms of an irreducible, heterogeneous multiplicity.

Moreover, Koselleck layers of time are not only "of differing duration and of differentiable origin," but also "present and effectual at the same time." This identification of the stratigraphic model with "the simultaneity of the non-simultaneous" is as remarkable as fundamental because it is based on a very selective interpretation of "the geological example." Koselleck's interpretation of time layers ignores the fundamental distinction in geology between "deformed" and "undeformed" layers and takes the "deformed" situation as the "exemplary," paradigmatic situation—or at least that is what I will argue below. For reasons of simplicity, I will focus on sedimentary layers and leave layers of igneous and metamorphic origin aside.

In geology, sedimentary layers are the result of two basic processes: erosion and deposition, otherwise known as sedimentation. Every layer on the Earth's surface—including sedimentary rock itself—is constantly subject to erosive forces, and the products of erosion are constantly being transported and deposited elsewhere in the form of horizontal layers. As long as they are not deformed, these layers form a linear series producing the (ideal-typical) "pile of pancakes" model of stratigraphy. There are no *a priori* reasons to assume with Koselleck that these layers cannot be (more or less) identical, because many geological layers are in fact deposited cyclically. This "undeformed," horizontal model is exemplified paradigmatically by two instances: first (Figure 17.1), the sedimentary strata that have been produced by the successive Ice Age floods in Washington State, in which over forty different layers have been identified that were deposited cyclically between 15,000 and 13,000 years ago, many of them (approximately) equally thick; second (Figure 17.2), the horizontal strata making up much of the Grand Canyon and accounting for deposition over the last six hundred million years.

The essential characteristic of a linear series is that new layers are always located on top of older ones. The horizontal order of the layers is identical to the order of their chronological origin, while *only* the last layer is visibly "present" because it is on top, covering the others. In

FIGURE 17.1 Hanford Reach, State of Washington, USA (Bruce Bjornstad).

geology, the linear structure of layers is the "undeformed" situation of sedimentary rocks.

Now, as I pointed out earlier, in Koselleck's view, the historical past does *not* exhibit the horizontal linear structure that the nineteenth-century model of periodization and the geology of "undeformed" sedimentary rocks suggest: geology only helps historians to conceptualize and visualize the *non*-linear character of "the simultaneity of the non-simultaneous." We must conclude that Koselleck apparently had only the "deforming" forces in geology in mind that undo the "original," horizontal structure of sedimentary layers by effects like rockfolding, superposition, and intrusion, because only then is Koselleck's phenomenon of "the simultaneity of the unsimultaneous" present and able to be observed as such.

Only when geological layers are in a "folded" condition (Figure 17.3) do layers with different origins in time come to the surface in the present simultaneously, just as Koselleck posited for layers of time *in general*. As a consequence of this "folded" condition, the present surface is no longer the last layer in a linear horizontal series (the last pancake on the pile), but consists of a composite of layers with various origins in time. "Folding" (and other processes of deformation) disturbs the linear chronology of the successive layers: chronologically older layers may move on top of

Era	Supergroup	Group	Formation	Value
MESOZOIC			Chinle Formation	0.0
MESOZOIC			Moenkopi Formation	0.3
PALEOZOIC			Kaibab Formation	0.8
PALEOZOIC			Toroweap Formation	2.1
PALEOZOIC			Coconino Sandstone	4.5
PALEOZOIC			Hermit Formation	4.9
PALEOZOIC		Supai Group	Esplanade Sandstone	11.4
PALEOZOIC		Supai Group	Wescogame Formation	15.0
PALEOZOIC		Supai Group	Manakacha Formation	15.0
PALEOZOIC		Supai Group	Watahomigi Formation	20.2
PALEOZOIC			Suprise Canyon Formation	
PALEOZOIC			Redwall Limestone	23.3
PALEOZOIC			Temple Butte Formation	37.7
PALEOZOIC			Unclassified Dolomite	35.1
PALEOZOIC		Tonto Group	Muav Limestone	37.0
PALEOZOIC		Tonto Group	Bright Angel Shale	46.9
PALEOZOIC		Tonto Group	Tapeats Sandstone	58.2
PROTEROZOIC	Grand Canyon Supergroup	Chuar Group	Sixtymile Formation	68.5
PROTEROZOIC	Grand Canyon Supergroup	Chuar Group	Kwagunt Formation	65.5
PROTEROZOIC	Grand Canyon Supergroup	Chuar Group	Galeros Formation	63.0
PROTEROZOIC	Grand Canyon Supergroup	Chuar Group	Nankoweap Formation	74.8
PROTEROZOIC	Grand Canyon Supergroup	Unkar Group	Cardenas Lava	65.5
PROTEROZOIC	Grand Canyon Supergroup	Unkar Group	Dox Formation	63.0
PROTEROZOIC	Grand Canyon Supergroup	Unkar Group	Shinumo Quartzite	74.8
PROTEROZOIC	Grand Canyon Supergroup	Unkar Group	Hakatai Shale	76.2
PROTEROZOIC	Grand Canyon Supergroup	Unkar Group	Bass Limestone	77.0
PROTEROZOIC				77.5
PROTEROZOIC			Vishnu Schist	Zoroaster Granite

Colorado River

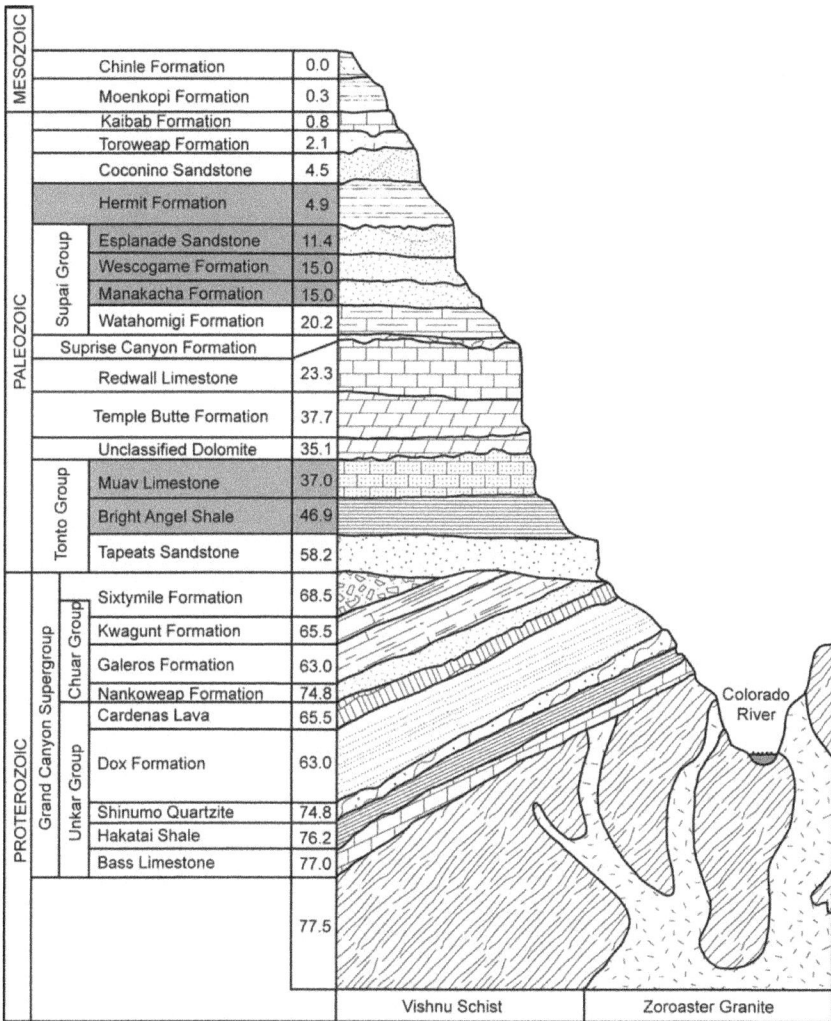

FIGURE 17.2 Geologic Column of the Grand Canyon. Credit to Peter G. Griffiths/ Robert H. Webb/Theodore S. Melis, "Frequency and Initiation of Debris Flows in Grand Canyon, Arizona," *Journal of Geophysical Research* 109 (2004): F04002, doi: 10.1029/2003JF000077.

younger ones (superposition), intrude on them (intrusion), or cut through them (cross-cutting), producing what Koselleck called "the simultaneity of the unsimultaneous."

On closer analysis, Koselleck's geological metaphor turns out to be based on a "halved" picture of geology, namely the "deformed" half of stratigraphy; my "unpacking" is intended to make this fundamental

FIGURE 17.3   Folded rocklayers at Agia Pavlos, Crete (Panther Media at Alamy).

limitation explicit (see Gould 1987 for the role of metaphors in geological time). And although *all* use of metaphor is obviously selective *by definition*, in representations connected to factual truth claims this selection may come with serious "cognitive costs" if the metaphor is not "right" or "fitting" (Lorenz 1998 and 2004: 54–63; Fermandois 2003). In the following section, I will explore another fundamental problem in Koselleck's theory of layers of time that as yet has not been addressed in the exponentially growing Koselleck reception.

The solution as a problem, part 1: What is a *Zeitschicht* in history anyway?

The problem I am referring to is as basic as it is baffling, because it concerns both the temporal *identification* and the *explanation* of the layers of time. The problem I see in using the stratigraphic model in history is this: geologists have not only developed a whole range of methods for identifying and determining the age of geological layers in both relative and absolute terms in, respectively, chronostratigraphy and geochronology (Zalasiewicz et al. 2013), but also established explanatory principles concerning the position of the layers in geology (superposition, folding, intrusion, etc.). Historians, in contrast, have not even begun to develop such a conceptual and methodological toolkit for identifying and measuring historical layers of time outside the domain of linear chronology (e.g., decades, centuries, etc.). Therefore, it is by no means accidental that history has nothing equivalent to the International Commission on Stratigraphy—a global body of geological experts that decides on all stratigraphic issues within the discipline of geology based on standardized criteria (of physical, chemical, and biological character) and standardized methods of measurement (Ellis 2018: 34–52; Zalasiewicz et al. 2019: esp. 11–31). The same holds for the formalized geologic time scale (GTS), divided into eons, eras, periods, epochs, and ages, for which there are no equivalents in historical time. In human history, periodization remains inextricably connected to issues of subjectivity and normativity (Lorenz 2017), as the discussions about the Anthropocene also demonstrate (see the "Capitalocene").

Let me illustrate the fundamental differences between geology and history as far as layers of time are concerned with the example of relative dating because it is fairly simple. In geology, it is the principle of superposition that helps to determine the relative age of flat-lying sedimentary rocks (the "pancakes"): the rocks at the bottom of the pile are the oldest and the rocks on top are the youngest. Next to this rule there is the principle of original horizontality, meaning that sedimentary rocks are always originally deposited flat—that is, horizontally. In history, however, there are no general principles that help historians to date layers of time relative to each other. Did capitalism "supersede" slavery and feudalism diachronically in time (assuming all three somehow qualify as complex "layers of time," of course), as Marx thought? Or do they still co-exist synchronically, as Wallerstein and Braudel argued? And can the "confrontational" politics of the Second German Empire (1871–1918) be explained by its combination of an "untimely" ("absolutistic") political system and a very "timely" (modern-capitalistic) economic system—that is, by the "simultaneity" of two "unsimultaneous" layers of time—as the "Bielefeld School" argued for some time?

Now, my problem is not that questions like these were and are debated in history. My problem is that Koselleck's geological metaphor is not only unhelpful in answering these kinds of questions, but is fundamentally misguided because it claims that the "deformed"—folded— situation is the "normal" condition of layers of time (by identifying them with "the simultaneity of the unsimultaneous"). Contrary to this claim, we saw that geological layers may remain in an "undeformed"—horizontal— position for hundreds of millions of years, as in the rock formations of the Grand Canyon. Moreover, when horizontal rocks are folded, overturned, or intruded by igneous rocks, the principles of superposition and of original horizontality still allow geologists to reconstruct the sequence of events that explain the order of the layers. The "undeformed" situation of strata in geology is normally the clue to the "deformed" situation—in complete contrast to what Koselleck's interpretation of the stratigraphic model suggests.

Since the eighteenth century, historians have most certainly developed reliable methods for establishing the chronological date of their objects and events in a global frame, but they did not develop theories and methods for identifying and explaining layers of time. Koselleck did not produce much clarity concerning layers of time in the first place, nor did he apply the stratigraphic model of time in his own historical investigations. Consider what he wrote about time layers and modern history (*Neuzeit*) in his famous article "How Modern is our Modern Age?":

> In order to know how modern our modern age is we have to know how many layers of past history are included in our present. Maybe more than we can observe directly. This is a task of historical reflection and its results cannot be found beforehand in the sources. (Koselleck 2000: 239)

According to Koselleck, layers of time can be observed and counted, although not in the sources. Apparently, "historical reflection" is needed to do so: this is a matter of historical theory. Koselleck, however, never developed a historical theory of time layers, as Christian Meier (2007) and Lucian Hölscher (2011), among others, have remarked in their obituaries of Koselleck, although such a theory was also at the very heart of his project to formulate the features of "possible histories"; this long-awaited book, however, did not see the light of the day. Therefore a fundamental question in history and historical theory remains how to identify and explain layers of time.

The solution as a problem, part 2: The case of the Anthropocene

The sobering conclusion that on closer analysis Koselleck's stratigraphic model does not enable historians to identify and explain layers of time leads me to the *only* discussion in which (especially global) historians are actually looking for help and orientation from geologists concerning the issue of time and periodization. I am referring to the debate over whether the human (*anthropos*) and the planet it is (mis-)using have entered the so-called Anthropocene—and by implication have produced a caesura with the Holocene (the latest geological period that began after the last Ice Age ended, some twelve thousand years ago). The reason why geological time and geological periodization have recently become an issue of interest for historians is the circumstance that human influences (the anthroposphere) on the Earth System (consisting of the anthroposphere, the atmosphere, the biosphere, the hydrosphere, and the lithosphere, including their interactions) have acquired such a magnitude and force that they have become traceable in the geological record (Zalasiewicz et al. 2019: 41–101). The proponents of the Anthropocene thesis argue that for the first time in history humankind has turned into a geological factor itself—thereby producing "unprecedented change" (Simon 2019) and erasing the nature–culture/history divide literally (Ellis 2018: 16–24; Zalasiewicz et al. 2019). The most well-known phenomena in question are a human-induced mass extinction of species and global warming, the latter of which is changing the climates globally in such a way that also the long-term conditions of survival of humanity appear to be increasingly at risk. Several prominent global historians like John McNeill (2001) and Dipesh Chakrabarty (2009, 2018) are arguing that the Anthropocene question is not only at the top of the agenda in geology, climate science, and Earth science, but in history too, because the future existence of history is also at stake.

Now that the question of whether the specifically human influences on the Earth System satisfy the criteria for distinguishing geological periods from each other is on the table of both geologists and historians, one would expect that Koselleck's stratigraphic model could be helpful in at least framing this question and bridging the gap between geological and historical thinking. However, nothing of the sort is happening (as far as I can see): the debate about the caesura between the Anthropocene and the Holocene as distinct geological periods has as yet been conducted without any recourse to Koselleck's model of *Zeitschichten*, although Juhan Hellerma (2020: 202) recently suggested that this could and should be used. This absence of connection is all the more remarkable because in the discussion about the onset of the Anthropocene—and thus its caesura with the Holocene—the "Great Acceleration" hypothesis has found most support among geologists and Earth System scientists, locating the beginning of the Anthropocene in the "dramatic mid-20th-century change in anthropogenic global environmental change" (Ellis 2018: 53). The affinity between the "Great Acceleration" and Koselleck's ideas about "acceleration" in modern history is so obvious that connecting them seems the most logical track to follow for those who see a future for the stratigraphic model in history. However this may be, as long as all these questions are not even addressed, the stratigraphic model will remain at best a seductive metaphor in history.

References

Bevernage, B., and C. Lorenz (2013), "Introduction," in C. Lorenz and B. Bevernage (eds.), *Breaking up Time: Negotiating the Borders between Present, Past and Future*, 7–35, Göttingen: Vandenhoeck.

Bouton, C. (2016), "The Critical Theory of History: Rethinking the Philosophy of History in the Light of Koselleck's Work," *History and Theory* 55(2): 163–84.

Chakrabarty, D. (2009), "The Climate of History: Four Theses," *Critical Inquiry* 35(2): 197–222.

Chakrabarty, D. (2018), "Anthropocene Time," *History and Theory* 57(1): 5–32.

Ellis, E. C. (2018), *Antropocene. A Very Short Introduction*. Oxford: Oxford University Press.

Esposito, F. (2017), *Zeitenwandel. Transformationen geschichtlicher Zeitlichkeit nach dem Boom*. Göttingen: Vandenhoeck & Ruprecht.

Fermandois, E. (2003), "Kontexte erzeugen. Zur Frage der Wahrheit von Metaphern," *Deutsche Zeitschrift für Philosophie* 51 (2003): 427–42.

Gould, S. J. (1987), *Time's Arrow, Time's Cycle. Myth and Metaphor in the Discovery of Geological Time*. Cambridge, MA: Harvard University Press.

Jordheim, H. (2011), "'Unzählbar viele Zeiten': Die Sattelzeit im Spiegel der Gleichzeitigkeit des Ungleichzeitigen," in H. Joas and P. Vogt (eds.), *Begriffene Geschichte. Beiträge zum Werk Reinhart Kosellecks*, 449–81, Berlin: Suhrkamp.

Jordheim, H. (2012), "Against Periodization: Koselleck's Theory of Multiple Temporalities," *History and Theory* 51(2): 151–71.

Jordheim, H. (2017), "In the Layer Cake of Time: Thoughts on a Stratigraphic Model of Intellectual History," in T. Goering (ed.), *Ideeengeschichte heute. Traditionen und Perspektiven*, 195–214, Bielefeld: transcript.

Hellerma, J. (2020), "Koselleck on Modernity, *Historik*, and Layers of Time," *History and Theory* 59(2): 188–209.

Hoffman, S-L., and S. Franzel (2019), "Introduction. Translating Koselleck," in R. Koselleck, *Sediments of Time: On Possible Histories*, ix–xxxi, Stanford, CA: Stanford University Press.

Hölscher, L. (2011), "Abschied von Reinhart Koselleck," in H. Joas and P. Vogt (eds.), *Begriffene Geschichte. Beiträge zum Werk Reinhart Kosellecks*, 84–94, Berlin: Suhrkamp.

Koselleck, R. (2000), *Zeitschichten—Studien zur Historik*. Berlin: Suhrkamp.

Lorenz, C. (1998), "Can Histories Be True? Narrativism, Positivism and the 'Metaphorical Turn'," *History and Theory* 37(3): 309–29.

Lorenz, C. (2004), "Kann Geschichte wahr sein? Zu den narrativen Geschichtsphilosophien von Hayden White und Frank Ankersmit," in J. Schröter and A. Eddelbüttel (eds.), *Konstruktion von Wirklichkeit. Beiträge aus geschichtstheoretischer, philosophischer und theologischer Perspektive*, 33–63, Berlin and New York: De Gruyter.

Lorenz, C. (2017), "The Times They Are a-Changin'. On Time, Space and Periodization in History," in M. Carretero, S. Berger, and M. Grever (eds.), *Palgrave Handbook of Research in Historical Culture and Education*, 109–33, Houndmills: Palgrave.

Lorenz, C. (2019), "Out of Time? Critical Reflections on Francois Hartog's Presentism," in M. Tamm and L. Olivier (eds.), *Rethinking Historical Time. New Approaches to Presentism*, 23–43, London: Bloomsbury.

McNeill, J. (2001), *Something New under the Sun: An Environmental History of the Twentieth-Century World*. New York: Norton & Co.

Meier, C. (2007), "Gedenkrede auf Reinhart Koselleck," in N. Bulst and W. Steinmetz (eds.), *Bielefelder Universitätsgespräche und Vorträge*, 7–35, Bielefeld.

Olsen, N. (2012), *History in the Plural: An Introduction to the Work of Reinhart Koselleck*. New York: Berghahn.

Osterhammel, J. (2006), "Über die Periodisierung der neueren Geschichte," in *Berlin-Brandenburgische Akademie der Wissenschaften, Berichte und Abhandlungen* (Bd. 10), 45–64, Berlin: De Gruyter.

Pomian, K. (1984), *L'ordre du temps*. Paris: Gallimard.

Rohbeck, J. (2020), *Integrative Geschichtsphilosophie in Zeiten der Globalisierung*. Berlin and Boston: De Gruyter.

Rudwick, M. (2014), *Earth's Deep History. How It Was Discovered and Why It Matters*. Chicago, IL: University of Chicago Press.

Simon, Z. B. (2019), *History in Times of Unprecedented Change: A Theory for the 21st Century*. London: Bloomsbury.

Wallerstein, I. (1974), *The Modern World-System I: Capitalist Agriculture and the Origins of the European World-Economy in the Sixteenth Century*. New York: Academic Press.

Zalasiewicz, J., M. B. Cita, F. Hilgen, B. R. Pratt, A. Strasser, J. Thierry, and H. Weissert (2013), "Chronostratigraphy and Geochronology: A Proposed Realignment," *GSA Today* 23: 4–8.

Zalasiewicz, J., C. N. Waters, M. Williams, and C. P. Summerhayes (eds.) (2019), *The Anthropocene as a Geological Time Unit. A Guide to the Scientific Evidence and Current Debate*. Cambridge: Cambridge University Press.

Zammito, J. (2004), "Koselleck's Philosophy of Historical Time(s) and the Practice of History," *History and Theory* 43(1): 124–35.

CHAPTER EIGHTEEN

Against the historicist tradition of historical understanding

Jörg van Norden

Historical understanding is the objective historians typically try to accomplish. The notion is, however, notoriously elusive and plagued by difficulties. The first difficulty arises from its different meanings in German and Anglo-American discourse, despite the fact that at the same time they are deeply entangled. In this chapter, I want to discuss this ambivalent relation. To capture the argument in a few words: the Anglo-American concept of "historical understanding" seems much broader, since it is used as an equivalent to "historical thinking," while in the German tradition it is something like "historical empathy" or "intuition," but both discourses—and this is the second difficulty—generally use the expression "historical understanding" as something self-evident, without specifying it.

Historical understanding, in both the aforementioned cases, derives from a long tradition that has been nearly forgotten. Understanding, *Verstehen*, was born in the work of Johann Gustav Droysen ([1857] 1977) in German historicism, and in the philosophy of Wilhelm Dilthey ([1889] 1968, [1898] 1968, 1968a, 1968b) in the *Geisteswissenschaftliche Schule*. It survived the change of political systems, and one can find it in the twentieth century in Robin George Collingwood's *The Idea of History* (1966) or in John Lukacs's

Historical Consciousness or the Remembered Past (1968), and most recently also in Jörn Rüsen's *Historik* (2013). This historicist tradition has been institutionalized in the departments of humanities in Anglo-American universities, while in Germany, where the history of historical understanding began in the nineteenth century, it has been at the center of historiographical debates.

In exploring the problematic assumptions of historical understanding, my chapter engages in historical semantics. The first section is dedicated to the German discourse, and the second looks at the Anglo-American context. In my conclusion, I argue for the necessity of bidding farewell to "historical understanding" in its historicist denotation.

From divinity to humanity: The German context

The nineteenth-century tradition of *Verstehen* is based on the assumption that there is something substantially human in every person, in human agency and its material artifacts. Notwithstanding the differences of culture, place, or time, this human substance enables us to understand each other. The concept dates from the ancient Greek philosophers, who were convinced that phenomena are the externalization of eternal ideas. Christian theology adapted this tradition and believed in the almighty God within every part of his creation: God formed the first human from mud and enlivened him with his breath. That divine essence in every human being was considered as the basis of understanding each other and the whole world around us, regardless of cultural or historical differences. By relying on this argument, sixteenth-century Jesuits defended South American natives against their fellow conquerors, while in Europe, creationist Catholicism became gradually secularized and man replaced God. In the latter case, the essence was no longer God within, but humanity, which connects not only coevals, but also present and past peoples, in spite of cultural and temporal differences.

Nevertheless, humanism did not deny heterogeneity. People in Europe and in Asia were not regarded as the same, and nor were the medieval clergyman and the Renaissance philosopher. But the differences have become related to the particular context in which humanity became externalized. This was the approach of Ranke, the historicist founding figure of professionalized historical writing, who requested that historians understand the past from the past itself, drawing epistemologically on Christian theology. Yet enlightened historicist humanism traced back all the differences to the cultural or historical context only in the second step. First of all, one had to understand what everybody has in common: humanity as the essence of mankind. If this constituted no problem for enlightened humanism, it was due to assuming the possibility of understanding through intuition. In historicist humanism, all human beings in the present and the past were considered to be on the same wavelength because of that human essence in everyone (Jaeger and Rüsen 1992; Steenblock 2000).

Outside the German context, Thomas Paine's "Common Sense," the title of his memorandum in favor of North American independence and a democratic government geared to human rights, is a prime example of this, as is the coeval philosophy of the so-called Scottish School, with its similar focus on "common sense" (Buhr and Klaus 1976: 245). In the German context, in the mid-nineteenth century, Droysen adapted humanism to historiography and substantiated the historicist tradition of a specifically historical understanding which lasts to the present day (Droysen 1863, [1857] 1977).

This historicist tradition combines intuitive understanding, hermeneutics, and narration. In nineteenth-century hermeneutics as a method of textual interpretation, reason and intuition work together in aiming to unearth the partial facts which historians need for composing their narration as a whole. Dilthey named the process of constantly oscillating between the part and the whole in developing understanding the "hermeneutic circle." In distinguishing natural sciences and humanities, *Naturwissenschaften*, and *Geisteswissenschaften*, he argued that explanation is not reserved to the natural sciences: the *Geisteswissenschaften* also explain, but they focus on understanding as the common spirit in everything human beings think, do, and produce (Dilthey [1889] 1968, [1898] 1968, 1968a, 1968b). The *Geisteswissenschaftliche Schule*, the school of thought committed to the historicist mode of historical understanding, was convinced that the more manifestations of that spirit are intuitively understood and experienced, the better we know humanity and the more human we become. Accordingly, writing the history of humanity appeared to also be a moral project (Nobira 2006).

The enormous potential of the *Geisteswissenschaftliche Schule* derived from its combination of individuality and community, of continuity and change, of collective identity and individual difference. In its view, each human being represents a special and unique externalization of the human essence, and, at the same time, is an integral part of humanity because of that essence. The human community, the secularized communion in the spirit, guarantees mutual understanding, solidarity, respect, and harmony. At a later stage, I will return to this point and question this approach, but for now, let's stay with the promises the *Geisteswissenschaftliche* philosophy makes.

Following its tune, historians felt safe to find the truth: by writing history, they assumed they would recover the past from the sources which were considered to be the ashes of what had happened. Their human intuition works like the divine breath of the creator in Christian theology, to the extent that the dead relics of the past can come to life again. *The Geisteswissenschaftliche Schule* was metaphysical in its nature, and it had legions of followers among educationists and historians. In Germany during the Weimar Republic, it equally impressed right and left: fascists like Dietrich Klagges, Max Wundt, and Ernst Anrich; racists like Ernst Krieck, Harold Steinacker, Erich Rothacker, Rudolf Stadelmann, Philipp Hördt, Gerhardt Giese, and Reinhard Wittram; and democrats and socialists such as Siegfried Kawerau, Kurt Sonntag, Theodor Litt, and Richard Koebner (van Norden 2018: 9–80). Although by 1945, following the Second World War, it had become difficult to imagine something human that the fascist murderers and their victims in the concentration camps could have in common, the *Geisteswissenschaftliche Schule* remained in a dominant position in Germany. While it became impossible to venerate one's own nation as the privileged externalization of the human in a chauvinist way as Klagges and Wundt did, it was still quite acceptable to find the universal human, for example, in the discourse on human rights.

In addition, the intuitive element of the historicist mode of historical understanding stayed alive, and not only among conservative historians. Left-leaning scholars such as Anna Siemsen, Fritz Lucas, and Ernst Weymar also argued on the assumption of a common human spirit in humankind. The difference between right and left was the intention to stabilize the political institutions or to transcend them in support of emancipation (van Norden 2018: 88–119). Whereas the majority of German historians rejected those emancipatory tendencies in the windfall of 1968, the assumed harmony of understanding was criticized by a small group of history didacts—Annette Kuhn, Klaus Bergmann, and Hans-Jürgen Pandel—on the basis of critical theory. Their criticism, however, had no chance against a broad current in school and university, and against the coalition of mainstream in historiography, history didactics, and philosophy of history, as represented by Rudolf Vierhaus,

Karl-Ernst Jeismann, and Jörn Rüsen in the central meeting of German historians in 1976 in Mannheim, where the conflict was fought (van Norden 2018: 159–63).

Rüsen played an ambivalent role in this controversy. On the one hand, he remained committed to the premises of the *Geisteswissenschaftliche Schule* throughout his scholarly career. Even in his recent *Historik* (2013), he keeps defending it against those who criticize the ideal of human understanding as Eurocentric universalism. On the other hand, Rüsen cooperated with the emancipatory movement in its new journal, *Geschichtsdidaktik*. But back to the 1976 controversy on history education, the different theoretical approaches concerning historical understanding seemed to be irreconcilable. Yet what really mattered for all involved was the continuing existence of history as a school subject. In line with a general conservative roll-back in society and politics, Jeismann, Rüsen, and Vierhaus, alongside most historians in school and university, successfully defended history against a new subject called *Gesellschaftslehre* (social sciences). With their victory, the theoretical debate about historical understanding faded out, but not the unreflected use of the concept (van Norden 2018: 159–221). Humanist historicism stayed alive implicitly—and, with Rüsen, more and more explicitly, too.

The implicitness of understanding: The Anglo-American context

A similar explicit controversy is absent in the English-speaking discourse. Here, historical understanding seems to be a container of everything that deals with the past, and the concept is used quite arbitrarily. It is symptomatic that *The Wiley International Handbook of History Teaching and Learning* does not dedicate a chapter to "historical understanding," but reserves ones for "Historical Thinking," "Historical Reasoning," "Historical Consciousness," and "Historical Empathy," for example. In their chapter on "Historical Consciousness," Anna Clark and Maria Grever do not go beyond the statement that defining "the concepts and skills of historical understanding is a complicated and continuously evolving process, … there is considerable overlap and confusion between the seemingly synonymous terminology of historical thinking, understanding, and literacy" (Clark and Grever 2018: 186).

At the same time, the Anglo-American discourse professes its dedication to humanity as borrowed from German historicism, as discussed above. Collingwood (1966: 287, 298), for instance, refers to rational thinking as the "humanum" which bridges the gulf between past and present and different cultures. The rationality of thoughts, he claims, do not depend on time and place, and today's historians are able to identically rethink what was thought a long time ago. By doing so, historians re-enact and understand the past. What historians apprehend "is the act of thought itself, in its survival and revival at different times and in different persons: once in the historian's own life, once in the life of the person whose history he is narrating" (Collingwood 1966: 302–3). Only reflective thoughts—that is to say, those recognized by people of the past—can be rethought, meaning that Collingwood (1966: 308) considerably reduces the variety of historical subjects. Historians do not deal with unconscious thinking, nor emotions or nature, but only with acts "we do on purpose" (308–9). In addition to rationality, Collingwood bases understanding on the assumption that the past is an integral part of the present because the latter is the result of what has happened before (334). Because of the presence of the past in the present, the historian's mind is "pre-adapted," "congenial" with the mind of historical actors whose thoughts the historian rethinks (304–5). Perhaps not coincidentally, the same idea can be found in Jörn Rüsen (2013) in the German context.

To mention another example, John Lukacs critically describes Collingwood as neo-idealist and characterizes his own position as "'post-materialistic' idealism" (1968: xxi, 152, 229). But, just like Collingwood, he posits that the historian forms part "of the entire human race, of all history" (236). Besides, according to Lukacs, "in history the observer and the observed belong to the same species," and "understanding … involves a kind of sympathetic participation in the observed." Lukacs is convinced that "human nature does not change" and that there is no difference between present and past knowledge: "we are human repositories of all mankind's historical experiences in the past," while past and future are "overlapping … through our minds" (248). History tells us about human nature and the past is a variation of human behavior. Like Collingwood, Lukacs is convinced that "the past remains latent in the present" (Lukacs 1968: 251), and believes in a common sense which allows understanding always, everywhere. When he admits potential misunderstanding, he does not explain what may impair understanding (Lukacs 1968: 247–8, 251, 268).

Whereas Collingwood and Lukacs are explicitly historicist, many texts in history education invoke historicist ideas implicitly. The examples are plenty: Denis Shelmit claims that history "should contribute to adolescents' understanding of their humanity" (see Seixas 2017: 594); Peter Seixas wonders "where the boundary lies between the historically malleable and humanly universal" (2017: 601); Levisohn is convinced that history "calls us back to our innate humanity" (2017: 619). Furthermore, Peter Lee and Rosalyn Ashby (2001) appeal to common sense; Clark and Grever (2018: 179) speak about "a relatively unchangeable human nature"; and Wineburg (2001: 5–7, 12) wishes that history would "allow … us to take membership in the entire human race," and, following Carl Degler, "expand our conception and understanding of what it means to be human."

On a diverging note, although Wineburg claims that there is some connection, something similar between past and present in spite of all the differences, he also emphasizes that we cannot see through the eyes of past people and that it is quite difficult to understand what happened back then. Understanding, therefore, is something "unnatural": you have to learn it in order to be able to do it. Wineburg stresses that historical understanding has to abandon our present ways of thinking and avoid presentism. In his view, learning to deal with the foreign past helps us to open ourselves to our present's strangeness (Wineburg 2001: 22, 24). But epistemologically, presentism is unavoidable and should be welcomed in the way of pragmatic constructivism. It is the condition of problem-solving by narration.

Breaking with "historical understanding"?

In the German and Anglo-American discourse, historicist humanism based on "historical understanding" survived only implicitly because its metaphysical foundation became obsolete after the horrors of the Holocaust. Only a few continue defending the idea explicitly, such as Jörn Rüsen, who has been severely criticized as a Eurocentric on this ground (Rüsen 2011).

There are, I think, two ways to cope with the difficulties of "historical understanding" as entailed by the historicist view. The first, somehow smaller one is to work out a new definition of that old concept with a new theoretical foundation. I wonder if this is possible without a new essentialism. Perhaps an existentialist philosophy of value enables a new way to hold on to a historicist notion of "historical understanding" (Stern 1967). But I would rather prefer rupture to reform. Hence, the second and more consequent option is that of pragmatic constructivism (Rorty 1991), which rejects understanding and whatever interpersonal intersection it might be based on. Inasmuch as human beings need to cooperate to manage the problems of survival and have to negotiate over what to do in times of crisis, understanding is less important than cooperation. Although it is not easy to find agreements across the differentiations of multiple structures of race, class, and gender that may impair balanced communication, there is no better alternative I can think of than the process in which the past is brought to the present by shared narratives which go alongside decision-making. To construct narrations, historical thinking is necessary. It combines our questions of the present with our imaginations of the past in designing a future which is worth living. Historical thinking constructs time passages by means of such narrations. We do not have to explain the world or find the ultimate truth; rather, we need to construct our narratives und strategies of problem-solving. So let us use the potential of our historical thinking to enable a sustainable and agreed way if there are problems to cope with. If there is no human essence in history, as historicism promised but was proven wrong by history, then past, present, and future are just our responsibility.

References

Buhr, M., and G. Klaus (1976), *Philosophisches Wörterbuch*, 12th edn. Westberlin: Das europäische Buch.

Clark, A., and M. Grever (2018), "Historical Consciousness: Conceptualizations and Educational Applications," in L. M. Harris, S. Metzger, and S. A. Metzger (eds.), *The Wiley International Handbook of History Teaching and Learning*, 177–201, Hoboken, NJ: Wiley.

Collingwood, R. G. (1966), *The Idea of History*, 7th edn. Oxford: University Press.

Dilthey, W. ([1889] 1968), "Archive der Literatur in ihrer Bedeutung für das Studium der Geschichte der Philosophie," in H. Nohl (ed.), *Wilhelm Dilthey: Gesammelte Schriften*: 555–75, 4th edn, Stuttgart, Göttingen: Teubner; Vandenhoeck & Ruprecht.

Dilthey, W. ([1898] 1968), "Die drei Grundformen der Systeme in der ersten Hälfte des 19. Jahrhunderts," in H. Nohl (ed.), *Wilhelm Dilthey: Gesammelte Schriften*: 528–54, 4th edn, Stuttgart, Göttingen: Teubner; Vandenhoeck & Ruprecht.

Dilthey, W. (1968a), "Einleitung in die Geisteswissenschaften: Versuch einer Grundlegung für das Studium der Gesellschaft und der Geschichte," in H. Nohl (ed.), *Wilhelm Dilthey: Gesammelte Schriften*, 4th edn, Stuttgart, Göttingen: Teubner; Vandenhoeck & Ruprecht.

Dilthey, W. (1968b), "Vom Aufgang des Geschichtlichen Bewusstseins: Jugendaufsätze und Erinnerung," in H. Nohl (ed.), *Wilhelm Dilthey: Gesammelte Schriften*, 4th edn, Stuttgart, Göttingen: Teubner; Vandenhoeck & Ruprecht.

Droysen, J. G. (1863), "Die Erhebung der Geschichte zum Rang einer Wissenschaft," *Historische Zeitschrift* 9: 1–22.

Droysen, J. G. ([1857] 1977), *Historik*, Band 1: Rekonstruktion der ersten vollständigen Fassung der Vorlesung. Grundriß der Historik in der ersten handschriftlichen (1857/58) und in der letzten gedruckten Fassung (1882). Stuttgart: Frommann-Holzboog.

Jaeger, F., and J. Rüsen (1992), *Geschichte des Historismus: Eine Einführung*. München: Beck.

Lee, P., and R. Ashby (2001), "Empathy, perspective-taking, and rational understanding," in O. L. Davis, Jr., E. A. Yeager, and S. J. Foster (eds.), *Historical Empathy and Perspective Taking in the Social Studies*, 21–50, Lanham: Rowman and Littlefield.

Levisohn, J. A. (2017), "Historical Thinking: and Its Alleged Unnaturalness," *Educational Philosophy and Theory* 49(6): 618–30.

Lukacs, J. (1968), *Historical Consciousness or the Remembered Past*. New York: Harper & Row.

Nobira, S. (2006), "Zum kritischen Potenzial der Pädagogik Wilhelm Diltheys," in D. Gaus and R. Uhle (eds.), *Wie verstehen Pädagogen?: Begriffe und Methoden des Verstehens in der Erziehungswissenschaft*, 17–39, Wiesbaden: VS Verlag für Sozialwissenschaften.

Rorty, R. (1991), *Contingency, Irony, and Solidarity*. Cambridge: Cambridge University Press.

Rüsen, J. (2011), "Umriss einer Theorie der Geschichtswissenschaft," *Erwägen-Wissen-Ethik. Streitforum für Erwägungskultur* 22(4): 477–90.

Rüsen, J. (2013), *Historik: Theorie der Geschichtswissenschaft*. Köln, Weimar, Wien: Böhlau.

Seixas, P. (2017), "A Model of Historical Thinking," *Educational Philosophy and Theory* 49(6): 593–605.

Steenblock, V. (2000), "Vom Sinn der Geschichte nach dem Ende der Geschichtsphilosophie: Ein Plädoyer für Historische Bildung," in S. Jordan (ed.), *Zukunft der Geschichte: Historisches Denken an der Schwelle zum 21. Jahrhundert*, 35–47, Berlin: trafo.

Stern, A. (1967), *Geschichtsphilosophie und Wertproblem*. München: Ernst Reinhardt.

Van Norden, J. (2018), *Geschichte ist Bewusstsein: Historie einer geschichtsdidaktischen Fundamentalkategorie*. Frankfurt am Main: Wochenschau.

Wineburg, S. S. (2001), *Historical Thinking and Other Unnatural Acts: Charting the Future of Teaching the Past*. Philadelphia, PA: Temple University Press.

CHAPTER NINETEEN

Historical understanding and reconciliation after violent conflict

Berber Bevernage and Kate E. Temoney

Introduction

With the exception of an occasional dissident voice, a quasi-consensus exists among policy makers, activists, and academics that actively "dealing with the past" and achieving a certain historical understanding are necessary to foster reconciliation after violent conflict or historical injustice. However, underlying this consensus, there are divergences, confusions, and even contradictions regarding how best to achieve reconciliation in the first place—independent of whether this reconciliation is conceived as a mere non-violent co-existence, as a more profound mutual respect or civic solidarity, or as the highly ambitious goal of interpersonal harmony or even forgiveness between former enemies. In this chapter, we conceptually delineate three ways of dealing with the past and the correlative historical understanding that theorists and practitioners *believe* can foster reconciliation. We emphasize "believe" because there is regrettably very little measurable proof for a causal relation between historical understanding and reconciliation. Consequently, we will not try to answer the question of which ways of dealing with the past (if any) actually work to foster reconciliation. Rather, we are interested in the way the widespread preoccupation with reconciliation gives rise to important discussions on the nature, function, and value of historical understanding and how these can challenge conventional historiography.

We argue that there are at least three ways of dealing with the past and outline the kinds of historical understanding these demand. The first approach—which is typically favored by more conventionally trained academics—is that of the Cognitive Recovery of Truth, which relies upon the efficacy of objectivist historical knowledge and the indispensability of a single and shared reality. Alternatively, the second approach, (Inter) subjective Reframing, stresses the importance of the active re-emplotment of historical narratives and favors a metahistorical understanding for reconciliation. This approach aims to assist victims and perpetrators alike in not recovering reality but seeing this reality and their own identities in it in a new way. Embracing the possibility of irreconcilable narratives and realities, the third approach, Ethical Recognition, emphasizes the need for a recognition of oppressed historical experiences of peoples and their culturally different ways of relating to the past. This approach tends to be highly critical of historicism, contending that a traditional form of historical understanding—and the epistemological framework of objectivist historicism that undergirds it—at the very least cannot authentically accommodate their stories and at worst is politically damaging and perpetuates elite histories.

Ultimately, we argue that the preoccupation with reconciliation has not always resulted in approaches to historical understanding that easily align with the views of more positivist-leaning historians. Especially in the cases of the (Inter)subjective Reframing and Ethical Recognition approaches, advocates of reconciliation have favored ways of dealing with the past and forms of historical understanding that do not prioritize the aim of Cognitive Recovery of Truth and thus can profoundly challenge classic academic history. In what follows, with two caveats due to space restrictions, we briefly elaborate upon and compare the three different ways of dealing with the past and the historical understandings of reconciliation that facilitate these ways, with a few criticisms of each of these approaches. We will not address the multivalence of "reconciliation" (for an overview, see Bloomfield 2006; Meierhenrich 2008); for the purpose of this article, we adopt "sociopolitical reconciliation" (Cole 2007), as it focuses on an inter-communal rather than an interpersonal or personal level of reconciliation. Moreover, we broadly sketch different positions in the reconciliation debate, which inevitably means that our discussion is neither exhaustive nor finely nuanced.

Cognitive Recovery of Truth: Truth-telling and "objective" historicist understanding

Likely due to the popularity of Truth and Reconciliation Commissions (TRC)—quasi-judicial bodies that cannot sentence or punish but can offer official "truth-telling" as an alternative—reconciliation is often associated with neo-positivist rhetoric. This has culminated in perceiving the preoccupation with reconciliation as confirmation of the societal value of objective historical research. In turn, this created high hopes among some historians for a renewed public role for their profession and, for the most optimistic, the belief that this engagement could be combined with their traditional academic epistemological standards: a classic objectivist historical understanding that gets the facts straight and uncovers the past as it really was (e.g., Barkan 2005; Ingrao 2009).

Although remaining empirically untested, the enthusiasm for "historical" truth-telling is often based on the presumption that people can only reconcile if they share the same historical reality, if they accept that the past is really past rather than treating it as continuously present, and/or if they come to understand that history is inherently complex and nuanced, leaving no space for collective or transgenerational guilt. In this context, the historical understanding that seems required for reconciliation is an objectivist and historicist one. If the goal is tying former antagonists to the same historical reality so as to create political consensus via historical consensus—which many see as tightly linked (e.g., Teitel 2000: 89)—then the objective reconstruction of the bare historical facts seems the best way forward. From this perspective, the great attraction of the objective truth is that there is only one version of it.

A historicist understanding can also seem attractive because of its tendency to treat the past as a "foreign country" and posit a distance between past and present (see Bevernage 2011). The hope of some historians is that proper "historicization" will pacify the past and "draw a line under victimhood" by taking victims out of their state of "extra-temporality," in which the past seems to "remain present" and historical atrocities are experienced as if they "only happened yesterday or even today" (de Graaff 2006; see also Rousso 1998).

The tendency of historicist understanding to focus on the particular and the unique in history, furthermore, seems very fit for deconstructing the notion of collective guilt and helping to individualize it. Indeed, the hope of many seems to be that the objective study of history will yield a "moderating truth" based on a "mutual acknowledgement of complicity in past conflict" and "dismantling understandings of the Other as an essentially evil and intractable foe" (Aiken 2014: 54).

Striving for a mere objective historicist understanding as an effective means to foster reconciliation is not without its critics. A historicizing approach that distances past from present and stresses the "pastness of the past" can lead to overlooking "enduring injustices" (Spinner-Halev 2012) and hamper reconciliation by ignoring how contemporary (group) identities often continue to be informed by legacies of historical injustice. In addition, the hope that an objective study of the past will yield a "moderating truth" can never be guaranteed, and can also hamper a just process of reconciliation when becoming an *a priori* presumption about what Anat Biletzki (2013: 39) calls "symmetry" in historical conflict or the idea that there are always "two sides to every [hi]story." The historicist focus on the particularity and unicity of actors and events can be used to deny the structural character of historical injustices or help communities absolve themselves from having to assume any collective responsibility. According to David Mendeloff (2004: 368), the assumption of a certain collective responsibility, in contrast, can facilitate reconciliation, as illustrated by the German–Israeli case.

Moreover, the capacity of the recounting of "objective" historical facts to wed former enemies to a shared historical reality may also be more limited than hoped. The reason is that the meaning attributed to historical facts is always dependent on larger sociocultural frames that are often highly tenacious and have a great capacity to neutralize "new" facts by incorporating them into an already established view of historical reality. The latter is, for example, one of the main conclusions of historian David Engel (2009: 926) in his reflections on a Polish–Jewish historical reconciliation initiative.

Seemingly, the connection between objective historical truth and understanding, on the one hand, and reconciliation, on the other, is ambiguous at the very least. As Bert van Roermund (2001: 177) avers: "Acknowledging the oppressive facts of the past seems a precondition of reconciliation," yet at the same time "reconciliation seems incompatible with a persistent pursuit of what things have happened, how they have happened, who was to blame for it and who had an excuse. If reconciliation would be the concluding ceremony of a Historikerstreit, it would never occur."

(Inter)subjective Reframing: Re-emplotment, identity transformation, and metahistorical understanding

Contra the positivist stress on objective historical truth, many believe that effective reconciliation initiatives require a certain (inter)subjective reframing or reworking of history and the identities in the present which are based on it. As Aletta Norval (1999: 514) puts it: "[the]assumption that knowledge of the past will lead to a change in attitude, is at best misleading, and at worst, disastrous. … Change is brought about, not by appealing to 'reality', as if it existed unmediated, but by changing the very framing of that reality." In order to try to provoke the change that is needed for reconciliation, many theorists and practitioners focus not on truth-telling but rather on narratives or "story-telling," and their alleged potency for (re)constructing identity and as an "instrument for cultural negotiation" (Bruner 1991: 17). At the core of narrative-based reconciliation theories and practices is the idea that narratives can be "re-emplotted," thereby leading to what is at times referred to as "hermeneutic relocation", "revelation" or "narrative revision."

South African "narrative theologist" Charles Villa-Vicencio (1997) believes that "stories, memories, symbols and culture are at the root of the alienation that exists between most whites and most black" and argues for the creation of new stories and the democratic rewriting of history. This has the potential of "revelation," in the sense of putting things in a radically new light, "gaining an understanding from the perspective of another's lived experience. It is a process that involves more than empathy. It involves hermeneutical relocation whereby we see, hear and understand in a different way" (ibid.: 34). Notice how Villa-Vicencio's approach to reconciliation has strong religious or spiritual overtones. He acknowledges that the South African Truth and Reconciliation Commission "clearly defined political objectives and legal parameters." However, he argues that the Commission was "*ultimately* … a deeply spiritual, theological, and moral endeavor" (38, emphasis ours) and that the very process of forging, maintaining, and recreating community identities is a spiritual one. "Spirituality is the process through which a community creates itself and keeps itself in existence" (33), and at times new "stories override the importance of established sacred symbols; at times they give established religious stories new vitality and contextual meaning" (34).

(Inter)subjective Reframing is not always embedded in religious or spiritual language, however. Susan Dwyer (1999), for example, describes reconciliation in non-theological terms as an "epistemological task that involves strategies of 'narrative revision'" (ibid.: 99) and "narrative incorporation" (98) whereby the involved parties try to bring "apparently incompatible descriptions of events into narrative equilibrium." Yet, Dwyer warns, to be "realistic," narrative reconciliation should "not [require] that all parties settle on a single interpretation, only that they are mutually tolerant of a limited set of interpretations" (100).

Nadim Khoury (2018) has a similar narrative-based theory. Particularly inspired by Hayden White (1973), Khoury argues that post-war historical reconciliation requires very specific types of re-emplotment: it requires warring parties to give up on the "mutually exclusive romantic plots" through which they often represent their conflict histories and move toward "tragic," "comic," or "satiric" plots (for a further explanation, see Khoury 2018: 6–15). Like Dwyer, Khoury agrees that historical reconciliation does not require former enemies to opt for one shared emplotment of their histories; instead, he believes their historical narratives should not mutually exclude each other and be brought into what he calls "counterpoint"—a term Khoury borrows from classical music composition, preferring this to Dwyer's "equilibrium" because it is less static.

Clearly, the stress on the need for an (inter)-subjective reframing of the past by means of its "re-emplotment" for reconciliation sits uncomfortably with the Cognitive Recovery of Truth approach: truth-telling via objectivist historicist understanding. The (Inter)subjective Reframing approach does not favor the denial or ignoring of historical facts but asks for a historical understanding that goes beyond the mere (cognitive) knowledge of historical facts and produces an insight into how the interpretation of these facts can change by being emplotted differently. This approach often asks for a historical understanding that is "meta-historical" in the sense that Hayden White (1973) construes it—that is, requiring an understanding of how histories are being emplotted, which types of rhetoric and "tropes" are being used, and what sociopolitical implications these can have. Occasionally, theorists also plead for forms of historical understanding that are metahistorical in another sense—forms that encourage people to find meaning in history beyond or above the level of mere historical facts or events and thus break with the conventional objectivist historical understanding that reduces the significance of events to their position in a chronologically organized sequence tied together by causes and effects. Khoury (2017) is quite clear on this point when he pleads for a critical re-engagement with "grand narratives"—including their typical teleological and universalist features. He argues that by rejecting and deconstructing all grand narratives, modern historical understanding also destroyed the reconciliatory potential that often came with older grand narratives, whether of a theological (e.g., Christian) or secular (e.g., Marxian or Hegelian) nature.

Although not involving an explicit call for a return to a grand-narrative-style philosophy of history, a similar plea to find meaning (or a deeper "truth") in history that is beyond, against, or despite the mere historical facts can be found in Bert van Roermund's (2001) theory of reconciliation. Remarkably, he argues that supporters of reconciliation should not focus so much on factual historical understanding but on a "counterfactual" historical understanding. Reconciliation should be based on the insight that "there is a counterfactual reciprocity in wrongdoing"; "[the] recognition involved is that of the counterfactual possibility that the victim could have been the perpetrator but for the actual course of history" (183).

The main criticisms of the (Inter)subjective Reframing approach are that it has an all too optimistic and voluntarist conceptualization of how changes in (national) identities can be rendered and often bases its views of historical conflict on an idealist and anti-materialist ontology (for a more elaborate discussion, see Bevernage 2018).

Ethical Recognition: Identity restoration and acknowledging the limits of historicist understanding

A third strand of theories revolve around the notion of recognition rather than truth or narrative re-emplotment. Although they should be analytically distinguished, reconciliation and recognition, as Eric Doxtader (2007: 120–1) remarks, are two "relation-making goods" which are often appealed to "in the same breath." "Both an action and judgment," Doxtader explains, drawing inspiration from Paul Ricoeur, "recognition ... is an event that may grant a kind of status, attribute worth to historical experience or interest, commend a form of life, engender dignity, confess transgression, or honor an individual's (intrinsic) value" (122). Recognition-based approaches to historical reconciliation are often, although not exclusively, proposed to address tensions between communities (e.g., indigenous vs. non-indigenous) and issues of diversity, multi-culturalism, or decolonization in "consolidated democracies" as opposed to major political transitions.

A good illustration of the drive toward the recognition of others' historical experiences can be found in some of the state-sponsored reconciliation initiatives toward the Aboriginal population in Australia. Most notable was the 1997 "Bringing Them Home Report" about the "stolen generations," which, as Bain Attwood (2005) argues, led to increased attention on different historical experiences in the forms of testimonies, oral histories, and affective styles of writing. Recognition-centered approaches primarily conceive of dealing with (painful) pasts as a means of mending identity wounds that are created by "historical oppression" or securing the authentic identities that are believed to be threatened by it (Taylor 1994; Bashir 2012). The Ethical Recognition approach to reconciliation resembles the (Inter)subjective Reframing approach in that it also often stresses the importance of narratives and identity. Yet, recognition does not demand a radical transformation of identities—or at least it does not see this transformation as a condition of reconciliation. The politics of recognition and corresponding approaches to reconciliation generally embrace identity difference or diversity rather than trying to transform these identities or reorganize them into a more universalist identity such as a civic or cosmopolitan one.

The challenge of reconciliation projects which involve indigenous peoples or other people with "subaltern pasts" is that such peoples often recount their stories in ways that do not easily fit with the epistemology underpinning traditional historical understanding. Because recognition-based reconciliation turns on the values of esteem, dignity, and equality, it is deemed critical not to reproduce historical oppression on an epistemic level by forcing others to rewrite their histories (or past relations) according to the modern Western "master-discourse" of the discipline of history (Chakrabarty 2001: 8). Recognition-based reconciliation, therefore, demands a historical understanding that has an insight into the (ethical) limits and potential negative political effects of historicization.

Moreover, it demands an understanding that historicism is only one possible way of engaging with past relations that stands alongside many other equally valuable ways of relating to the past; this is what Ashis Nandy (1995) coined as "history's forgotten doubles." Forgetting these "doubles" and advocating modern historicism as the only valid approach to the past, according to Nandy, has not only eclipsed the possibilities for reconciliation in alternative approaches to the past, but has at times catalyzed conflict (e.g., between Muslims and Hindu nationalists in India).

Despite addressing some of the shortcomings of the other two approaches, the Ethical Recognition approach has also received criticism. The stress on recognition-centered historical narratives possibly leads to dangerous forms of identity politics which fossilize identities and identity differences rather than transform or transcend them (see Fraser and Honneth 2003). Professional historians have also often been quite critical of the way these narratives often tend to blur history with memory or focus too heavily on subjective testimonies and affect or "the evidence of experience" (Scott 1991). The extent of the challenges that recognition-centered reconciliation creates for a conventional "objectivist" historical understanding differs by case and very much depends on the degree of difference between the "historical cultures" of the parties to be reconciled. These challenges can be profound, however, and exceed a mere openness to the role of oral histories or testimonies in the writing of historiography (Chakrabarty 2001, 2007; Attwood 2005).

Conclusion

Which historical understanding as the basis for reconciliation is most effective remains an open and empirically elusive question. All three approaches engage documented events. While the Cognitive Recovery perspective privileges the agreed-upon facts of history as the crux of reconciliation, the (Inter)subjective Reframing and Ethical Recognition models focus on transformative story-telling and dignity-restoring, authentic narratives, respectively. The theoretical as well as the practical-political preoccupation with sociopolitical reconciliation has yielded interesting debates about how to manage the past after conflict and the value of different types of historical understanding—seriously challenging conventional academic historiography in the process.

References

Aiken, N. (2014), "Rethinking Reconciliation in Divided Societies: A Social Learning Theory of Transitional Theory," in S. Buckley-Zistel, T. K. Beck, C. Braun, and F. Mieth (eds.), *Transitional Justice Theories*, 40–65, New York: Routledge.

Attwood, B. (2005), "Unsettling Pasts: Reconciliation and History in Settler Australia," *Postcolonial Studies* 8(3): 243–59.

Barkan, E. (2005), "History on the Line. Engaging History: Managing Conflict and Reconciliation," *History Workshop Journal* 59(1): 229–36.

Bashir, B. (2012), "Reconciling Historical Injustices: Deliberative Democracy and the Politics of Reconciliation," *Res Publica* 18(2): 127–43.

Bevernage, B. (2011), *History, Memory, and State-Sponsored Violence: Time and Justice*. New York: Routledge.

Bevernage, B. (2018), "Narrating Pasts for Peace? A Critical Analysis of Some Recent Initiatives of Historical Reconciliation through 'Historical Dialogue' and 'Shared History'," in S. Helgesson and J. Svennungsson (eds.), *The Ethos of History*, 70–93, New York: Berghahn.

Biletzki, A. (2013), "Peace-less Reconciliation," in A. MacLachlan and A. Speight (eds.), *Justice, Responsibility and Reconciliation in the Wake of Conflict*, 31–46, 39, Dordrecht: Springer.

Bloomfield, D. (2006), *On Good Terms: Clarifying Reconciliation, Report No. 14.* Berlin: Berghof Research Center for Constructive Conflict Management.

Bruner, J. (1991), "The Narrative Construction of Reality," *Critical Inquiry* 18(1): 1–21.

Chakrabarty, D. (2001), "Reconciliation and Its Historiography: Some Preliminary Thoughts," *The UTS Review* 7(1): 6–16.

Chakrabarty, D. (2007), "History and the Politics of Recognition," in K. Jenkins, S. Morgan, and A. Munslow (eds.), *Manifestos for History*, 77–87, London: Routledge.

Cole, E. (2007), "Reconciliation and History Education," in E. Cole (ed.), *Teaching the Violent Past*, 1–30, Lanham: Rowman and Littlefield.

De Graaff, B. (2006), *Op de klippen of door de vaargeul: De omgang van de historicus met (genocidaal) slachtofferschap*. Amsterdam: published oration.

Doxtader, E. (2007), "The Faith and Struggle of Beginning (with) Words: On the Turn Between Reconciliation and Recognition," *Philosophy & Rhetoric* 40(1): 119–46.

Dwyer, S. (1999), "Reconciliation for Realists," *Ethics & International Affairs* 13(1): 81–98.

Engel, D. (2009), "On Reconciling the Histories of Two Chosen Peoples," *The American Historical Review* 114(4): 914–29.

Fraser, N., and A. Honneth (2003), *Redistribution Or Recognition?: A Political-Philosophical Exchange*. London: Verso.

Ingrao, C. (2009), "Introduction," in C. Ingrao and T. A. Emmert (eds.), *Confronting the Yugoslav Controversies: A Scholars' Initiative*, 1–11, Washington: United States Institute of Peace Press.

Khoury, N. (2017), "Political Reconciliation: With or Without Grand Narratives?" *Constellations* 24(2): 245–56.

Khoury, N. (2018), "Plotting Stories after War: Toward a Methodology for Negotiating Identity," *European Journal of International Relations* 24(2): 367–90.

Meierhenrich, J. (2008), "Varieties of Reconciliation," *Law & Social Inquiry* 33(1): 195–231.

Mendeloff, D. (2004), "Truth-Seeking, Truth-Telling, and Postconflict Peacebuilding: Curb the Enthusiasm?" *International Studies Review* 6(3): 355–80.

Nandy, A. (1995), "History's Forgotten Doubles," *History and Theory* 34(2): 44–66.

Norval, A. (1999), "Truth and Reconciliation: The Birth of the Present and the Reworking of History," *Journal of Southern African Studies* 25(3): 499–519.

Rousso, H. (1998), *La hantisse du passé: entretien avec Philippe Petit*. Paris: Les éditions Textuel.

Scott, J. W. (1991), "The Evidence of Experience," *Critical Inquiry* 17(4): 773–97.

Spinner-Halev, J. (2012), *Enduring Injustice*. Cambridge: Cambridge University Press.

Taylor, C. (1994), "The Politics of Recognition," in A. Gutmann (ed.), *Multiculturalism: Examining the Politics of Recognition*, 25–73, Princeton, NJ: Princeton University Press.

Teitel, R. (2000), *Transitional Justice*. Oxford: Oxford University Press.

Van Roermund, B. (2001), "Rubbing Off and Rubbing On: The Grammar of Reconciliation," in E. Christodoulidis and S. Veitch (eds.), *Lethe's Law: Justice, Law and Ethics in Reconciliation*, 175–90, Oxford: Hart Pub.

Villa-Vicencio, C. (1997), "Telling One Another Stories: Toward a Theology of Reconciliation," in H. Wells and G. Baum (eds.), *The Reconciliation of Peoples: Challenge to the Churches*, 105–21, Maryknoll: Orbis Books.

White, H. (1973), *Metahistory: The Historical Imagination in Nineteenth-Century Europe*. Baltimore, MD: Johns Hopkins University Press.

CHAPTER TWENTY

The cross-cultural appeal of the "mirror" metaphor—History as practical past

Q. Edward Wang

The mirror of the Yin is not too remote to see,
it was shown in the fate of the previous Xia.

Introduction

This saying was found in the *Shijing* (Classic of Poetry), the oldest text surviving from ancient China. Here the legendary King Wen (1112–1050 BCE), a vassal under the Yin dynasty (otherwise known as the Shang dynasty, 1600–1046 BCE), predicted that the dynasty would quickly follow the same wicked fate as the previous Xia dynasty. Indeed, no sooner had he offered the prophecy than the Yin was replaced by the Zhou dynasty (1046–256 BCE), founded by his son King Wu (r. 1045/46–1043 BCE).

King Wen's prediction, which was both correct and self-serving, was the first instance in China in which the knowledge of history was compared to a mirror, reflecting not only the past but also foretelling the future. In the following centuries, the mirror metaphor became widely used among the Chinese in expounding the use of history: lessons from the past should serve a practical purpose. The reason for this, if we can rely on Hayden White's analysis, is rather simple: not only are pasts plural, but also the past historians could reconstruct, or the "historical past," "has to be distinguished from the past as a constantly changing whole or a totality of which it (the historical past) is only a part" (White 2014: xiii). Since it is only a partial past, the past historians hoped to recover, to simplify White's thesis, is often and ought to be a "practical past," or a useful mirror.

A cross-cultural survey of history as a mirror

The notion that history-writing is useful as a mirror was by no means popular only in ancient China. Rather, the "mirror for/of princes," or *Fürstenspiegel*, has been an influential genre of writing in many cultures around the world, including those of the West and the Middle East. Concerning the origin of the "mirror-for-prince" genre in ancient times, some have pointed our attention to the prophecy of Samuel in ancient Israel. Like King Wen of China, Samuel (*c.* 1070–1012 BCE) expressed his belief that the monarchic excess of power observed from the kings' behaviors in Babylon and Assyria were useful lessons for educating future rulers (Kaplan 2012). In ancient Greece, Socrates, too, made a similar admonition to his sovereigns, which was elaborated by his disciple Xenophon (431–354 BCE) in *Cyropaedia*, establishing Cyrus the Great (*c.* 600–530 BCE), founder of Achaemenid Persia, as an ideal ruler with exemplary deeds for future princes (Gray 2020).

A few centuries later, in Han China (206 BCE–220 CE), the term *Yinjian* (mirror of the Yin) had become a stock phrase repeatedly employed by historians and other savants to refer to an object lesson drawing on past experience: a licentious ruler would face the dire consequence of losing his power if his behavior was not corrected in time. And the word *jian* (mirror) in the phrase was used even more frequently. While referring foremost to a physical mirror made of bronze in those times, it also carries the metaphorical meaning of "history" and appeared in nearly all historical texts from the Han period onward—used as a verb by Han historians like Sima Qian and Ban Gu in their works: "to reflect (history)," "in view of (history)," and "considering (history)."

The mirror metaphor also received an endorsement from the imperial court. The following remark was attributed to the great Taizong

Emperor of the Tang dynasty (618–907) upon the death of his most-trusted counsel, Wei Zheng (580–643):

> Bronze as mirror to straighten one's clothes and caps; the past as mirror to illuminate dynastic rise and fall; and individuals as mirror to rectify our judgment—we have always known these three mirrors. … Now that Wei Zheng is gone, one of these mirrors has disappeared. (Quoted in Ng and Wang 2005: 108)

During the Tang dynasty, Chinese historians working at the imperial court indeed churned out a half-dozen dynastic histories that purported to "illuminate dynastic rise and fall." During the Song dynasty that followed (960–1279), the minister-cum-historian Sima Guang (1019–86) compiled the well-known *Zizhi tongjian* (Comprehensive Mirror of Aid for Government) in approximately three hundred fascicles, representing the culmination of the history-as-mirror tradition in middle imperial China. A lesser-known work, which was equally ambitious in scope and encyclopedic in coverage, was called *Tongzhi* (General History) in two hundred fascicles, compiled singlehandedly by Zheng Qiao (1104–62), a recluse in South China, on the eve of the Mongol conquest.

In the medieval West, concomitantly, the height of the mirror-for-prince genre also occurred in the eleventh and twelfth centuries. Vincent of Beauvais's (*c.* 1184/94–1264) *Speculum maius* was a prime example. It comprised four parts (one incomplete), of which *Speculum historiale* was most pertinent. Like his Chinese/Asian counterparts—the mirror metaphor was also commonly accepted and used by historians to name their works in medieval Japan (Foot and Robinson 2012: 71–3)—Vincent of Beauvais believed that "history was at one and same time a mirror and a teacher; people cannot only see themselves, but they can learn from the image as well."[1]

An equally important phenomenon was that, by this or that time, the mirror-for-prince had been developed into a diverse, mature, and well-regarded genre in the Middle East, too, with an origin tracing back to pre-Islamic Persia. Some were preserved in the work of Ibn al-Muqaffa (?–757), who, as a Persian serving the Umayyads, introduced prose narrative to Arabic literary culture. In the eleventh century, Nizam al-Mulk (1018–92), another Iranian who acted as the *de facto* ruler of the Seljuq dynasty for two decades, produced *Siyasatnama* (Book of Statecraft), which became an exemplary work of the genre in Persian. There were several other similarly intended works appearing in the time, such as *Nasihat al-Muluk* by Al-Ghazali, *Qabus-Nama* by Keikavus, and *Kutadgu Bilig* by Yusuf Balasaguni; together they gave rise to a boom of mirror-for-prince literature in the Middle Eastern tradition. It might also be named as the genre of "mirror-of-prince," as some of the works, like *Siyasatnama* and *Qabus-Nama*, were written by the princes, or rulers, themselves.[2]

From the subsequent centuries through the early modern period, the genre, or the notion that history serves as a mirror in which one could see both admirable and abhorrent human behavior, remained attractive and continued to evolve and expand. In China, Sima Guang's mammoth *Comprehensive Mirror* inspired many to produce its sequel. For instance, Zhu Xi (1130–1200), a key figure in propagating Neo-Confucianism, revised it into the *Tongjian gangmu* (Outline and Details of the Comprehensive Mirror), which was most consequential. Together with other Neo-Confucian texts, Zhu's reworking of Sima Guang became a must-read in Confucian education across East and Southeast Asia. In the Middle East when the Ottoman Empire ruled in dominance, the mirror-for-prince writing flourished further and acquired a larger readership. Ibn Khaldun (1332–1406), the fourteenth-century Tunisian, authored *Muqaddimah*, which was indebted to the mirror-for-prince tradition, as Khaldun shared the same interest in drawing valuable lessons from history.

From the High and Later Middle Ages well into the Renaissance period, Europe saw an impressive development in mirror-for-prince writing. Thomas Aquinas (1225–76), a contemporary of Vincent of Beauvais and a dominant intellectual figure of the period, authored *De Regno*. And *De Regimine Principum*, another key text in the genre, written by William Perault (*c.* 1190–1271), was also formerly attributed to Thomas Aquinas, who might have contributed a part to the book. In Renaissance Italy, Niccolo Machiavelli's (1469–1527) *The Prince* was a well-known example, suggesting that the influence of Vincent of Beauvais was far-reaching. Yet to a notable degree, *The Prince* also deviated from the mirror-for-prince tradition, in that it significantly downplayed the importance of religiosity in the tradition. As such, the text was a renovation that reflected the development of Renaissance culture. Erasmus's (1466–1536) *Institutio principis Christiani*, appearing approximately at the same time, was another interesting example, representing the attempt to combine secular and religious values and concerns in education, not merely for the prince.

To a degree, the same could be said about Baldassare Castiglione's (1478–1529) *The Book of the Courtier*. During the period, the best-studied work that demonstrated Vincent of Beauvais's durable influence was the voluminous *Mirror for Magistrates* in England from the mid-sixteenth century. Compiled and edited by generations of scholars over the course of a century, this work became a landmark in the development of English literary culture, one that witnessed the transformation of the genre from medieval to early modern times.[3] To varying degrees, this transformation also occurred in the similarly purported works appearing across continental Europe, such as in Spain, the Netherlands, and Wallachia (Romania); the latter also extended and rejuvenated the Byzantine tradition of the genre (Tilmans 1991; Kerlin 2009; Goina 2014).

The mirror metaphor as a mode of historical understanding

The above contour, while brief, should probably be sufficient for us to have the impression that the mirror metaphor, or imagery, had had not only a long tradition, but also a cross-cultural appeal. Thus, it was a rare example for us to choose as a basis for a comparative study of the worldwide appreciation of the wisdom of history. Granted, the writings included in the genre were not historical per se, but boasted a wide variety, as many of the works were considered poetic, political, religious, and philosophical rather than historiographical. But this wide range in fact enables us to appreciate the diverse forms in which historical consciousness was expressed across many civilizations. Indeed, just as White argued forcefully in his *The Practical Past*, the form of historical writing advanced by professional historians from nineteenth-century Europe was but one style of representing the past. While purging "ethical content" from historical writing, it served "nation-states as custodian of its genealogy" (White 2014: 9).

   If the genre always serves a "practical past," then have its practitioners ignored the need to ensure truthfulness in their writings? The answer, perhaps surprisingly to some, is a resounding yes. Despite the versatility in ways of expression, the writings in the genre shared a common goal, which was to establish an accurate and truthful mirror, not a distorted and broken one, for their intended readers. China's Sima Guang described his intention for the *Comprehensive Mirror*, as well as the method he used, as follows:

> I have devoted all my energy, day and night, to the work with full dedication. It used not only previous official histories, but also many unofficial ones, letters and documents, piling up like the sea. We explore the truth of history in the most secret places, and correct every word for its mistakes. ... Reviewing the rise and fall of preceding dynasties, we can see the gains and losses of political measures of the present; praising the good, eliminating the evil, upholding justice and correcting the mistakes, we can trace the prosperity of the ancient times and bring the country into a state of peace that never existed before. (Sima 1982: 152–3, translation is mine)

By quoting Cicero, Vincent of Beauvais of Europe also shared his firm belief that "History is the witness to time, the light of truth, the road of memory, the teacher of life, the messenger from antiquity" (Weber 1965: 107). If history were to play such a role "to instruct and admonish," then, in the words Eckenrode (1984: 347), his modern interpreter, Vincent maintained that "it is imperative it [history] be calmly impartial in the pursuit of truth."

Needless to say, the motivation for pursuing a truthful presentation of the past in the mirror-for-prince writing apparently differed from that of modern historians. Religion was an instrumental factor. To most Christian writers, human history was an embodiment of God's providence. It required them to offer the most accurate description, lest their writing failed to fully represent the divine will and work. Vincent of Beauvais believed that as God created humans, human actions and their interactions with nature invariably constituted and reflected the providence (Weber 1965: 58–62). This faith in God was also shown in the Middle Eastern practice of the genre: rulers were second only to the Prophet, for they carried the sacred responsibility for ruling the society for God. In a ninth-century Arabic piece of the literature, for instance, we found the following admonition:

> Hold fast to all the good fortune which God has bestowed on you, at the same time remembering the ultimate destination towards which you are inevitably traveling, the duties to which you are obligated, and the responsibilities which you now have. ... God has been gracious to you and has accordingly made it incumbent upon you to show tenderness toward those of His creatures over whom He has appointed you shepherd. (Bosworth 1970: 30–1)

In the Eastern Asian tradition, Heaven was an equivalent to God in the West, whose mandate was the source of power for a ruler. It required him to carefully uphold it lest it was withdrawn from him, as had happened to the irresponsible rulers of Xia and Yin dynasties in antiquity and many others in subsequent eras. According to the followers of Confucianism in China and around Asia, the *tiandao* (Way of Heaven) ruled the universe, so the primary responsibility of a ruler was to observe and abide by the Way, or the Dao. This notion was thus comparable to the Christian belief in God's providence in human history. It motivated Asian historians to make a continuous effort over the millennia to establish historical writing as a reliable mirror that could honestly reveal and reflect Heaven's mandate so that rulers could straighten their behaviors accordingly. In a sense, according to Robert Eno (1990) who wrote about the notion of Heaven in Confucianism, the Confucian practice of the Dao could mean "a coherent teaching," comprising "practices and statements," in ancient China.

While religious faith was a seemingly important motivating factor in the various traditions of the writing, we also need to note that the *raison d'être* for the mirror-for-prince writing was secular. The mirror-for-prince genre, in fact, advanced the notion that past human behavior would help guide that of the present and also improve it in the future. It was a philosophy of human history, one that saw historical movement as more cyclical than linear. Meanwhile, the process of the cyclical movement was for achieving a progressive and better end. The above quote of Sima Guang was a clear illustration: Sima strongly believed that if the emperor to whom he presented his work would learn from the past, then he could improve his rulership to the best extent the world had ever seen. As religious as Vincent of Beauvais was, he also clearly saw the importance of human behavior, which was one of the four parts that constituted his idea of history: "God, creation, man and providence." He spent his energy on making the *Speculum maius* as comprehensive as it could be because he wanted to preserve the knowledge of the past, since "it is worthy of admiration and of imitation" (Weber 1965: 53, 37–8).

In medieval Europe, the underlying idea sustaining the work of mirror-for-princes, as Bee Yun (2007: 16) observes in his study of a visual image of the genre in a mural, was "the concept of man as microcosm. Man is understood as part of the homogeneous order encompassing all beings in the universe; in himself, he embodies all its principles." In the Middle East as well as in the Byzantine tradition of the writing, there was ample discussion on comparing the role of the king to that of religion or God's providence, as the two served a common function and thus were on a comparable rank. Nizami Aruzi (fl. 1110–61), a follower of Nizam al-Mulk, contended that "kings and prophets were equally important players in a balanced universe." The writing of Neagoe Basarab (1459–1521) in Wallachia was an example of the Byzantine practice of the genre: Expanding on the idea of Eusebius of Caesarea (260/265–339/340), it promoted the emperor as a god on Earth who played a central role in keeping together the world order (Dahlén 2009: 21; Goina 2014: 31–2).

Notably, this secular interest in turning history into a repertoire of practical and useful wisdom also characterized its writing as an intercultural endeavor and exchange. As mentioned above, the prophecy of Samuel in ancient Israel had drawn on the historical experiences of Babylon and Assyria, representing a genre of diverse discourses. The mirror metaphor for history advanced by Chinese historians also exerted a broad and lasting influence across the Sinitic world, exemplified by the number of works bearing the "mirror" in their titles in medieval Japan. In the Middle East, the early development of this style of writing was indebted to Hellenistic cultural influence from Europe. Meanwhile, as research has shown, influences also originated from South Asia—some exemplars established in the writing were modeled on historical figures in ancient India. In fact, in Persian, Greek, and Sanskrit writings, there was a common theme of comparing a society to a human body in order to illustrate the importance of justice to God's grace. An ideal society was perceived as a balanced human body whose mutually dependent limbs and organs were likened to the equation of justice demonstrated in God's earthly balance. More interestingly, if in its formative age the Middle Eastern form of the genre was inspired by similar literature in Europe, then through Islamic rule of Spain, it exerted its influence in developing the European mirror-for-prince writing in the High and Later Middle Ages (Tor 2011; Marlow 2013: 16; Yun 2015).

Conclusion

Due to the various sources of influence, the mirror-for-prince genre, invariably, was heterogeneous in style; some have thus questioned if the different forms of the writing could be placed under one rubric (Jonsson 2006). From the nineteenth century, when historical writing became professionalized around the world, this traditional genre received more criticism than commendation. Needless to say, there were concerning issues uncovered in all forms of the mirror-for-prince writing. For one, despite its diversity, its purported readers were rulers rather than the ruled or the society as a whole, which reflected an outdated notion of history that mainly considered rulers as the makers of history. As its main purpose was hortatory, the fruits that sprang from the tradition, despite such titles as the *Comprehensive Mirror* and/or the *Speculum maius*, might also have been much less general and comprehensive than their producers had wished. Be that as it may, reviewing this long and rich tradition, in which the history's relationship with the past was metaphorized as a useful mirror (Dakhlia 2002), ought to be a worthwhile exercise in our times.

As the tradition remains alive in certain cultures, I believe our examination of it would not only help open our minds to the variety of historical mindedness in the world, past and present, but also lead us to realize that while helping turn historical study into an academic profession, the historiographical model established in late-nineteenth-century Europe, which remains prevalent in historical communities worldwide, contained obvious limits. If historians only study the past for its own sake, or, to borrow White's words, if studying the past is "constructed as an end in itself," then it "possesses little or no value for understanding and explaining the present, and provides no guidelines for acting in the present or foreseeing the future" (2014: 9). It is time for today's historians to aspire and achieve more in their pursuit.

Notes

1   Quoted in Eckenrode (1984: 347). A comprehensive study of Vincent of Beauvais hitherto remains Weber (1965).
2   See Bosworth (1970); Marlow (2013); and Dahlén (2009). A more general survey of the literature is Richter (1932).
3   Budra (2000: 21) observes that "in broad terms, we may argue that early sixteenth-century history emphasized first causes of events, the intervention of God into history. Late sixteenth-century history, under the influence of Guicciardini, Machiavelli, and Bodin, became concerned with second causes, with the intervention into men into history."

References

Bosworth, C. E. (1970), "An Early Arabic Mirror for Prince: Tāhir Dhū I-Yamīnain's Epistle to His Son 'Abdallah (206/821)," *Journal of Near Eastern Studies* 29(1): 25–41.
Budra, P. (2000), *A Mirror for Magistrates and the* De Casibus *Tradition*. Toronto: University of Toronto Press.

Dahlén, A. P. (2009), "Kingship and Religion in a Medieval *Fürstenspiegel*: The Case of the *Chāhar Maqāla* of Nizāmī 'Arūzī," *Orientalia Suecana* LVIII: 9–24.

Dakhlia, J. (2002), "Les Miroirs de princes Islamiques: une modernité sourde?" *Annales. Histoire, Sciences Sociales* 57(5): 1191–1206.

Eckenrode, T. R. (1984) "Vincent of Beauvais: A Study in the Construction of a Didactic View of History," *The Historian* 46: 339–60.

Eno, R. (1990), *The Confucian Creation of Heaven: Philosophy and the Defense of Ritual Mastery*. Albany, NY: State University of New York Press.

Foot, S., and Robinson, C. F. (eds.) (2012), *The Oxford History of Historical Writing. Vol. 2*. Oxford: Oxford University Press.

Goina, M. (2014), "Medieval Political Philosophy in a Sixteenth-century Wallachian Mirror of Princes: The Teachings of Neagoe Basarab to His Son Theodosie," *The Slavonic and the Eastern European Review* 92(1): 25–43.

Gray, V. J. (2020), *Xenophon's Mirror of Princes: Reading the Reflections*. Oxford: Oxford University Press.

Jonsson, E. M (2006), "Les 'Miroirs aux Princes': Sont-Ils un Genre littéraire?" *Médiévales* 51: 153–65.

Kaplan, J. (2012), "1 Samuel 8: 11-18as 'A Mirror for Princes'," *Journal of Biblical Literature* 131(4): 625–42.

Kerlin, G. M. (2009), "A True Mirror of Princes: Defining the Good Governor in Miguel De Luna's 'Verdadera Historia del Rey Don Rodrigo'," *Hispanófila* 156: 13–28.

Marlow, L. (2013), "Among Kings and Sages: Greek and Indian Wisdom in an Arabic Mirror for Princes," *Arabica* 60(1–2): 1–57.

Ng, O., and Wang, Q. E. (2005), *Mirroring the Past: The Writing and Use of History in Imperial China*. Honolulu: University of Hawaii Press.

Richter, G. (1932), *Studien zur Geschichte der Älteren Arabischen Fürstenspiegel*. Leipzig: J. C. Hinriches'sche Buchhandlung.

Rosenthal, F. (1968), *A History of Muslim Historiography*. Leiden: Brill.

Sima, G. (1982), "Jin *Zizhi tongjian* biao" (Presentation of *A Comprehensive Mirror of Aid in Government*), in Lei Gan (ed.), *Zhongguo lishi yaoji xulunwen xuanzhu* (Annotated Selections of Prefaces to Key Historical Texts in China), 152–5, Changsha: Yuelu shushe.

Tilmans, K. (1991), "The Origin of the Empire and the Tasks of the Prince: Neglected Renaissance Mirrors-of-Princes in the Netherlands," *Humanistica Luvaniensia* 40: 43–72.

Tor, D. G. (2011), "The Islamisation of Iranian Kingly Ideals in the Persianate *Fürstenspiegel*," *Iran* 49: 115–22.

Yun, B. (2007), "A Visual Mirror of Princes: The Wheel on the Mural of Longthorpe Tower," *Journal of Warburg and Courtauld Institutes* 70: 1–32.

Yun, B. (2015), "The Representation of An Indian Prince in the Great Chamber of Longthorpe Tower and the Intercultural Transfer of Political Ideas in the Middle Ages," *Source: Notes in the History of Art* 34(3): 1–6.

Weber, R. K. (1965), *Vincent of Beauvais: A Study in Medieval Historiography*. Ph.D. thesis, University of Michigan.

White, H. (2014), *The Practical Past*. Evanston, IL: Northwestern University Press.

Histories

CHAPTER TWENTY-ONE

Mouse-eaten records

Erica Fudge

Gnawing away at humanity

In his *A Defence of Poetry* of *c.* 1579 (first published 1595), Sir Philip Sidney ([1579] 1966: 29) argued that knowledge should lead to "virtuous action," its aim being "well-doing and not ... well-knowing only." Of all kinds of writing, he proposed, poetry could achieve this best because it was able to go beyond nature: it could represent worlds in ways that were not limited to what was present in reality, and so could inspire new possibilities. The poet, Sidney (ibid.: 82) wrote, "makes a Cyrus" ("a figure of manly virtue"), not in order to reproduce the Cyrus of ancient reality, but to represent him in a way that "make[s] many Cyruses" in the present (24). In this way, the imaginative depiction of heroes and heroic actions, he believed, could lead readers to virtuous emulation.

Sidney set poetry against history, stating that, unlike the poet, who is "freely ranging only within the zodiac of his own wit," the historian is "tied, not to what should be but to what is" (24, 32). That is, where imaginative work can depict heroism achieving greatness and show villainy defeated, a study of the past has to stick to what actually happened, and so must sometimes show malign forces coming out on top. Sidney doesn't name him, but it is easy to read Niccolo Machiavelli as hovering in the background here. In *The Prince* (1513), Machiavelli offered Lorenzo de Medici, as a guide to future rule, examples from the past to illustrate how earlier leaders had succeeded or failed. Sometimes those successes were far from virtuous. In Chapter XVIII, "*How princes should honour their word*," for example, Machiavelli ([1513] 1961: 99) began by noting that "Everyone realizes how praiseworthy it is for a prince to honour his word," but went on to state: "nonetheless contemporary experience shows that princes who have achieved great things have been those who have given their word lightly, who have known how to trick men with their cunning, and who, in the end, have overcome those abiding by honest principles." He concluded by arguing that history shows that appearing to possess integrity is, in the end, more important than actually possessing it: this is hardly a prompt to "virtuous action," and his human subjects are far from heroic as Sidney would understand that term.

Elizabeth Story Donno (1975: 277) has suggested that Sidney's position on history in *A Defence of Poetry* was a "tactical device" rather than a reflection of his true opinion. But whether or not he actually held the position he took in that text, his discussion opens up a way of thinking about an aspect of current historical understanding which also challenges the conception of humanity as heroic and transcendent. This is reinforced in Sidney's description of the study of the past, where he speaks of the historian as "laden with old mouse-eaten records" ([1579] 1966: 30). He places real, historically situated actions in opposition to imagined feats that transcend time.

Animals are not Sidney's concern, of course: his focus is on the virtuous actions of humans (or more specifically, men). But I want to suggest that his use of the phrase "mouse-eaten," as well as his representation of history in *A Defence*, offers a productive starting point for thinking about what the inclusion of animals in history can do. The idea of the defeat of human heroism, juxtaposed with the image of records being consumed and destroyed by a tiny, apparently insignificant creature, offers a way of thinking about both humanity's limits and history's possibilities. Where I differ from Sidney is in my belief that the image of history as made up of mouse-eaten records might not have negative implications, but might be a route into another kind of "well-doing."

Bringing in the animals

Over the past thirty years, animals have entered history in very different ways to Sidney's conception of the mouse's relation to the writing of the past. Rather than only adjectivally present (and so being simply an attribute of the main subject), animals are becoming a focus in themselves. This development has not been a singular or static one. The history of animals has shifted, and continues to shift.

Keith Thomas's 1983 *Man and the Natural World: Changing Attitudes in England 1500–1800* is often cited as a foundational text in the emergence of this new modern interest, and Thomas's engagement with a vast range of materials in addressing the shifts in human relationships with the non-human world has certainly laid an important foundation. But this work can also be read as coming toward the end of a particular tradition, which includes Dix Harwood's *Love for Animals and How It Developed in Great Britain* ([1928] 2002) and E. S. Turner's *All Heaven in a Rage* ([1964] 1992). These works offered histories of ideas about animals, tracing what people thought about them and how their thought impacted behavior toward them. In such works, while clearly not adjectivally present—that is, not "accessory" to the subject (the *OED*'s definition B2 of "adjective")—animals are still not the true center of attention. The active subjects remain the humans who are having the ideas, changing their attitudes and behavior, while the animals themselves are figured as unchanging—or, if they do change, those changes are understood to be created by humans.

These studies differ from works of natural history in that they do not look specifically at the development or habitat of a natural world "out there"—a place that was visited, observed as if from the outside. Rather, the historical studies by Harwood, Turner, and Thomas all focus on animals as creatures in their direct relationships with humans in various (human) contexts: sport, science, labor, consumption. In these works, the history that includes animals is crucially social, cultural, and political. Indeed, Nigel Rothfels (2002: 6) has called such works "unnatural histories" to draw out the distinction between studies of animals in their "native haunts" and those that look at animals "in such human environments as museums, books, circuses, zoos."

A subsequent crucial development in the history of animals, following Thomas's study, was marked by Harriet Ritvo's 1987 *Animal Estate: The English and Other Creatures in the Victorian Age*, a book that showed the ways in which animals were, importantly, real (the dogs in the dog shows she studied were actual dogs), but were also used to represent something more abstract. Ritvo linked them to questions of empire, nation, and class. My own *Perceiving Animals: Humans and Beasts in Early Modern English Culture* (2000) and Karl Steel's *How to Make a Human: Animals and Violence in the Middle Ages* (2011) are just two examples of work that followed this lead, tracing in earlier periods the ways that people understood themselves and their worlds through animals, which were understood as prompts to think with as well as real beings to be baited, hunted, killed. Such recognition challenges previously unexamined assumptions that allowed the human to be figured in isolation from animals; it lays bare the crucial role that non-human beings had, and continue to have, in that thing we call, in all its varieties, human culture.

As this work began to challenge the "splendid isolation" of the human, it can no longer be assumed that humans are the only actors in history. This crucial shift in historiography has been outlined succinctly in an autobiographical moment in an essay by historian of horses Peter Edwards. He notes that while his 1988 book *The Horse Trade of Tudor and Stuart England* dealt "with horses as a commodity to be bought, sold, and used solely in the interests of humans," his 2007 *Horse and Man in Early Modern England,* influenced by work in animal studies, recognized horses as "intelligent, sentient creatures, who interacted with their environment and could even change it through the exercise of agency" (Edwards 2018: 89). The question of agency, as Philip Howell (2018) has recently shown, is one that raises a variety of important questions for history. Crucially, as a number of recent historians have shown, assigning agency does not require the need to assume intention on the part of the agent which, in turn, allows animals to be recognized as actors in ways that they were not before. In the works by Thomas, Harwood, and Turner, for example, the only agents were the humans. So, where Edwards's early work was written under the influence of Joan Thirsk, whose invaluable agricultural histories present animals as objects of trade, the focus of human labor, sources of food (see, e.g., Thirsk 1984), his more recent studies reflect a shift that is clearly evident in "Settler Stock?", Sandra Swart's 2014 essay which traces negotiations between Dutch settlers and the Khoisan people at the Cape in the mid-seventeenth century, noting how significant animals were in them. What is important in her study is that the humans who are doing the negotiating remain the active subjects, but the animals are more than objects, and by recognizing this, new histories can be written. Indeed, what is clear from "Settler Stock?" is that taking animals as a focus can also chip away at certain established historical assumptions. In tracing evidence that the Dutch "were in need of two vital commodities—not only animals but knowledge about how to keep those animals alive," when they arrived at the Cape, Swart shows how this need "invert[s] the triumphalist narrative of conquest," locating power with the Khoisan people, who possessed the animals and the knowledge to maintain them (Swart 2014: 258–9).

Taking animals seriously

Swart's essay exemplifies the way that taking animals seriously, as presences in the past, can change how we understand that past, and the documents used to do that can be the very documents that have been used before. So, Jonathan Saha (2015) has brought what he calls "the felt encounters" between humans and animals to the center of his study of colonial Burma to produce a new and more complex understanding of some horribly familiar images. In his study he shows how the imperial dehumanization of Burmese people is constructed through their closeness to their animals, which is illustrated in the early-twentieth-century photograph of a Burmese woman breast-feeding an elephant calf. Refusing to take the image at face value, Saha (ibid.: 9) recognizes it as "staged and posed," arguing that it "is *producing* the practice by moving it from the anecdotal to the evidential." The photograph is orientalism made real, you might say. But Saha does something else: alongside this imperial will to dehumanize the Burmese, he traces the "ample evidence of British intimacy with animals in Burma," revealing "unacknowledged tension" in British attitudes. This is a tension that would be missed if the presence of animals was not taken seriously and is one that has the potential to offer new ways of thinking about the imperial endeavor (5, 11).

Saha presents this new reading by thinking about animals, and thinking about the historical importance of touch in human relationships with those animals. As such, he is emphasizing not simply the visual (how things look, with their potential—as Machiavelli knew—to look somewhat different from the truth) but the tactile: he is bringing into his history another way of experiencing the world. Saha is not alone in making this move: like him, Swart also reveals the important relationship that is emerging between sensory studies and the history of animals, and there is good reason for this connection. As the anthropological work brought together in David Howes's *Empire of the Senses* (2005) reminds us, being in the world involves sensory engagement with it, and those sensory engagements are experienced differently and have different meanings in different cultures. Alain Corbin and others have shown that these differences are also historical: Corbin ([1982] 1996) has studied the olfactory world of nineteenth-century France, and Bruce R. Smith (1999), to offer just one more example, has looked at changing soundscapes of early modern England. Such work has opened up new ways for historians of animals to think, not only about the visual presence of animals in the past, but about the olfactory, auditory, and tactile, and to contemplate what those animals' own experiences of their worlds were. Swart has reminded us, for example, that, alongside historians' tendency to "deodorize" the past and so to evacuate the presence of animals in that way, recognizing the species specificity of sensory engagement also leads us to consider that there is not only one way of looking at the world. "Horses and Humans would write very different histories," she writes (2010: 245, 256). We can't know those histories, of course; but contemplating their existence can be productive, and can offer new insights (see Fudge 2017).

In another essay that focuses on touch, Sarah Cockram (2018) has used current studies of the positive physiological and psychological impacts of proximity to animals to consider what the inclusion of pets in Italian Renaissance portraits might allow us to understand about the human and animal worlds they represent. In doing this, her work signals another important move in the history of animals over the last few years. In the past decade, the relationship between historical and current scientific research has changed. Ethologists (those who study animals in their own environment) have advanced new ways of understanding animal behavior and culture that open up our understanding of animals' complex social worlds, and this has impacted work by historians by offering a foundation from which to consider animals not as objects of human interest but as makers of their own worlds. Environmental historian Mahesh Rangarajan (2013: 126), for example, traces the history of the lions of the Gir forest in India through records of their interactions with the forest's human residents, arguing that the changes in the lions' behavior over time offer the possibility that these lions and humans have "a shared past," that they have learned to live alongside each other, and that "each and both have interacted and shaped that history, not equally, not as each lion (or herder or cultivator or prince or official) pleases but in time-specific ways rooted in a particular context." Such a history can only be written when the lions are themselves considered to be subjects—the focus, but also the agents of change.

Developing out of ethology over the past forty years, Animal Welfare Science (AWS) has challenged the previously held view "that domestic animals were completely modified by man [*sic.*] and therefore scarcely biological and not comparable with their wild equivalents" (Broom 2011: 125). Instead, studies have revealed animals such as cows to have complex social worlds, and to thrive in challenging environments (see, e.g., Špinka and Wemelsfelder 2011). As such, where work in ethology has opened up new ways of understanding wild animals' behavior and so has impacted our understanding of how past encounters with those animals might have been experienced by all parties, work in AWS has offered a way of reconceptualizing some of the mundane historical encounters that took place in the past. Milking, for example, can be read not just as a human process whereby a valuable commodity is produced, with price and marketability a focus. Instead, it becomes an engagement between two parties—one human and the other animal. It can be read as being founded upon mutual understanding as well as relations of dominance and submission that can tell us much about the worlds of all the participants (see Fudge 2018). Recognizing animals' agency—their capacity to be changed by, and change, their own worlds—means that animals can enter history as co-workers to be negotiated with, not only as objects to be counted, weighed, killed, consumed.

The power of a hungry mouse

So how does all this link to Sir Philip Sidney's relegation of the value of history because of historians' reliance on "old mouse-eaten records"? Whether they are influenced by developments in anthropology, ethology, AWS, or some other area, what all these works in the history of animals show is that being in the world is historical for all species; and that human lives are lived in constant interaction with non-human animals— whether in direct relationships, such as in animal agriculture, or through attempts at avoidance, such as in the Gir Forest. What follows from this is that the histories that attempt to understand and include this are inevitably undermining the idea that the human is the only world-shaping force, and as well as that, they are opening up the possibility that just as humans have been shaped by their interactions with animals throughout the past, so there might be another way of being human in the future. Like Machiavelli, we might look to the past to understand how, and how not, to act in the future. But we might do this with an eye not to maintaining human power, but to exploring other ways of being, other ways of exercising our agency in a multi-species world.

For Sir Philip Sidney, human endeavors (by which, of course, he meant male endeavors) were the only ones worth contemplating. And those human endeavors were utterly separate from animals, except where the animal was trained, ridden, or killed—made object. But his negative description of history, it turns out, might actually offer a possibility that is much more like current work in the history of animals than is initially apparent. If we think in another way about those hungry mice—if we focus on their agency to change their own world as well as ours—we might read them, in fact, as figures of the "anti-humanist" position that is visible in many histories of animals (Saha 2015: 910).

In their destruction of human endeavors, Sidney's mice are not simply undermining the human capacity to *know* the past—to tell its story clearly, cleanly; they are revealing themselves, in fact, to be agents who shape how that past can be understood. Attending to the presence of a mouse—or a cow, a horse, an elephant, a dog, a lion—can reveal the limits of humanity and open up new ways of thinking about the past. The mouse might not be a prompt to virtuous action (with its etymological root in the Latin "*vir*," man), but recognizing its presence might, perhaps, allow us to see history in a way that Sidney refused to. Here, acknowledging the "mouse-eaten" nature of the human record might offer a path to another way forward that could include recognition of the presence of animals, and through that allow for "well-doing and not … well-knowing only" in a way that Sidney had not foreseen.

References

Broom, D. (2011), "A History of Animal Welfare Science," *Acta Biotheoretica* 59: 121–37.

Cockram, S. (2018), "Sleeve Cat and Lap Dog: Affection, Aesthetics and Proximity to Companion Animals in Renaissance Mantua," in S. Cockram and A. Wells (eds.), *Interspecies Interactions: Animals and Humans between the Middle Ages and Modernity*, 34–65, London: Routledge.

Corbin A. ([1982] 1996), *The Foul and the Fragrant: Odour and the Social Imagination*. Basingstoke: Macmillan.

Donno, E. S. (1975), "Old Mouse-Eaten Records: History in Sidney's *Apology*," *Studies in Philology* 72(3): 275–98.

Edwards, P. (2018), "The Tale of a Horse: the Levinz Colt, 1721–29," in S. Cockram and A. Wells (eds.), *Interspecies Interactions: Animals and Humans between the Middle Ages and Modernity*, 89–106, London: Routledge.

Fudge, E. (2017), "What was it like to be a Cow? History and Animal Studies," in L. Kalof (ed.), *The Oxford Handbook of Animal Studies*, 258–78, Oxford: Oxford University Press.

Fudge, E. (2018), *Quick Cattle and Dying Wishes: People and their Animals in Early Modern England*. Ithaca, NY: Cornell University Press.

Fudge, E. (2000), *Perceiving Animals: Humans and Beasts in Early Modern English Culture*. Basingstoke: Palgrave.

Harwood, D. ([1928] 2002), *Love for Animals and How It Developed in Great Britain*. Edited by R. Preece and D. Fraser. Lewiston, NY: The Edwin Mellen Press.

Howell, P. (2018), "Animals, Agency, and History," in H. Kean and P. Howell (eds.), *The Routledge Companion to Animal-Human History*, 197–221, London: Routledge.

Howes, D. (ed.) (2005), *Empire of the Senses: The Sensual Culture Reader*. Oxford: Berg.

Machiavelli, N. ([1513] 1961), *The Prince*. Trans. George Bull. London: Penguin.

Rangarajan, M. (2013), "Animals with Rich Histories: The Case of the Lions of Gir Forest, Gujarat, India," *History and Theory* 52(4): 109–27.

Ritvo, H. ([1987] 1990), *The Animal Estate: The English and Other Creatures in the Victorian Age*. London: Penguin.

Rothfels, H. (2002), *Savages and Beasts: The Birth of the Modern Zoo*. Baltimore, MD: Johns Hopkins University Press.

Saha, J. (2015), "Among the Beasts of Burma: Animals and the Politics of Colonial Sensibilities, c.1840-1940," *Journal of Social History* 48(4), 910–32.

Sidney, P. ([c.1579] 1966), *A Defence of Poetry*. Edited by J. A. Van Dorsten. Oxford: Oxford University Press.

Smith, B. R. (1999), *The Acoustic Worlds of Early Modern England: Attending to the O-Factor*. Chicago, IL: University of Chicago Press.

Špinka, M., and F. Wemelsfelder (2011), "Environmental Challenge and Animal Agency," J. A. Mench, A. Olsson, and B. O. Hughes (eds.), *Animal Welfare: Second Edition*, 27–44, Wallingford: CAB International.

Steel, K. (2011), *How to Make a Human: Animals and Violence in the Middle Ages*. Columbus: Ohio State University.

Swart, S. (2010), "'The World the Horses Made': A South African Case Study of Writing Animals into Social History," *International Review of Social History* 55(2), 241–63.

Swart, S. (2014), "Settler Stock? Animals and Power in Mid-Seventeenth-Century Contact at the Cape, circa 1652–62," in P. F. Cuneo (ed.), *Animals and Early Modern Identity*, 243–67, Farnham: Ashgate.

Thirsk, J. (1984), *The Rural Economy of England: Collected Essays*. London: Hambledon.

Thomas, K. (([1983] 1984), *Man and the Natural World: Changing Attitudes in England 1500–1800*. London: Penguin.

Turner, E. S. ([1964] 1992), *All Heaven in a Rage*. Fontwell: Centaur Press.

CHAPTER TWENTY-TWO

Lines of sight: The historical certitude of digital reenactment

Vanessa Agnew

Introduction

On the edge of a town not far from Berlin is a small hill crested by a house that dates from the 1930s. The house has the wood siding typical of the period; it is double-storied with a balcony leading from a room that was once the children's nursery; there is a chimney issuing from an open fireplace in the sitting room. If the ceilings are low and the rooms small, there are additions to the house that must have contributed to the well-being of its former inhabitants—a sizable kitchen, a pantry, and a bathroom with a tub. The now-peeling wallpaper and the cheery pink and yellow paint suggest that this was a house where a family could live comfortably—sustained by a kitchen garden, attending school in the nearby town, boating and fishing on the lake (the Schwedtsee), and making excursions by train to the capital.

Yet, obscuring the view from the house is a stand of fir trees and the pitched roofs of some imposing administrative buildings. Partially hidden is the perimeter wall of the largest female camp in the Nazi prison system, Ravensbrück concentration camp, a complex that was erected in 1939 and gradually expanded to include satellite camps for men and children. In this place, some 140,000 people were incarcerated, tens of thousands killed, and their ashes disposed of in the lake.[1] Today, the site encompasses a commemoration and education center. Exhibitions explain the history of the site and its role in the larger apparatus of Nazi ideology, as well as its repurposing by the Soviets after the Second World War. Here visitors can learn about the prisoners' everyday lives and working conditions, the medical experiments inflicted upon them, their suffering and resilience, and their deaths. Visitors are also informed about the camp leadership and camp guards, their daily lives and how they were accommodated, and their motivations and actions. Objects on display provide a glimpse into this tenuous co-existence. Visitors are directed to the buildings that concretize the structural organization of camp life—dormitories, workshops, an infirmary, guard stations, an assembly ground, execution site, gas chamber, crematorium.

Elsewhere, museum signage informs visitors about not only what can be seen at the site, but also what cannot be seen. Specifically, this vista of apparent invisibility can be tested by visitors to the so-called *Führerhaus*. Stepping out onto the camp commandant's balcony, visitors can look eastward and gauge for themselves the extent of the view from the house. Is it possible to look into the prisoners' compound, see from the nursery or the kitchen the gas chamber and crematorium, the burial grounds, and the lake? It is this looking that prompts visitors to reflect on what can and cannot be seen today and, as a result, speculate about what might have been known or not known in the past. But this little experiment raises other questions. Was the unusual turbidity of the Schwedtsee, redolent with the dead, not observed by those living and working locally at the time? Did the murky contrast with nearby lakes go unremarked—other pellucid lakes where the fish are so abundant that to scoop a handful of water is to catch a fish? And what of the other senses? Did the sounds—of the workhouses, rail transports, forced marches, and executions—not carry over the water toward the nearby town where the church steeple rises over the trees? Did the sounds not carry over the balcony railing to trouble the sleep of the camp commandant's very own children?

This prompts us to inquire into these lines of sight and the knowledge that follows from what is, and was, visible. For the museum practitioners and exhibition designers of the Ravensbrück memorial center, the implication is that a direct line of sight from the camp leadership's balconies, sitting rooms, and nurseries to the scenes of suffering in the camp would have exposed the horror of the Nazi apparatus not only to others, but to the perpetrators themselves. Committing the crimes of the Holocaust was, to follow this logic, contingent upon a kind of invisibility—whether partial or pretended—that enabled both Nazi perpetrators and local people to feign ignorance of what was happening beyond the stands of fir trees and behind camp walls. Testing the visible, it is implied, is what will provide visitors today with access to this historical insight. By reinhabiting the life world of the prisoners, but also that of the camp leadership and guards—a comparatively new development in Holocaust education—visitors today will gain some understanding of the genocidal past.

This chapter examines the basis upon which we claim to know things about the past. In addition to the example above—one that implies that we can gain historical knowledge by seeing and "reexperiencing" the limits of what people saw and experienced in earlier times—the chapter examines examples in which reenactment, machine-learning classifiers, and immersive virtual reality (VR) are used to produce historical adjudications. Institutions making practical use of this technology include the Detmold District Court, which draws on digital visualizations and reconstructions developed by the Bavarian Zentrale Fototechnik und 3D-Tatortvermessung (Office of Central Photo Technology and 3D Crime Scene Mapping), and Forensic Architecture, the University of London-based research group headed by Eyal Weizman, which uses architectural and media research techniques, artificial intelligence, and immersive technologies to expose and display human rights abuses and instances of state-sponsored violence. Both are underscored by an assumption that machine-enabled, "perfect" vision facilitates an interrogation of past events and places and produces historical knowledge that is qualitatively new and unassailable.

The immersive character of VR allows participants to seemingly inhabit other worlds and other times. Participants can, for example, interact with holograms in the University of Southern California Shoah Foundation project and conduct an apparently one-to-one conversation with a Holocaust survivor (Leuski et al. 2016: 360–2). Simulated first-person experiences can likewise be gleaned from initiatives like the Gedenkstätte Hohenschönhausen's 360° film, *Was wollten Sie in Berlin?* (What Were You Planning on Doing in Berlin?), in which the viewer assumes the dehumanizing role of a prisoner of the German Democratic Republic's state security services. By exploring these kinds of new medial possibilities, participants can occupy alternative subject positions and acquire affective experiences that seem authentic and real (Agnew and Tomann 2020).

VR's increasingly sophisticated simulations operate on the promise of an inductive approach to historical knowledge production—gathering vast amounts of data, observing its operations, formulating hypotheses, and generating specular scenes within which hypotheses about the past can be tested. By discussing the trial of a former SS guard in which VR was central to the prosecutorial case, however, this chapter takes the contrary position. First, it questions whether machine-learning and high-tech immersive simulations can, in fact, be deemed inductive modes of knowledge production if historical postulates drive data collection, observation, and simulation, rather than being derived from them. Second, and contrary to much historical reenactment, the chapter argues for retaining a degree of epistemic uncertainty with regard to the past and what we claim to know of it. Open inquiry about the past, conducted in good faith, cannot be taken as a given at a time of resurgent right-wing extremism, growing anti-Semitism, the proliferation of misinformation, and a careless dismissal of the factual. And so, third, it makes a case for stimulating the public desire for rigorous historical knowledge through processes that lay bare the actual modes of evidentiary knowledge production. Finally, the chapter concludes by asking how we can go about sparking the moral rectitude that is needed to respond to the historical injustices and ongoing legacies of suffering that are, in fact, visible to us all, anyway.

Digital reenactment's evidentiary claims

Historical reenactment is based on the idea that individual experience in the present has a metonymic relationship to experience in the past. Doing something over, in a way similar to the way it was done before, often in the same place, will elicit emotions, perceptions, and forms of bodily knowledge that have direct corollaries in the past. It is on the basis of this temporal parallel that the reenactor can testify, in a compelling and affective way, to bygone events, experiences, and lifeways. That this modus operandi is underscored by problems of evidence and interpretation has already been noted (Agnew 2007).

New developments in reenactment like high-resolution multidimensional scanning, virtual reality (VR), and machine-learning seem to offer a way out of the impasse created by an overreliance on individual testimony. Digital reenactment is a technologized means of establishing facts about the past and of uncovering and modeling the material conditions of prior experience. Digital reenactment suggests novel possibilities for investigating, representing, and "experiencing" the past through high-calibre simulations of built environments, the reconstruction of events and cultural practices through a range of evidentiary sources, and the possibility of virtually occupying different subject positions. Such technologies, increasingly used in museum settings, mark an important shift in reenactment because the individual reenactor's affective and authentic experience is no longer the primary basis upon which claims about the past can be made. By substituting big data, multiple viewpoints, and hyperreal simulations for the individual reenactor's self-report, immersive digital environments would seem to introduce a new level of objectivity: in place of introspective reports, we have an account of the past that appears to be multiperspectival, reliably evidenced, and testable—a form of historical extrospection that seems to provide third-person access to the past.

Digital reenactment already exerts a powerful presence in performance art and critical museology. Yet it also promises to transform judicial systems because of its capacity to make crime scenes accessible to investigators and courts long after crimes have been perpetrated (Ralf Breker quoted in Cieslak 2016). While mainstream historians are generally skeptical about reenactment, digital reenactment is seen by some as having the capacity to transform not only the field of historical studies but broader understandings of the past itself. Historian David Staley (2014: 131), for instance, goes so far as to predict that its tools will supersede traditional historical narratives for the very reason that traditional narratives "linearize concepts and ideas that are not inherently linear." Rather than thinking of history as a timeline of causal events, Staley suggests that digital environments will introduce forms of spatial complexity and simultaneity that allow for more nuanced forms of historical exegesis. Comparable arguments are made by the principal investigators of the digital humanities project "Transmission through Imitation" at the Swiss Federal Institute of Technology in Lausanne, aiming at the creation of motion data archives and the use of VR for transmitting embodied knowledge systems through imitation (Kenderdine and Hauw 2020).

As historian Paul Pickering (2020: 61–2) has pointed out, reenactment has long been used in courtroom reconstructions. However, *Nazi VR* (2017), directed by David Freid, documents the prosecution of a Nazi criminal in a case that marks a turning point in the use of digital technology to reconstruct and re-stage the past within the judicial context. Given the advanced age of the alleged perpetrators and the dearth of material evidence and surviving witnesses, the 2016 trial of the former SS guard, Reinhold Hanning, was seen as a last possible effort to bring a Holocaust perpetrator to justice. Changes to German law and a precedent-setting case in 2011 allowed prosecutors to charge low-level functionaries with having abetted rather than directly committed crimes during the Second World War. Central to securing Hanning's conviction was the use of digital media and VR reconstruction. The former SS guard at Auschwitz-Birkenau was found guilty of having been an accessory to the murder of 170,000 people and sentenced to five years' imprisonment. However, since the case was still on appeal when he died in 2017, the conviction did not stand under German law (Smale 2017).

Claiming to have witnessed neither the selections nor the gassing of victims at Auschwitz, Hanning's defense rested on the assertion that, although he had worked at the concentration camp, he possessed no firsthand knowledge of the crimes committed there. Freid's film points out that it was impossible to definitively prove what the defendant had done—no archival evidence demonstrated a direct link to the killings. It was determined by the court, however, that acting as a camp guard was tantamount to having been implicated in the machinery of mass murder. What needed to be established by the court was "merely" Hanning's liability as an accomplice. The prosecutors' case thus rested on a determination of what the defendant had actually seen in the camp. Laser scans, aerial photographs, witness testimony, and historical blueprints were used to digitally recreate buildings that had been destroyed at the end of the war. Equipped with this VR model, the court was able to virtually inhabit the simulated genocide site, examine it from multiple angles, and draw on this re-enactive experience to establish the defendant's guilt.

The 3D digital model was commissioned by public prosecutors and produced by the Office for Photo Technology and 3D Crime Scene Mapping. Laser scanning was conducted on site over a period of several days in 2015. Since most of the buildings no longer exist, the concentration camp infrastructure was digitally reconstructed from photographs, maps, and surveyors' records (Bayrisches Landeskriminalamt Zentrale Fototechnik und 3D-Tatortvermessung 2019). According to digital forensic expert Ralf Breker, this recording and reconstructive work resulted in an Auschwitz model of unprecedented exactitude: "It is much, much more precise than Google Earth … The advantage the model offers is that [it gives] a better overview of the camp and can recreate the perspective of a suspect, for example, in a watchtower" (Cole 2016). Looking through his headset at the model concentration camp, Breker claims to see "exactly what a security guard saw," making VR a tool that "objectively" establishes what was visible to the defendant at the time (Freid 2017).

According to the Office for Photo Technology and 3D Crime Scene Mapping, 3D modeling that draws on laser scans, photogrammetric technology, digital mapping, and image editing software renders the scene "precisely measurable and interpretable" and allows "inferences about the nature of external acts of violence" to be made (Freid 2017). The central perspective is replaced by infinite possible perspectives, allowing for greater verifiability. In the film, this claim to objectivity is taken up by the former US Ambassador-at-Large for War Crimes, David Scheffer, who says that Hanning represented "the common man in the killing machine"—and most like him never faced justice. "Virtual reality," he adds, "is a great tool to establish what was objectively visible to the defendant [and it] proves [that Hanning] was an accomplice to murder." "Technology," Scheffer concludes, "reveals the memory of what occurred 70 years ago" (Freid 2017).

Since Jeremy Bentham's innovation in the eighteenth century, the panopticon has been thought of as a *ne plus ultra* of information-gathering. To see things with a totalizing view is, apparently, to see things with ultimate clarity and reliability. Prisons built on a circular model, surveillance towers, CCTV, and face recognition allow the perpetual visibility and identification of the subject under a regime of asymmetric power relations and constant monitoring. The surveilled subject is unable to surveil in return. Yet, scholars like Lorraine Daston and Peter Galison (2007) have long drawn attention to problems associated with the dominance of the specular and its claims to objectivity, while other scholars draw attention to problems associated with visualizing big data, particularly within a judicial context. Legal scholars Mark Lemley and Eugene Volokh (2018), for example, argue that legal doctrine is based on conventional distinctions between reality and communication, perception and experience, physical presence and remoteness, conduct and speech, and physical and psychological harm—distinctions that VR undermines. Falling into uncharted legal territory are thus factors that include the influence of VR on the viewer's own thoughts and emotions, the proprietorship of VR experiences, the blurring of the real and the perceptually real, and the capacity of VR itself to generate memories (Nori 2018).

That said, employed in the courtroom, VR reconstruction based on high-resolution scanning has made it possible to bring historical cases to trial and achieve convictions where incriminating evidence would otherwise have been insufficient. In light of this, we can only welcome the prosecution of low-ranking Nazi criminals like Hanning—a gesture of historical reckoning that has been too little and come too late. Yet, a note of caution might be sounded. Digital reenactment posits truth as the inevitable outcome of massive data capture and 3D reconstruction, even if that digital data capture relies on 3D modeling in the first place. Here we find a co-mingling of the *a priori* and the *a posteriori*. Whereas the violent crime scene analysis profiled by forensic VR engineer Ralf Breker is one in which data capture is performed on an extant crime scene, data capture in the Hanning case is complicated by the partially ruined state of the Auschwitz-Birkenau complex. It was necessary to model Auschwitz-Birkenau *before* its sight trajectories could be ascertained. In other words, big data—upheld as the evidentiary basis for independent adjudication—has already been subject to processes of historical interpretation using conventional evidentiary sources: eyewitness testimony, aerial photographs, and architectural blueprints. The inherently reductive nature of the model seems to vanish when the model itself comes to stand in for historical reality. Thus, a method that appears to follow an inductive approach can, in fact, more properly be said to follow a deductive one.

Historical certitude supersedes the possibility of testing hypotheses about the past in a simulated environment. To be clear, this is not to suggest that the camp guard was not guilty of the crimes with which he was charged, nor that the courts did not make a good-faith effort to ascertain his guilt or innocence. Rather, the critique rests on the methodological obfuscation and lack of falsifiability that surround digital reenactment and the epistemological sleight of hand that ensues. Asserting the primacy and comprehensiveness of the visible begs the further question as to not only what cannot be seen and must therefore be virtualized, but also what cannot be heard, felt, tasted, or smelled. In reducing historical experience to the visible and re-enactable, the victims' suffering seems incidental to an enterprise that imbricates big data, digital reconstruction, and claims to total knowledge.

Conclusion

Knowledge claims are often predicated on what can be seen—what was visible historically, what is visible today, and what can, through technological or aesthetic means, be made re-visible, experientially accessible, and testable in the present. In the introductory example dealing with the house at Ravensbrück, it was the apparent invisibility of the camp from the house that was held to explain how the SS leadership was able to conduct everyday life within a short distance of the torture and killing of tens of thousands of people. Albeit indirectly, the museum plaque urges us to inquire into that which historical agents themselves refused to see. By exposing the feigned invisibility—and hence unknowability—of occurrences behind camp walls, the museum exhibit picks up a question oft-repeated in the film *Shoah*, a question posed by the director Claude Lanzmann to local townspeople and farmers near Chełmno extermination camp, "What did you see?" Yet, as the project *Unbekannte Orte. Ravensbrück*, directed by Kristin Witte, suggests, if remnants of the past do remain visible, such visibility is not in and of itself tantamount to legibility.[2] What is required for these decayed, repurposed, overgrown, torn-down, and half-forgotten remnants of a concentration camp, is that they be made intelligible. A story is to be told that serves a commemorative purpose by "supplementing the lost milieu."[3]

We can assume that the sounds and smells at Ravensbrück would have carried, the water in the lake would have been muddied by the deposition of ash from the crematorium, the poisoned fish would have floated to the surface. At Auschwitz-Birkenau, the avenues to understanding would also have been many—from the smell of charred bodies to the smoke-filled skies. Today, the obstacles to awareness—about governmental abuses of power, social inequality, racial injustice, genocidal killing, and environmental degradation—are not due to a paucity of evidence, per se, evidence that needs to be mass-collated, machine-learned, subject to hyperrealistic simulation, and experienced by re-enactors. Rather, we are beset by a failure to ask difficult questions, and to see and act upon that which lies arrayed before us already—what lies, in fact, in our direct line of sight.

Acknowledgements

A version was presented as "Lines of Sight: Excursions in Seeing, Feeling, and Knowing," Keynote Address, *Experimental Humanities*, ICI Berlin, November 14, 2019, and slightly reworked paragraphs appeared in the author's "'Suffering," *Reenactment Studies Handbook: Key Terms in the Field*, co-edited with Jonathan Lamb and Juliane Tomann, 213–18, London: Routledge, 2020.

Notes

1　Mahn- und Gedenkstätte Ravensbrück. Available online: https://www. ravensbrueck-sbg.de/en/history/1939-1945/ (accessed September 12, 2020).
2　*Unbekannte Orte. Ravensbrück*. Available online: https://unbekanntes-ravensbrueck.de/projekt/ (accessed September 12, 2020).
3　Aleida Assmann, 1999, quoted in *Unbekannte Orte. Ravensbrück*. Available online: https://unbekanntes-ravensbrueck.de/projekt/ (accessed September 12, 2020).

References

Agnew, V. (2007), "History's Affective Turn: Historical Reenactment and Its Work in the Present," *Rethinking History* 11(3): 299–312.
Agnew, V., and J. Tomann (2020), "Authenticity," in V. Agnew, J. Lamb, and J. Tomann (eds.), *Reenactment Studies Handbook: Key Terms in the Field*, 20–4, London: Routledge.
Bayrisches Landeskriminalamt Zentrale Fototechnik und 3D-Tatortvermessung (2019), Exhibition at Frankfurter Kunstverein. Available online: https://www. fkv.de/en/bavarian-state-police/ (accessed September 12, 2020).
Cieslak, M. (2016), "Virtual Reality to Aid Auschwitz War Trial of Concentration Camp Guards," *BBC News*, November 20, 2016. Available online: https://www. bbc.com/news/technology-38026007 (accessed September 12, 2020).
Cole, D. (2016), "Virtual Reality Helps Net Last Auschwitz Criminals," *The Times of Israel*, October 2. Available online: https://www.timesofisrael.com/virtual-reality-helps-net-last-auschwitz-criminals/ (accessed September 12, 2020).
Daston, L., and P. Galison (2007), *Objectivity*. Princeton, NJ: Zone Books.
Freid, D. (2017), *Nazi VR*, produced by Mor Albalak, Mel Films. Available online: https://davidfreid.com/portfolio/nazi-vr (accessed September 12, 2020).

Kenderdine, S., and D. Hauw (2020), "Transmission through Imitation". Available online: https://www.epfl.ch/labs/emplus/projects/page-155235-en-html/ (accessed September 12, 2020).

Lemley, M. A., and E. Volokh (2018), "Law, Virtual Reality, and Augmented Reality," *University of Pennsylvania Law Review* 166(5): 1051–138.

Leuski, A., et al. (2016), "How to Talk to a Hologram," *Proceedings of the 11th International Conference on Intelligent User Interfaces, IUI 2016, Sydney, Australia*, 360–2, New York: ACM.

Nori, F. (2018), *Perception is Reality. On the Construction of Reality and Virtual Worlds*. Exhibition, Frankfurter Kunstverein. Available online: https://www.fkv.de/en/exhibition/perception-is-reality-on-the-construction-of-reality-and-virtual-worlds/ (accessed September 12, 2020).

Pickering, P. (2020), "Evidence," in V. Agnew, J. Lamb, and J. Tomann (eds.), *Reenactment Studies Handbook: Key Terms in the Field*, 57–62, London: Routledge.

Smale, A. (2017), "Reinhold Hanning, Former Auschwitz Guard Convicted a Year Ago, Dies at 95," *The New York Times*, June 1, 2017. Available online: https://www.nytimes.com/2017/06/01/world/europe/reinhold-hanning-dead-convicted-auschwitz-ss-guard.html (accessed September 12, 2020).

Staley, D. J. (2014), *Computers, Visualization, and History: How New Technology Will Transform Our Understanding of the Past*, 2nd edn. New York: Routledge.

CHAPTER TWENTY-THREE

The DNA archive

Jerome de Groot

Genetic information is becoming a way of narrating historical experience and understanding the human in time. The collection of biological information and the reading, analyzing, and interpreting of this data is being experienced firsthand by millions of people around the world. Adam Rutherford suggests that DNA has "transformed into an historical source" (2017: 4). DNA data is both a means of recollecting the past and, possibly, a way of storing information for the future. Developing tools for reading and interpreting this huge new archive will be a challenge for historians in the next decade. In this brief meditation, I want to present several ways of approaching this body of data. In doing so, I also consider the problems and challenges for considering human DNA as a type of archive.

For the historian, the possible gains in using genetic information as a "source" are huge. As many archaeologists have already found out, the amount of data being produced—often in relation to areas in which evidence is lacking—can be a game-changer in terms of interpretation and understanding (see Kristiansen et al. 2017). Data can be used in ways hitherto unimagined, to transform our understanding of the human (of varying types of the subspecies *homo*) and its world. An indicative example, at present being discussed in some research groups, would be the study of DNA samples from saliva left on envelopes. This could add nuance, dimension, and inflection to our understanding of a physical archive and could solve many mysteries relating to the use of such materials. Yet the ethics of using samples of DNA from deceased individuals, let alone the logistics of curating, storing, interpreting, and organizing the information, might give us pause.

On a wider scale, new DNA information seems to suggest new things about the ways that humans moved around and interacted with each other (Clarkson et al. 2017). The growing availability of this big data suggests new avenues for investigation and innovative ways of conceptualizing human community (see Green 2014). The size of the archive now produced demands the development of methodologies and tools that are currently lacking. Like other historical approaches attempting to draw on contemporary scientific data, the growing DNA archive seems to offer a new way of interrogating historiographic assumptions as well as opening up new modes for investigations and templates for understanding (see Smail 2007; Malafouris 2013). For instance, the very idea of an "archive" is interrogated by scientific information and technical practice; new processes for dealing with, processing, and understanding data will need to be engaged with, theorized, and understood (Daston 2017). Furthermore, as historians of science have demonstrated, the ethical and procedural issues surrounding the use of and engagement with genetic information need to be considered thoroughly (see Nelkin and Lindee 1995; El-Haj 2012; Sommer 2016; Radin 2017).

The family history research archive

The primary way in which human DNA is being used in recognizably archival fashion is via family history research. Millions of "amateur" historians are beginning to use genetic information as a resource with which to construct and create "history" (de Groot 2015). Generally, family historians are a well-organized and self-sufficient group of practitioners. They are highly innovative in terms of their work, and were early adopters as a community of internet resources, social media, and other research tools. They keep and organize their own information, sometimes using commercial software. The standard structure for this is the GEDCOM database unit, an archive code template that was developed by the Church of Latter Day Saints (see Creet 2019). Often family historians will consider themselves the holders of the memory of their families, in self-appointed roles as curators of information and historical resources.

Since 2012 and the arrival of widespread, cheap, heavily marketed Direct-to-Consumer Genetic Testing (DTCGT) products from companies such as AncestryDNA, 23andMe, LivingDNA, and Findmypast DNA, family historians have had another archive to organize: genetic data. DTCGT services for family history and ancestry largely suggest a user's ethnic makeup and geographical origins. The databases for each company suggest connections between user information and accordingly attempt to "connect" customers to each other (see Harris, Wyatt, and Kelly 2013; Hogarth and Saukko 2017). Genetic testing for family history is presented as a tool to help break down "brick walls," leading to the solving of problems that might have persisted for decades. Family historians around the world use genetic information to understand their backgrounds in more depth and to connect with those who might be related to them. They also recognize that the information generated might severely change the way they think about their past, with unforeseen revelations becoming increasingly commonplace in the field.

The companies also enable a user to download their full dataset of raw DNA data. To "read" and use this information, family historians have created databases and spreadsheets, written bespoke software, or utilized sophisticated online crowdsourced or community-curated programs such as DNA Painter or the suite of facilities at GEDMatch.com. Tools enable the genetic data to be mined and interrogated. Such software includes GEDMatch's "Lazarus" program, which allows the user to postulate the genetic makeup of dead relatives, and "Promethease," which allows family historians to have their genetic information read for health purposes. Some similar tools are provided by the big companies as well, keen that users manipulate data within their ambit. The family historian will organize their own data and may also manage the information of others. They will often have access to the genetic information of many other participants (voluntarily given), and will be connected to many possible "matches" through the company interfaces.

DNA testing for ancestry is marketed as "lifestyle" genetics, allowing the user a sense of heritage connection to a community or a historical way of understanding "who they are." In recent advertising, for instance, MyHeritage DNA offers to "Uncover your unique ethnic origins and find new relatives" and AncestryDNA will help to "Uncover your family history. And discover what led to you." The marketing addresses novelty, revelation, and historical situatedness. Millions of leisure users have paid the companies to gain a sense of their ethnicity and connection to communities. The data produced is interpreted by the companies and communicated through their subscription websites. These websites package the DNA data, presenting timelines, pie charts, graphs, maps, and ethnicity estimates, all based on a reading of the user's genetic code.

Through the commercial generation of genetic information for family history, then, companies are compiling major data archives. These collections of information provide huge amounts of revenue for such organizations, who are largely private and often funded by hedge-fund and biotech venture capitalist investors. AncestryDNA currently has over fourteen million customer records in its database; other companies are smaller but still have between three and five million users. Evidently, some family historians use multiple test services, but this still leaves a large— and growing—amount of genetic data, tied to pedigree records. The ownership of this body of information, then, and the monetization of it via commercial bio-banking and data-banking in an era of data medicine, is a very profitable enterprise (see Stoeklé et al. 2016). The market for this information is growing fast, and expanding in unforeseen directions. Once sold on, the organization, reading, and interrogation of such genetic ancestry information by researchers and medical practitioners might be considered as a kind of historical practice.

Access to and exploitation of the human archive

An unforeseen consequence of the explosion in genetic genealogy is in the area of law enforcement and border control (see Scudder et al. 2018). These agencies are exploring the use of the genetic databases and their associated family history information in criminal investigation. In particular, the highly public case of the "Golden State Killer," seemingly identified through using the DNA archives at GEDMatch, introduces an entirely new ethical concern. The archives were not created for such a purpose, and the legal, procedural, and criminological basis for using them for investigation is not legislated for. Family historians often conceive of themselves as "detectives," seeking truth and some kind of renewed meaning in the murky clues of the past. This is part of their self-representation, and such a motif provides insight into the historiographical structuring of their work. The addressing of the genealogical genetic information archive by *actual* detectives to solve cold cases is clearly a historical practice of a kind, and accordingly needs to be considered quickly even as it is being absorbed into the popular historical imagination.

As this example suggests, ethics are central to any consideration of the new archival possibilities of DNA. The massive expansion over the past couple of years in the databases held by the major family history companies raises compelling ethical questions: What should happen to DNA data now, and how will it be kept, curated, preserved, and managed into the future? Where will this information be kept, and who will maintain it? Who owns the materials of the past, and access to those materials? The question of long-term storage and access is already becoming an issue as family historians who have had their DNA sequenced begin to die, or take over management of the data of those who have passed away. Where should this information be held? Who should have access to it? It is not "public" and not stored in any kind of public archive. Certainly, the movement to open up the DTCGT market has enabled the major companies to promote their product—genetic analysis—as equally important as the information generated by the state (census data, BMD data, education information). The companies commercialize access to the past through their subscription services. The development of the DNA archive, though, puts a value on individual genetic information. Clients become what are known as prosumers, contributing their data and providing the online company with content.

AncestryDNA and 23andMe have started to realize the potential of their database by publishing scientific papers. AncestryDNA's work links the information created by their family history users with genetic information generated by DNA customers, including "322,683 pedigrees linked to genotyped samples in the United States alone and over 20 million total pedigree annotations [that] allow us to infer detailed historical portraits of the identified clusters" (Han et al. 2017: 9). They are "reading" their two archives by linking the textual family trees with the genetic information, allowing them to infer and analyze. However, because of the nature of the information, their results are not replicable: "we cannot make the genealogical and genotype data widely available to the academic community in light of our commitment to our customers" (Hang et al. 2017: 9). This represents an interesting evolution of the family history companies, which are taking steps to read and interpret the archive that they manage. It also demonstrates the potential problems for historians using genetic information as historical data in the future, as commercial interest may bring a lack of transparency or accessibility.

Indeed, scientific communities of all kinds—from population geneticists to medical investigators—are interested in addressing genealogical DNA archives. The DTCGT company 23andMe, which gives users ancestry and family history genetic information as well as medical advice, recently announced a partnership with the pharmaceutical company GlaxoSmithKline. Family history has become interlinked with medical research, as the body's information becomes an item of contemporary use. It is important that we understand the ways in which the DNA archive is being used commercially and how data generated about the past might impact upon practices in the present.

Challenging the current archive

Family history had hitherto worked using state, national, and public archives found in and collected by local libraries and national institutions. Family history companies now sell *access* to the records of these bodies, as well as the use of their family-tree-building software and social network of millions of other customers. The practice is predicated primarily on public records. DNA genealogy, however, is based on aggregating data generated and stored by private companies. There is currently no "public" forum for this DNA heritage information, something that is extremely worrying for possible future work on this material. The future DNA archive may not be held in a state or public institution.

As this suggests, genetic data about the past challenges the ways in which information about individuals has been collected and kept over the past centuries. For several communities, the development of a DNA archive allows the possibility of their reinsertion into "history," and a challenge to the ways in which the past was constructed and narrated formerly. Henry Louis Gates, Jr., a famous advocate of DNA testing for family history, points out the potential for this new technology to provide those forgotten or erased by state and nation archives with a means of asserting their historical agency: "For the first time since the seventeenth century, we are able, symbolically at least, to reverse the Middle Passage" (Gates 2009: 10). He points out the power of DNA work: "when the paper trail would end, as it inevitably did, in the horrid darkness of slavery, we traced our African roots through our DNA" (11). This has a historiographical consequence, as a more diverse and complete picture of the past might be drawn using the additional data in the archive: "Restoring the stories of the lives of the members of our extended families can directly transform the way that historians reassemble the larger narrative of the history of our people" (12).

However, many indigenous communities in North America, Australia, and Mexico have been highly critical of DNA investigation linking genetics with heritage and identity. There are various compelling critiques of the linking of DNA, heritage, and ethnicity (TallBear 2013; Nash 2016; Nelson 2016). Indeed, the notion that DNA information is indicative at all is problematic within these contexts, given the ways in which genetics has been utilized in the past to impose meaning and articulate ethnicity. Those using genetic information in future historical work will need to address the concerns raised by these and other scholars about the ideological complexity of DNA and the ways in which it can be understood.

Ancient DNA and the archive of the human

At the other end of the temporal spectrum, although also inflected by discussions of race and ethnicity, ancient DNA (aDNA) investigation is changing our understanding of what it means to be human, and how the human develops in time. The genetic analysis of archaeological samples has been common since 2010. It has enabled new assertions to be made about the development of human groups, as well as revealing types of the *homo* family that had hitherto been unknown (Reich et al. 2010). Such research has seemingly transformed the fields of archaeology, and will shortly begin to impact upon more modern historical investigations: "Findings from aDNA research are currently transforming our understanding of human history at an ever-increasing pace" (Haber et al. 2016). The practitioners of such work suggest the potential that such recent innovation has for changing the ways in which the past is understood: "Genome-wide analysis of ancient DNA has emerged as a transformative technology for studying prehistory, providing information that is comparable in power to archaeology and linguistics" (Haak et al. 2015: 207). Ancient DNA investigation conceives of *homo* as data and considers ways of understanding, narrating, and articulating this data. The geneticist-historian produces the information—through sampling, sequencing, and considering the genetic materials—and then reads it. The amount of data being produced by a DNA investigation is vast. Such research makes interventions into debates about population, migration, cultural development, evolution, and the definition of the human (see Mathieson and Skoglund 2018). Having begun with archaic specimens, such work is increasingly being undertaken on more "modern" individuals.

These researchers understand the human sample as a repository of DNA information that might be "read" in order to make historical arguments.

The information being generated here needs to be read, interrogated, and understood by historians, who therefore need to develop the tools with which to do this. Again, this information is not necessarily being stored in a way that is easily accessible by a range of scholars. Again, this information enables a group outside of the institutions of history to make interventions and assertions about the nature of the past and the way it might be narrated. Again, the development, growth, and management of this archive is largely unaudited and under-theorized. The expansive claims of aDNA scholars are being contested within archaeology, while many within the genetic sciences are also concerned about the ethical and power implications of the rapid growth of the area (see Heyd 2017; Bardill 2018; Prendergast and Sawchuk 2018).

Questions for the future

DNA as *storage* is being discussed and debated by various technologists as a means of dealing with the "vast amounts" of information that will be generated in the future and "far eclipse today's data flows" (Zhirnov et al. 2016: 366). DNA has already been used to "write" poetry and, tentatively, to encode information such as music and animation (Bök 2015; Minsker 2017). This information is being stored without discussion with archivists, historians, or those who study the past. The storage of this information will impact upon the way in which history can be written in the future and change the modes of memorialization available to humans in the decades to come.

The wider challenges of genetic information are profound for humanities scholars. How is this material to be understood, read, manipulated, and taught? Where does genetic information sit in relation to historical investigation? What is the historiography of DNA? How might it be visualized, understood, manipulated, critiqued? In museums and archives, how is this information to be stored or displayed? What are the legal, aesthetic, ideological, social, affective, material, and evidentiary issues associated with genetics, and how can they be addressed? Who owns this material, and where will it sit in the future (indeed, how will it be stored)? What tools are needed in order to read these collections, and who will be the archivists that use them?

In order to be able to respond to these important questions, historians need to engage with the various aspects of the genetic archive as it is being generated. The DNA archives that are being generated need to be codified, modulated, understood, and moderated. If not, there is a risk of the information being lost, becoming irretrievable, being made inaccessible to the public, being wrongly interpreted, or getting misused. DNA archives are being created in many contexts, some institutional, some commercial. Historians need to develop methodologies and tools for engaging with the data being generated, submitting such technology to scrutiny, and understanding and addressing this information.

References

Bardill, J., et al. (2018), "Advancing the Ethics of Paleogenomics," *Science* 360: 384–5.

Bök, C. (2015), *The Xenotext: Book 1*. Toronto, ON: Coach House Books.

Clarkson, C., et al. (2017), "Human Occupation of Northern Australia by 65,000 Years Ago," *Nature* 547: 306–26.

Creet, J. (2019), *The Genealogical Sublime*. Amherst, MA: University of Massachusetts Press.

Daston, L. (ed.) (2017), *Science in the Archive*. Chicago, IL: University of Chicago Press.

de Groot, J. (2015), "The Genealogy Boom: Inheritance, Family History, and the Popular Historical Imagination," in B. Taithe and P. Ramos Pinto (eds.), *The Impact of History? Histories at the Beginning of the 21st Century*, 21–34, London and New York: Routledge.

El-Haj, N. (2012), *The Genealogical Science*. Chicago, IL: Chicago University Press.

Gates, Jr., H. L. (2009), *In Search of Our Roots: How 19 Extraordinary African Americans Reclaimed their Past*. New York: Random House.

Green, M. H. (2014), "Genetics as a Historicist Discipline: A New Player in Disease History," *Perspectives on History*, https://goo.gl/rDViQf (accessed September 13, 2021).

Haak, W., et al. (2015), "Massive Migration from the Steppe Was a Source for Indo-European Languages in Europe," *Nature* 522: 207–11.

Haber, M., M. Mezzavilla, Y. Xue, and C. Tyler-Smith (2016), "Ancient DNA and the Rewriting of Human History: Be Sparing with Occam's Razor," *Genome Biology* 17(1), doi: 10.1186/s13059-015-0866-z.

Han, E., et al. (2017), "Clustering of 770,000 Genomes Reveals Post-Colonial Population Structure of North America," *Nature Communication* 8 (14238): 1–12.

Harris, A., S. Wyatt, and S. E. Kelly (2013), "The Gift of Spit (and the Obligation to Return It)," *Information, Communication & Society* 16(2): 236–57.

Heyd, V. (2017), "Kossinna's Smile," *Antiquity* 91: 348–59.

Hogarth, S., and P. Saukko (2017), "A Market in the Making: The Past, Present and Future of Direct-to-Consumer Genomics," *New Genetics and Society* 36(3): 197–208.

Kristiansen, K., et al. (2017), "Re-theorising Mobility and the Formation of Culture and Language among the Corded Ware Culture in Europe," *Antiquity* 91(356): 334–47.

Malafouris, L. (2013), *How Things Shape the Mind*. Cambridge, MA: MIT Press.

Mathieson, I., and P. Skoglund (2018), "Ancient Human Genomics: The First Decade," *Annual Review of Genomics and Human Genetics* 19, doi. org/10.1146/annurev-genom-083117-021749 (accessed September 30, 2021).

Minsker, E. (2017), "Miles Davis' "Tutu" is One of the First Songs to be Encoded in DNA," *Pitchfork*, October 1. Available online: https://pitchfork.com/news/miles-davis-tutu-is-one-of-the-first-songs-to-be-encoded-in-dna/ (accessed September 13, 2021).

Nash, C. (2016), *Genetic Geographies*. Minneapolis, MN: Minnesota University Press.

Nelkin, D., and M. H. Lindee (1995), *The DNA Mystique: The Gene as Cultural Icon*. New York: W. H. Freeman.

Nelson, A. (2016), *The Social Life of DNA*. Boston, MA: Beacon Press.

Prendergast, M. E., and E. Sawchuk (2018), "Boots on the Ground in Africa's Ancient DNA 'Revolution': Archaeological Perspectives on Ethics and Best Practices," *Antiquity* 92: 803–15.

Radin, J. (2017), *Life On Ice: A History of New Uses for Cold Blood*. Chicago, IL: University of Chicago Press.

Reich, D., et al. (2010), "Genetic History of an Archaic Hominim Group from Denisova Cave in Siberia", *Nature* 468: 2053–60.

Rutherford, A. (2017), *A Brief History of Everyone Who Ever Lived*. London: Weidenfeld and Nicolson.

Scudder, N., J. Robertson, S. F. Kelty, S. J. Walsh, and D. McNevin (2018), "Crowdsourced and Crowdfunded: The Future of Forensic DNA?" *Australian Journal of Forensic Sciences* 51, doi: 10.1080/00450618.2018.1486456.

Smail, D. (2007), *On Deep History and the Brain*. Berkeley, CA: University of California Press.

Sommer, M. (2016), *History Within*. Chicago, IL: University of Chicago Press.

Stoeklé, H.-C., M.-F. Bruneel, G. Vogt, and C. Hervé (2016), "23andMe: A New Two-sided Data-banking Model," *BMC Medical Ethics* 17(19), doi: 10.1186/s12910-016-0101-9.

TallBear, K. (2013), *Native American DNA*. Minneapolis, MN: Minnesota University Press.

Zhirnov, V., R. M. Zadegan, G. S. Sandhu, G. M.G. Church, and W. L. Hughes (2016), "Nucleic Acid Memory," *Nature Materials* 15: 366–70.

CHAPTER TWENTY-FOUR

Doing history and the pre-conceptual

Suman Gupta

This chapter presents less an argument and more a couple of tentative hypotheses, in two parts. In the first part, I gradually dig my way down to a rather narrow sense of "history" which has been of little interest to historians. In the second, I ponder the future prospects for that particular sense of "history" and therefore for the scholarly pursuit of history. I will present this as a move from a pre-conceptual historiography toward a pre-conceptual anti-historiography.

Pre-conceptual historiography

Historians in various contexts have made concerted collective efforts, especially from the 1960s to the 1990s, to imbue the unnoted in history with noticeable historical significance: the ordinary individual or neglected population, the everyday event or activity, the unremarkable or ignored space. Those who joined such collective efforts—for instance, in "history from below" and History Workshop (Selbourne 1980; Schwarz 1993); the Dar es Salaam "School of History" (Ranger 1971; Kimambo 1993); microhistory (Ginzburg, Tedeschi, and Tedeschi 1993); *Alltagsgeschichte* (Lüdtke [1989] 1995); and the Subaltern History

Collective (Guha 1982; Chakrabarty 2002)—both considered their historiographical principles and historicized their endeavors. Despite differences in focus and ideological emphasis, these historiographical approaches and schools presented some overlapping features.

First, they extended the scope of historical agency where it had earlier been muted, if not denied, in doing history. These approaches sought to recognize the intentions and actions of unnoted persons and groups by doing history, by placing them within its evidenced narrative and thereby reconstituting history. Human intentions and actions in the broadest, smallest, and most inclusive scales were at the heart of these projects, to enrich and complicate longstanding concepts of historical agency and causality.

Second, historiography is, nevertheless, up to historians. So, these projects were dogged by suspicions that they ultimately express historians' agency more cogently than that of the unnoted. After all, historians set the objectives, found the neglected traces and sources, wove the narratives accordingly, mainly in conversation with each other. Emphatic though they were about acknowledging the unnoted, their own agency was confirmed in the process. With reference to the Subaltern History Collective, Gayatri Spivak (1985) made the influential argument that the deliberate elision of the subjectivity of historians in their research corresponded to a contradictory muting of subaltern subjectivity while ostensibly foregrounding it. Implicitly, and sometimes explicitly, such arguments troubled all the above-named efforts.

Third, consequently, to invigorate the agency of the unnoted through *cultivating* history, if not in *doing* history, these projects attempted to reach outside academia and engage wider (lay) constituencies. Setting up workshops, initiating conversations in public spaces and media, writing for popular outlets, and investing in school and general education were some of the means employed. The idea was that history may only be done in historians' terms, but at least the erstwhile unnoted could be courted to take possession of the historians' gift. Nevertheless, even historians who were most determined to delve into the muted corners of history could not but find a one-way street. Historians *do* history for passive reception, akin to an intellectual clerisy addressing the laity, whereby the erstwhile unnoted—the ordinary people, or, more inclusively, the public—are informed and, so to speak, activated as participants in history.

The turn outwards from academia took a life of its own under the banner of Public History, which referred to the professional aspect of doing and mediating history. As one of its early proponents put it: "the historian answers questions posed by others [outside academia]. He or she serves as a consultant, a professional, a member of the staff" (Kelley 1978: 18). As such, Public History was less ideologically driven than the collective efforts named above, and more in sync with existing corporate and public institutions. In the main, it worked to update and consolidate the existing establishment rather than to constitute new critical formations. Instead of the erstwhile unnoted, it was the policy makers, bureaucrats, and executives of established institutions, and their "audiences," "communities," "publics," "clients," "consumers," and "markets" who were courted. Public History also came with a reflexive drive to bolster academic institutional interests, with employment-targeted teaching programs and practice-based research (Stowe 2006; Conard 2018). With some critical edge, scholarly analyses of the institutional ideologies, means, products, and transactional practices of various strands of public (and popular) history have appeared (de Groot [2009] 2016).

In brief, then, these collective efforts have sought to take account of the muted in history and to take history to the general public, but they have stuck to a top-down direction: ultimately, agency-rich historians and professionals lend support to passive recipients, to help them realize their intentions and actions.

And yet, this is a cynical way of presenting the above efforts. Such history projects have underpinned claims of, and calls for, self-possession, self-determination, sovereignty, fulfillment, etc., from various constituencies—with more or less justification. But that is probably not just because historians reached out to passive and inert recipients of history and brought them to life. Much more likely, those collective efforts were met halfway by recipients themselves in terms of a habitual, not-quite-articulated, or pre-conceptual and pre-existing sense of history. In fact, "professional" efforts may well have been more effective if academic historians paid some attention to such a lay sense of history. I suggest that this lay sense of history is grounded in a *pre-conceptual historiography* which exists already among those who receive historians' well-articulated, rigorous narratives based on principled historiography. By "pre-conceptual" I have in mind the use of the term in relation to "experience" by Eugene Gendlin (1962: 11); by "pre-conceptual historiography" I mean something like "the common sense of history," but with an eye to the likelihood that "common sense" is not random but underpinned by certain pragmatic organizing principles (the philosophical applications of which are much discussed in, e.g., Coates 1996).

With proper circumspection, let me then propose a hypothesis: *What historians do works, insofar as it is received by those who are habituated to living and thinking as if they are amidst history—i.e., amidst processes where intentions and actions matter—irrespective of how vaguely or inadequately they conceptualize history.* The everyday lives of the recipients, their unremarkable and narrowly focused intentions and actions, may not seem to have a discernible place in academic history, but nevertheless those are conducted *as if* they might, or at least *as if* they cohere in a minuscule way with the larger dynamic of history. They live as if their little agencies might have some unreckoned—but reckonable—relation to the big agencies in the general historical unfolding, which is continuously unpacked and repacked. The minutiae of intentions and actions have, in this pre-conceptual historiography, a continuous relationship with the big intentions and actions that are, so to speak, historical. The preconceived historiography makes it possible to apprehend (various) precepts of historical causality and agency.

While this sounds plausible in theory, the historian in me asks: where's the evidence that such a pre-conceptual historiography exists? How can it be characterized and presented for the historian's contemplation? Would conceptualizing it not immediately undermine its pre-conceptual character?

Investigating whether such a pre-conceptual historiography can be pinned down is a larger task for the future. But it does behoove me to consider here potential ways of investigating it. A starting point might be to examine idiomatic phrases (or catchphrases) in ordinary-language usage, suggesting an implicit concept of history. In English, those include: "annals of history," "the historical record," "making history," "go down in history," "lessons of history," "learning from history," "doing history," "right/wrong side of history," "history will show/judge," "tide of history," "historical event." Such phrases offer implicit notions of teleology, causality, utility, and form. With a blunt but easily accessible tool like Google Ngram, patterns of usage can be discerned that might clarify (and historicize) the pre-conceptual historiography. For instance, between 1979 and 2019, why did the use of the phrases "right side of history"/"wrong side of history" rise steadily from 0.00000012/0.00000025 percent to 0.0000030/0.0000029 percent (more than a tenfold increase in frequency of usage)? Of course, it is the case that a corpus of published books like Google Books is of limited relevance here; nevertheless, in my experience, such corpuses give reasonable indicators for the rise and spread of catchphrases. With more diverse corpuses taking in everyday usage (e.g., the numerous proliferations from the Survey of English Usage from 1959 onwards), contexts of usage can be factored in (say, in specific user groups or text genres, at sentential and post-sentential levels) and more fine-grained patterns discerned. The task might then be to consider how such preconceived ordinary-language notions of history bear upon the reception of history, especially when directed outside academic circuits. Whether and how such pre-conceptual historiography interferes with doing academic research might also be worth investigating.

There are undoubtedly other ways of grasping this pre-conceptual historiography. The point is, exploring it may come to be salient for the continuing—and hopefully increasing— relevance of "doing" history.

Pre-conceptual anti-historiography

I can imagine some of my colleagues raising quizzical eyebrows at the suggestion that ordinary-language corpus analysis might clarify a pre-conceptual historiography and have some actual bearing on doing history. For them, such a suggestion puts me in the camp of revisionist "digital history." I am fairly enthusiastic about that camp, but doubt it would grant me membership. However, this is not quite the direction I want to stray toward. Advocates and practitioners of "digital history" do not seem to make inroads into pre-conceptual historiography either, at least not much beyond the level of non-academic audiences for Public History (e.g., Dougherty and Howrotzki 2013: Part 6; Leon 2017). Even if recipients of history are heard, it remains the case that the "audiences," "communities," "readers," "markets," "consumers," "clients," "the public," may only pose questions to professional historians.

I have offered the hypothesis of pre-conceptual historiography not to extol the virtues of digital tools, but to lead toward a contrary hypothesis. To state it succinctly, let me coin the term "anti-historiography"—that is, subscription to any set of principles which disables the consistent application of notions of agency and causality in accounting for the past. Given that, the hypothesis could be stated thus: *If a pre-conceptual anti-historiography were to become grounded in habitual living and thinking—whereby it was already held that happening rather than action and inevitability rather than intentionality prevailed—then doing history would become ineffective.* That is to say, inasmuch as recipients of history live and think *as if* they would not intend and act but go along with predetermined developments, all they can meaningfully receive is not history from historians but foregone conclusions from authority-bearing pronouncers. It is possible that such a pre-conceptual anti-historiography cannot actually be totalized; perhaps it is too counter-intuitive a position for this or any historical juncture. But if such a position did have enough *a priori* credence in habitual life and thought to be able to shoulder pre-conceptual historiography, doing history would become less effective. History would start slipping in degrees, being extirpated from significant areas of social life, confronted by a certain deafness.

This hypothesis, I admit, is stated in excessively abstract terms. Yet it might be amenable to testing too. At any rate, the resources of a pre-conceptual anti-historiography are familiar in restricted domains. In exploring them, let's begin with the most fundamental assumptions. To be clear, what I dub a pre-conceptual anti-historiography is distinct from philosophical investigations into concepts of "free will," "fatalism," "determinism," "providence" (represented well recently in Fischer and Todd 2015; List 2019). While the latter aim at conceptual analysis, the former is interested in the pre-conceptual, the habitually lived and thought, rather than in that which is argued. Some notion of the former may, however, be obtained through surveys of lay attitudes to those philosophical concepts (e.g., Stillman, Baumeister, and Mele 2011; Paulhus and Corey 2011; Abbott 2020). Of course, it may be argued that such survey terms are premised and results are analyzed in rigorously conceived ways. Nevertheless, between rigorously considered concepts and surveys of lay attitudes, one can find some obvious constituents of anti-historiography being thrown forth: religious fatalism (or revelation of providence) and scientific determinism bearing upon social causality (e.g., biogenetic and evolutionary determinism). Such resources of anti-historiography have considerable histories, and they obviously have not managed to significantly undermine the status of doing history. They have not quite overshadowed the pre-conceptual historiography which is necessary for history to be received seriously. We may surmise that recipients of history have found ways to keep their pre-conceptual historiography active in their habitual lives and thought, while making tractable spaces for the accommodation or relegation of anti-historiographical concepts—perhaps by situating the latter in the stratosphere of the *Geist*, at some distance from the materiality of the everyday.

However, it is widely considered now that a sort of technological (or perhaps technocratic) determinism, on the back of large and linked datasets and algorithmic applications, has penetrated into habitual social life to an unprecedented degree. The penetration appears top-down, structured through governance systems (themselves seemingly shorn of human agency), bearing upon all. These involve surveillance mechanisms premised more on how populations and individuals behave *despite themselves* rather than when acting *intentionally*, and also include ahistorical modes of economic engineering and financial management which have been extensively investigated, mostly with unease. The technocratic functionaries producing and regulating these systems focus on anti-historiographical resources at the expense of historiographical principles: genetic dispositions and evolutionary rationales play indispensable parts. The penetration also appears within the minutiae of life on the ground. The extent to which networked apps inform and enable daily actions—at home or work or leisure—may well be reconfiguring how individuals regard themselves and others in terms of accessing "data selves" and "data profiles." Arguably, intentionality and automaticity, motive and impulse, act and reflex, calculation and design are becoming gradually indistinguishable in everyday life, amid the pervasive technoscape that surrounds everything.

I have put these observations impressionistically. They do not need elaboration: if they seem at all familiar, the point is already made. Irrespective of the extent to which this condition is empirically grounded, it is possible that habitual living and thinking is coming to be conducted with conviction in the pre-conceptual anti-historiography of data determinism. Possibly, many are now leading their lives and thinking *as if* happening supersedes action because intentions are actually chimerical. They are doing so and are constantly exhorted to do so because it is convenient—and often compulsory—in the prevailing technoscape and technocratic power structure.

If the hypothesis stated above holds, a challenge to doing history meaningfully is probably already afoot and certainly imminent, and calls for a collective conceptual and practical effort from historians. That effort would not involve contributing to the ever-burgeoning (since Ladurie 1973) and largely celebratory study of how digital capacities aid doing history. While this indeed is an exciting field, circumspection does not go amiss in this respect: the logic of data analysis and historical analysis works in a tension that is productive and unproductive at the same time (as Boldizzoni 2011 observed for cliometrics).

What I have in mind is a different and somewhat more probing investigation of the relationship between doing history in the twenty-first century and data determinism. It seems to me that John Gaddis's (2002) arguments usefully articulate some predicates for such an investigation. Particularly suggestive is his positioning of the historian's methods apropos of social science (which offer explanations by setting unifying principles and modeling accordingly) and what he calls "hard" or natural science (which mathematically incorporate randomness, indeterminacy, and chaos in explanations). Gaddis argues that the kind of contingent and retrospective explanations of social junctures—based on available evidence and plausible narrative—that constitute history are close to "hard" science and (somewhat counter-intuitively) incommensurate with social science. In this framework, interestingly, data determinism would be more in the area of social science than "hard" science. Gaddis's account of both sciences is questionable, and he was cautiously upfront about his penchant for extended metaphors. In fact, he saw "hard" science as having a principally metaphorical relation to doing history. And, indeed, the work that metaphors do, as it is within the natural sciences, might well turn out to be critical to investigating the relationship between doing history and data determinism (possibly extending precepts proposed in Arbib and Hesse 1986). But this investigation would not be a rhetorical exercise; as Gaddis suggests, it would involve exploring analogies between the methods of doing "hard" science and doing history, possibly against the allure of social science explanations.

References

Abbott, R. P. (2020), "'Providence' or 'Religious Fatalism'? A Distinction without a Difference in Disaster Research?" *Practical Theology* 13(3): 233–45.

Arbib, M. A., and M. B. Hesse (1986), *The Construction of Reality*. Cambridge: Cambridge University Press.

Boldizzoni, F. (2011), *The Poverty of Clio: How Economists are Abusing the Past*. Princeton, NJ: Princeton University Press.

Chakrabarty, D. (2002), "A Small History of Subaltern Studies," in *Habitations of Modernity: Essays in the Wake of Subaltern Studies*, 3–19, Chicago, IL: University of Chicago Press.

Coates, J. (1996), *The Claims of Common Sense: Moore, Wittgenstein, Keynes and the Social Sciences*. Cambridge: Cambridge University Press.

Conard, R. (2018), "Contemplating Origin Stories: The Making of Public History into an Academic Field in the United States," in D. M. Dean (ed.), *A Companion to Public History*, 19–32, Malden, MA: John Wiley.

Dougherty, J., and K. Howrotzki (eds.) (2013), *Writing History in the Digital Age*. Ann Arbor, MI: University of Michigan Press.

Fischer, J. M., and P. Todd (eds.) (2015), *Freedom, Fatalism and Foreknowledge*. Oxford: Oxford University Press.

Gaddis, J. L. (2002), *The Landscape of History: How Historians Map the Past*. Oxford: Oxford University Press.

Gendlin, E. (1962), *Experience and the Creation of Meaning: A Philosophical and Psychological Approach to the Subjective*. Evanston, IL: Northwestern University Press.

Ginzburg, C., J. Tedeschi, and A. C. Tedeschi (1993), "Microhistory: Two or Three Things That I Know about It," *Critical Inquiry* 20(1): 10–35.

de Groot, J. ([2009] 2016), *Consuming History: Historians and Heritage in Contemporary Popular Culture*. Abingdon: Routledge.

Guha, R. (1982), "On Some Aspects of the Historiography of Colonial India," in R. Guha (ed.), *Subaltern Studies 1: Writings on South Asian History and Society*, 1–8, Delhi: Oxford University Press.

Kelley, R. (1978), "Public History: Its Origins, Nature, and Prospects," *The Public Historian* 1(1): 16–28.

Kimambo, I. M. (1993), *Three Decades in the Production of Historical Knowledge in Dar es Salaam*. Dar es Salaam: Dar es Salaam University Press.

Ladurie, E. L. (1973), "L'historien et l'ordinateur," in *Le territoire de l'historien*, 11–14, Paris: Éditions Gallimard.

Leon, S. M. (2017), "Complexity and Collaboration: Doing Public History in Digital Environments," in J. B. Gardner and P. H. (eds.), *The Oxford Handbook of Public History*, 44–67, Oxford: Oxford University Press.

List, C. (2019), *Why Free Will is Real*. Cambridge, MA: Harvard University Press.

Lüdtke, A. ([1989] 1995), "Introduction: What Is the History of Everyday Life and Who Are Its Practitioners?" in A. Lüdtke (ed.), *The History of Everyday Life: Reconstructing Historical Experiences and Ways of Life*. Trans. W. Templer, 3–40, Princeton, NJ: Princeton University Press.

Paulhus, D. L., and J. M. Corey (2011), "The FAD-Plus: Measuring Lay Beliefs Regarding Free Will and Related Constructs," *Journal of Personality Assessment* 93(1): 96–104.

Ranger, T. (1971), "The 'New Historiography' in Dar es Salaam: An Answer," *African Affairs* 70:278: 50–61.

Schwarz, B. (1993), "History on the Move: Reflections on History Workshop," *Radical History Workshop* 57: 202–20.

Selbourne, D. (1980), "On the Methods of the History Workshop," *History Workshop* 9: 150–61.

Spivak, G. C. (1985), "Subaltern Studies: Deconstructing Historiography," in Ranajit Guha (ed.), *Subaltern Studies 4: Writings on South Asian History and Society*, 330–63, Delhi: Oxford University Press.

Stillman, T., R. F. Baumeister, and A. R. Mele (2011), "Free Will in Everyday Life: Autobiographical Accounts of Free and Unfree Actions," *Philosophical Psychology* 24(3): 381–94.

Stowe, N. J. (2006), "Public History Curriculum: Illustrating Reflexive Practice," *The Public Historian* 28(1): 39–65.

CONCLUSION
Historical understanding today: Incidental remarks

Lars Deile

When we planned the layout of this volume, we had the idea of beginning with a problem sketch and ending with a summarizing conclusion. It turned out differently. While the introduction dissected the current state of historical scholarship with a careful eye and a sure hand to determine the place where the contributions to this volume take their starting point, it fell on me to arrange the many different voices that we were thankfully able to gather into a chorus, or at least to pick out a melody among them. But I freely confess: I see myself incapable of summarizing this volume in the sense of a conventional conclusion. As it was our clear intention right from the beginning of this enterprise not to provide a handbook, a textbook that gathers together the topics and methods of contemporary historiography in order to learn and copy them, it would be rather absurd to summarize the most important points at the end anyway (even though I will refer to articles in this volume exclusively).

This book must be appropriated by its readers. It should inspire, unsettle, repel, and encourage them. It should provide food for thought that could lead to lively debates and further developments in the field, but also in the practice of historiography in general. This contribution is, therefore, less a conclusion and more a collection of incidental remarks.

Old problems

We wanted to track down history where it has become questionable. There are plenty of reasons to do so. The authors of this volume, for all their polyphony, agree that history is no longer able to keep the promises that have sustained it for the last two hundred years. Ethan Kleinberg, Joan Scott, and Gary Wilder put it most sharply: "Listen, please, to our voices of rage. ... Academic history has never managed to transcend its eighteenth century origins as an empiricist enterprise." What is it that has become, or even always been, so problematic?

From the seventeenth century to the second half of the nineteenth century, history answered the great questions about the meaning of the world by assuming a direction to all change toward the improvement of the world. When the answers provided by religion no longer seemed acceptable and philosophy could no longer keep track of the course of events, history (in German with the definitive article: *die Geschichte*) stepped into the picture in an orderly manner. Asserting linearity and purposefulness, it ordered the life of the individual as well as the constitution of societies according to the teleological pattern of progress. Hermetic as a conspiracy theory, this concept functioned at every suitable opportunity. Inventions were typically seen as steps forward, just like every discovery of a new species of beetle or an island—hitherto unknown in the West. Wars and revolutions were either declared to be engines of developments or declassified into short-lived aberrations, as appropriate. This basic pattern manifested Western standards masquerading as universal ones. Victoria Fareld calls this "chronoschism."

In the meantime, however, this pattern of interpretation has lost its persuasive power as its foundations crumble (Jörg van Norden). Where faith in the future is lost, modern history also loses its persuasive power. François Hartog, with reference to Reinhart Koselleck, puts this quite emphatically in this volume: for a long time, history was able to close the gap between the horizon of expectations and the space of experience. But where expectations continue to increase and become detached from experience or even run counter to it, history in its long-successful form no longer succeeds in meaningfully coupling the two. What opens up more and more is an abyss that demands reorientation.

But this gap, which can no longer be questioned, is also the productive force underlying a wealth of contributions inside and outside this volume. The need for reorientation opens the laboratory in which history is broken open, reassembled, questioned again, tested, discarded, and rethought. What emerges is still uncertain and fascinating precisely in its multiplicity and diversity. At first glance, this may look like some unsettling postmodern or even post-postmodern confusion. But it unsettles above all those who had settled down well in this modernity and gives others, the marginalized, the excluded, the possibility of emancipation and agency, as Fareld and Moira Pérez in particular, but also Erica Fudge, thematize in this volume. What can be expected is a *posthistoire*, not in the sense of Fukuyama's standstill in the perpetual completion of the project of modernity, but as work on alternatives to the linearity, directionality, hegemony, and chronology of modern history.

New approaches

This desire and necessity for the new sometimes has the lightness of an invitation to dance (Helge Jordheim), sometimes the seriousness of a reflection (Hartog), sometimes an emancipatory determination (Fareld, Pérez) and even an academic indictment (Kleinberg/Scott/Wilder, to some extent also Marnie Hughes-Warrington).

The productive power and depth of historical reflection that is uncovered in this process can be seen, among other things, in the analysis of metaphors with which the past is represented (Chris Lorenz on stratigraphic models, Q. Edward Wang on mirroring). It is revealed in the insistence on stories in the plural (as in Jordheim, Fareld, Pérez, Hughes-Warrington, and the joint piece of Berber Bevernage and Kate Temoney). It is also exciting to observe how productively the changed media conditions can be addressed. Instead of breaking out into lamentations about the loss of the golden olden past, Jo Guldi, Jerome de Groot, Silke Zimmer-Merkle, and Vanessa Agnew demonstrate how historians change with their subjects and how their methods can be fruitful when dealing with new and completely different material.

What is striking in the overview is that historical practice refers less and less to the past. There is a tendency for historians to increasingly turn to topics and questions related to the present and the future. This may be due precisely to the growing gap between the realm of experience and the horizon of expectation mentioned above, while "the present is our place and our environment" (Hartog). The assumption that history is concerned with the finite is widespread, but—according to Hughes-Warrington—it is simply wrong. If one lets oneself in for this change of perspective, completely new topics come into view. And this is probably an absolutely necessary process in order to get out of the embarkment of the present and to open up alternatives (Zoltán Simon, Marek Tamm, Patrícia Vieira, David Staley, Cornelius Holtorf, Suman Gupta). The concept of the Anthropocene places humans in a different relationship to their environment and the planet as a whole. The contemplation of a post-human world breaks down the seeming inevitability of our own present and forces humans to look behind their self-centered order of the world. A particular challenge here seems to be the development of a new serenity toward the infinite (Hughes-Warrington), contingency (Stefanos Geroulanos), and openness to the future (Franz-Josef Arlinghaus, Lars Deile). Yet, all authors in this volume pay special attention to the practice of historicizing, debating its use, its limitations, and its potential modes.

Theory in history

The authors of this volume have—quite predictably—no doubt about the "need for theory in the discipline of history" (Koselleck 2002: 1). On the contrary: it is demanded where it seems underdeveloped, which is one of the major concerns of the provocatively formulated *Theses of Theory and History* (Kleinberg, Scott, and Wilder). Historical theory has a special position within historical scholarship. It is neither a subdiscipline like medieval history nor a *Hilfswissenschaft* like numismatics, but a kind of metadiscipline that permeates the entirety of historical scholarship. This creates a difficult communicative situation in which there is a constant peril of disconnection. When things get uncomfortable, empirically focused historical researchers tend to accuse the questions historical theory deals with of being so abstract that they no longer have anything to do with the historical practice carried out in the dust of archives and libraries. Historical theory, in return, oftentimes complains about the unreflective naïvety of a purely positivist approach. The game could go on like this, but in the end, it would be to the detriment of both partners. Whereas theoretically unreflective practice is in danger of losing social and political relevance, isolated theory runs the risk of degenerating into an intellectual pastime of a closed circle.

The relationship between the theory and history must necessarily be uncomfortable in order to remain fruitful and innovative. But it also requires the willingness to engage in this adventure. This volume has a lot to offer in terms of provocations and adventurous spirit: while Guldi's contribution asks if historians can be replaced by algorithms, Zimmer-

Merkle demonstrates the importance of the historical in the context of new technologies. In the same spirit, Fudge underlines the importance of a history that breaks away from anthropocentric assumptions, de Groot reaches for the strictly patrolled boundaries between sciences and humanities, Hartog, Simon, and Tamm detach history temporally and spatially from its relation to constellations close to human beings, and so forth. Some people may gulp at first. And this unsettled pause is precisely the moment when things can be rearranged and, if necessary, put in a different order.

New relevance

More than a century ago, Georg von Below (1898: 239) declared that it was the task of historical observation to "descend into the detail [… and deal] predominantly and primarily with the varieties." His words were directed against Karl Lamprecht's quest for the typical and the regular, holding against this the importance of the free and creative individual. This insistence on *homo sapiens* and *homo faber* may have become a beautiful and edifying gamble, but it is increasingly giving historical scholarship the niche existence into which it is being forced and into which it is withdrawing with self-absorption. At least in parts of the world. The contributions by Bevernage and Temoney on truth commissions, by Vieira on global pandemics, or by Pérez and Fareld on chronopolitical issues, among others, demonstrate that things can be different. Temporality "powerfully fuels social conflict." For Hartog, this points to the necessity of re-establishing the "genuine circulation between the three categories of past, present and future and thus enabl[ing] us to properly face the present in order to act on it." This volume demonstrates, in its diverse variety of contributions, the possibilities and limitations of what history may have to offer.

References

Koselleck, R. (2002), "On the Need for Theory in the Discipline of History," in *The Practice of Conceptual History: Timing History, Spacing Concepts*, 1–19, Stanford, CA: Stanford University Press.

Von Below, G. (1898), "Die neue historische Methode," *Historische Zeitschrift* 81: 193–273.

INDEX